LARCENY & OLD LEATHER

LARCENY & OLD LEATHER

THE MISCHIEVOUS LEGACY OF MAJOR LEAGUE BASEBALL

Eldon Ham

ACADEMY CHICAGO PUBLISHERS

Published in 2005 by
Academy Chicago Publishers
363 West Erie Street
Chicago, Illinois 60610

Printed in the U.S.A.

Library of Congress Cataloging-in-Publication Data

Ham, Eldon L., 1952-
  Larceny & old leather : the mischievous legacy of major league baseball /
Eldom Ham.
    p. cm.
  Includes bibliographical references and index.
  ISBN 0-89733-533-3 (hardcover : alk. paper)
  1. Baseball--United States--Anecdotes. 2. Baseball--United States--Humor.
3. Baseball--United States--History. I. Title: Larceny and old leather. II.
Title: Mischievous legacy of major league baseball. III. Title.

  GV873.H26 2005
  796.357'64'0973--dc22
                                    2005003359

To Happiness and Family,
especially our children and salt-of-the-earth
grandmas and grandpas

CONTENTS

Part IV:
Had Satchel Been White:
The Truth About Racism and Baseball

Part V:
The Great Baseball Conspiracy

INTRODUCTION:

THE PRODIGAL GAME

You are remembered for the rules you break.
—Gen. Douglas MacArthur

EVERY BASEBALL PLAYER FROM little league to the big leagues knows it is illegal to steal signs, yet every Major League team assigns someone to do just that.

Baseball thrives on trickery and deception. And this larcenous legacy of our oldest major team sport goes much deeper than the field of play. Not only signs and bases are stolen in baseball: it has been known to snatch a bit of law, bully the Supreme Court, and pilfer more than a little history from the likes of Hank Greenberg, Jackie Robinson, Bobby Thomson and Roger Maris. That, in the truest sense, is baseball: a uniquely American game founded in the spirit of Yankee competition and played with larcenous abandon.

One of the most famous home-run cannon shots in Major League history was Bobby Thomson's long ball pennant winner against the Dodgers in 1951. According to the *Wall Street Journal* and others, it may have been stolen, the illicit product of signs pilfered from the Giants' center-field telescope. Over fifty years later, during the Chicago Cubs' near-pennant run of 2003, Cubs advance man Joe Housey spent his time scouting—that is to say, spying—with a clipboard and radar gun. Housey, and dozens of others, are shamelessly deployed to watch the actions of opposing managers, catchers, pitchers and runners in the hope of finding a subtle advantage, if not a way to steal hand signals outright.

Cheating has been a romanticized part of baseball since the late nineteenth century when every game had only one umpire who could not monitor everything on the field. The players learned quickly how to gain a fair or unfair advantage over the competition. In the old days, fielders would trip opposing players, hold the belts of tagging runners, and even take shortcuts home if they could. And somehow much of that cheating still seems perfectly kosher, even in the new millennium.

George Bernard Shaw once said, "There is no reason why the fielder should not try to put the batsman off his stroke at the critical moment by neatly timed disparagements of his wife's fidelity and his mother's respectability." Today's players don't rely on insulting wives and mothers, but the modern game nonetheless draws upon its mischievous roots, be they from 1951, 1927 or the 1890s.

Baseball skullduggery may have been invented on the field with spitballs, corked bats, stolen signs, framed pitches, slow grass, greased bats, the hidden ball trick and much more, but those pale when compared to the behavior of the likes of Pete Rose, Ty Cobb, Peter Ueberroth, and most of all, of Kenesaw Mountain Landis, the tyrannical first baseball commissioner, who, until the day he died in office, doggedly kept black ballplayers out of the big leagues. The question thus becomes not whether there are precedents for cheating in baseball, but rather, when is such behavior simply romantic mischief, a part of the guts and glory of the game, and when does it cross the shadowy line into actual corruption?

Baseball is a game of rugged infamy immortalized by the words of Ring Lardner, Damon Runyon, Red Barber and Yogi Berra, and fascinating to such diverse souls as Ernest Hemingway, George Will, Roger Kahn, Mark Twain, and Dwight Eisenhower.

We love the game itself, but it may be its no-holds-barred legacy that appeals to our national gut as no other sport does. Unconstrained by time clocks, the particular shape of a uniform field, or the self-indulgence of instant replay, baseball may be the only major team sport that understands what it is—a *game*. Armed with that singular understanding of itself, baseball has retained enough flexibility, grace and even dignity to overcome its shortcomings, wink at itself, tweak a bit of history, steal a few hits, and, above all, kick more than a little dirt on posterity.

The popularity of the game may ebb and flow; it may prosper on some days and suffer on others. But despite distractions, from racism to lost home-run records, broken hearts and more recently to the monster of steroids, baseball always finds its way home. We love the swashbuckling persistence of this great original pastime, not just for its drama, its players, and its endless statistics, but also for its history and its soul and because, above all else, baseball *is* us—its humor, its faults, and especially its colorful larcenous side—as American as Yogi Berra.

PART I
STEAL THIS GAME!

I

LUMBER!

Cheating is baseball's oldest profession. No other game is so rich in skullduggery, so suited to it or so proud of it.
—Thomas Boswell, *Inside Sports*

CARVED FROM ONE SOLID billet of ash, maple or hickory, Major League bats are a near mystical extension of those ballplayers who ever savored a fling at big league glory. As premier tools of the hitter's trade, they are the object of care and attention ranging from the meticulous to the mysterious, sometimes salted with more than a dash of big league mischief.

In 1923, when the great Babe Ruth hit a record-setting fifty-nine home runs, almost three times the number (twenty-three) hit by the Giants' George Kelly, all the Babe's lumber answered to one beloved name: Black Betsy. Ruth was not alone in this. Major League bats are often nurtured, sometimes given lifelike personae not unlike the kind of respectful affection sailors bestowed upon their tall ships. Americans have a long history of respect for their important possessions, including cars, boats and airplanes, often honoring them with affectionate or even mysterious names: "Spirit of St. Louis," for instance. Davy Crockett called his musket "Betsy" and Robert E. Lee named his horse "Traveler." It is no wonder, then, that big league ball players would do the same for the premier tools of their trade, thus contributing to baseball's uniquely American character.

3

Some players anointed their bats with biblical names, while others gave them more practical appellations. The Dodgers' Jay Johnstone, for instance, chose perhaps the most appropriate name of all: "Business Partner." By the time Ruth was launching sixty rockets into Major League posterity for the 1927 Murderers' Row Yankees, his bat had evolved from Black Betsy to be called Big Bertha or Beautiful Bella. But some of these fixations on the tools of the trade go beyond the quirky. White Sox legend Shoeless Joe Jackson not only swung lumber with such colorful names as Big Jim or Caroliny, he virtually lived with his bats and even took them home to South Carolina for the winter. The immortal Ty Cobb, a notable baseball misanthrope, took to rubbing his bats down with tobacco juice. Joe DiMaggio coated his with olive oil, and slugger Ted Kluszewski pounded nails into his big league lumber. But the strangest custom of all may belong to old-timer Eddie Collins who buried his bat in piles of cow dung, a practice that may not have influenced opposing pitchers as much as opposing catchers—not to mention home plate umpires.

Smelly or not, something clearly worked for the bats of Hall-of-Famer Collins. He may not sport a big name like Shoeless Joe or Ty Cobb, but Eddie Collins played second base for twenty-five years in the big leagues, much of it during the Jackson-Cobb era, garnering 3,311 hits with a lofty .333 lifetime average. A prodigious base stealer who set a post-1900 record with six steals in a game—which he did twice in one month—Collins was the marquee player in Connie Mack's "$100,000 Athletics infield," winning five pennants in six years, from 1909 to 1914.

The cliché about hitting a baseball being the most difficult action in sports may be overstated, but it certainly explains the predictable frustration when even the most efficient batters fail seven of ten plate appearances, thus opening the door to one of the great human weaknesses: temptation. The relentless search for a competitive edge has forever been a part of baseball, even more than in most other sports. Whether throwing the curve ball, knuckler or spitter, pitchers seek to deceive, and the batters they face likewise yearn for the hidden advantage.

Contemporary players use relatively light bats, usually in the range of thirty-one to thirty-three ounces. The power hitters of old preferred heavy lumber like Ruth's forty-two-ouncers or Cobb's forty-four-ounce bat. Some accounts suggest Ruth may have used even heavier bats in the range of forty-eight to fifty-two ounces, especially in his earlier years. Lou Gehrig swung a Louisville Slugger model "GE69" with a 2 1/2-to-2 5/8 barrel. It weighed a hefty thirty-eight ounces. As the era of Mantle and Maris began in the late 1950s and early '60s, the power hitters were down to about thirty-two ounces with spray-hitting infielders sometimes wielding even lighter thirty-ounce bats.

Don't the laws of physics suggest that the ball will rebound further from a bat of greater mass? According to Dr. Robert K. Adair, Sterling Professor Emeritus of Physics at Yale University and author of *The Physics of Baseball*, the answer is "yes." Given similar bat speed and motion, Adair calculated that a forty-six-ounce bat will launch a baseball about eight feet further than a thirty-two-ounce bat. In 1962, *This Week* magazine conducted an experiment with Roger Maris slugging balls with various bats weighing from thirty-three to forty-seven ounces. As the weight increased, the ball traveled further on average, though with a fairly wide standard deviation.

But there is one fundamental problem: to smash a four-hundred-foot home run, the player has in fact to hit the ball, and therein lies the challenge of offensive baseball. Swinging a forty-four-ounce chunk of lumber takes powerful arms and strong hands, while catching up to a big league fastball or adjusting to a sweeping curve requires bat speed and acuity. Dilemmas such as these frequently produce a quirky neurosis in players seeking to defy physics by swinging a heavier bat faster while still retaining enough versatility to adjust either to a low slider or hanging curve.

These fundamental dilemmas lead to miscreant behavior as players resort to trickery and a concealed advantage. Batters soon learned that by illegally hollowing out portions of the bat and replacing the wood with a lighter substance, often cork, they could make their heavier bats lighter by about one-to-two ounces. Although baseball rules have varied over the decades, they have consistently banned substances other than wood in the bats—thus no aluminum or composite bats have been allowed, although there have been occasional allowances for certain coatings and laminates. Still, rules or no rules, cheating with cork and other substances has been around for most of baseball's modern era, up to and including superstar Sammy Sosa's notorious broken-bat misadventure on June 3, 2003, perpetuating what has become part of the game's colorful image.

Paradoxically, those cheaters of yesteryear and today may have defied the rules, but they could never really cheat physics itself. A heavy bat made lighter with illegal cork becomes, well, lighter—a simple condition that could be accomplished by four different, notably legal, means. First, the bat could be hollowed out at the end, a process known as cupping. Or the barrel could be shaved down as long as its circumference remains consistent with the rules. Third, the hitter could simply swing a lighter bat in the first place. Or, simplest of all, the player could just choke up on the grip, which would not lighten the bat, but would change the fulcrum and accomplish a similar result without changing the bat at all.

Nevertheless, there have been hitters throughout baseball history who have chosen to cheat rather than to simply use the lighter—legal—means to the same end. Their decision might reflect a fear of somehow admitting inadequacy, complicated perhaps by a touch of superstition.

Many sports historians believe the greatest of all baseball records may have been Joe DiMaggio's famous 1941 hitting streak of fifty-six games for the Yankees. It was a streak of great skill and occasional luck, but it was not without its unnerving moments. After the fortieth game, for example, a fan stole DiMaggio's favorite bat, of all times, between games of a double-

header. Although emergency bats were available—one of his
teammates was using the same model—DiMaggio went into a
panic, because the purloined bat had been customized with
shaved-down wood to lighten it and increase the speed crucial
to nailing big league fast balls. A skeptic might wonder whether
the magical bat had been doctored in more clandestine ways,
but legal or not, the point was clear—DiMaggio's bat was special, not just physically, but perhaps metaphysically, too.

DiMaggio's shaving technique was legal under the rules, and
although his panic could have been evidence of further tampering, it is just as likely to have been caused by an affinity for the
occult that has haunted ball players for more than a century.
What with effective hitting at such a premium, it is no wonder
that superstition, eccentric habits, and Major League bat treat-
ments have enjoyed a colorful legacy from the nineteenth century well into the new millennium.

The Cubs' fateful pennant chase of 2003 was a roller coaster
ride that ended in catastrophe for Chicago when a lifelong Chicago fan robbed a foul ball out from Cubs left fielder Moises
Alou. Although finishing in fatal misfortune, the 2003 Cubs
campaign had begun with its red-hot slugger Sammy Sosa batting .333 with twenty home runs in the first three weeks. Then
Sosa was beaned by a pitch that shattered both his helmet and
his hitting rhythm, sending him into a six-week funk. Exacer-
bated by a painful sore toe that put him on the disabled list for
the first time in seven years, Sosa slumped to a .244 pace and
knocked in a woeful four runs in the next few weeks.

Then came panic, temptation—and the cork. When Sosa
returned from the DL on May 30, 2003, he had compiled only
six total home runs in 137 plate appearances. Four days later
he had the added misfortune of shattering his bat in a game
against the Devil Rays, ripping the barrel open to expose a portion of the shaft stuffed with cork in full view of an astonished
baseball world. Sosa was promptly suspended and, though he
issued an apology of sorts, he never admitted using the bat in-

tentionally, stressing that it had been altered for batting practice only.

Sosa's remaining bats were ceremoniously X-rayed, including those already tucked away in the Hall of Fame. When no other cork showed up and memories began to fade, Sosa had moved well down the path of atonement. He finished the year with forty homers and set a new Major League record for total home runs in a ten-year span, besting the immortal Ruth and nearly—but not quite—exorcising the cork ghost. Sosa's unfortunate rendezvous with fate, cork and history—and especially the ease of his atonement—tells us much about baseball itself, but particularly reaffirms the mischievous legacy of ball players and the big league sticks they love, nurture, and sometimes even illegally alter.

Sosa's easy forgiveness suggests one of the lasting tenets of big league lore: even the fans exhibit a willingness to overlook baseball shenanigans. Sosa was "back," and he would soon be proving home-run physics again, especially when he launched a mammoth moon-shot home run on national television during the 2003 National League Championship Series against the Florida Marlins. Almost certainly without the aid of cork, Sammy's blast rushed all the way into Wrigley Field history, thumping the dead-center television shed by the distant scoreboard, close to where the great Roberto Clemente once drilled a similar legendary shot.*

Over the course of many baseball eons, the long ball was sometimes preferred, and sometimes out of style, due to dominant pitching. It had enjoyed a profound resurgence with the neck-and-neck 1961 duel between Mickey Mantle and Roger Maris, then drifted for decades until the 1998 home-run barrage of Sosa-McGwire. Since then much talk and print have been expended

---

* That Sosa's bat was by then duly corkless was a near certainty: in a few earlier playoff games, his bat had shattered almost on cue for the world to see, inspiring cork-induced complaints by Braves fans, but exposing no actual cork.

on the sweeping home-run explosion of modern baseball.

When the old timers were wielding forty-to-forty-eight-ounce mini-trees, it made partial sense to cheat with hollowed barrels stuffed with cork, because even those baseball icons had discovered that lighter bats produce greater bat speed, hits and homers, although somehow it never occurred to them to swing lighter bats in the first place. With the likes of Mantle, Maris, McGwire, Bonds, and Sosa wielding thirty-two or thirty-three-ounce bats, cork itself should be reduced to a counterproductive joke, weakening the bats and interfering with the natural trampoline effect of the ball-bat collision.

Bat speed makes the difference, even more than heavy lumber or bats doctored with cork, motor oil or cow dung. Swing the bat faster and the ball will go farther. Maris knew it and Sosa perfected it. Remarkably, it seems that the great Ruth knew little about the Newtonian physics of launching baseballs with lighter lumber, even though he rocketed more than anyone until Hank Aaron broke the all-time career record on April 8, 1974, against Dodger lefty Al Downing. One can only wonder what Ruth could have done with lighter, speedier bats—unless they were corked in the first place and *were* speedier, an intriguing speculation supported by no empirical evidence whatever.

Heavy lumber or not, one thing those old-timers did better than the modern player was to hit for average, often exceeding the vaunted .400 mark, but, except for Ruth, many of the old guard did not hit much for power. In 1900, Honus Wagner led the National League in hitting at a lofty .381, but the home-run leader, Boston's "Germany" Long, clubbed only twelve dingers all year. In 1901, Nap Lajoie (pronounced "La-Zwah"), one of the premier turn-of-the-century players, led the American League in both batting average (a staggering .426) and home runs (a mere fourteen). The immortal Ty Cobb topped the American League in hitting at .420 in 1911, but the home-run leader that year smashed only eleven round-trippers—and his power was so prodigious that he was called "Home Run" Baker. It seems

Baker earned his nickname smashing two home runs during the 1911 World Series, but it was a miracle he could hit any at all with the weighty fifty-two-ounce cannon he used for a bat.

In the early days of baseball, the game was played with less emphasis on power and more attention to the finer points of timely hitting, bunts, and moving runners over. But power, though deployed sparingly, was thought to come from heavy lumber, those cumbersome bats that outweighed today's models by as much as fifty percent. Since then, Major League bats have continued to become much lighter over the generations, including Sosa's thirty-two-ounce, thirty-four-inch stick. Moreover, as the season wears on, some players may even drop an ounce to make up for the fatigue of a long year and the typically hot, draining summer.

Major League players achieve typical bat speeds around seventy miles per hour. Estimates suggest that for every one mile per hour faster, the average ball will travel five extra feet. Presumably lighter bats are easier to control as well, increasing the likelihood of connecting with certain difficult pitches. However, at some point there are diminishing returns. To achieve lighter bats, and hence greater bat speed in the swing, the barrel can be narrower, the bat could be shorter, or the bat might be hollow. But a slender barrel, even one within the rules, makes it harder to connect squarely with big league pitches and produces more pop-ups and easy fly balls, while a short bat obviously lacks both reach and leverage.

The hollow or corked bats are most problematic, not only because they are blatantly illegal, but since they are smaller and lighter to begin with, their hollow cavities produce excessive weakness. A check of contemporary Major League rules reveals that a legal bat must be smooth, rounded, not more than forty-two inches long, and have a barrel not greater than two-and-three-quarter inches. It also has to be one piece of solid wood under current rules, although in years past certain composite woods and even laminates were allowed. In the old days, one slight but common modification was to "bone" each bat, preferably with an old ham bone, rubbing the grain to seal the pores. Such a practice was and is decidedly legal, but is no longer used because of improved manufacturing technology.

But it is the illegal bat that produces some of baseball's most compelling history. Since 1970, only five Major League players have actually been caught with corked or similarly doctored bats, but each incident was high profile, if not entertaining and even comic. Norm Cash, who led the American League hitters in 1961 with .361 for the Tigers, reportedly adopted the corked bat technique during his batting crown season. Amos Otis of the Royals used corked bats over most of his career, a practice exposed in 1971 when he shattered a bat and spewed not only cork but also superballs over the infield. After he retired, Otis, a five-time All-Star, admitted, "I had enough cork and superballs in there to blow away anything."

In 1974, Yankee Graig Nettles busted a bat, spraying around the bases six superballs that were dutifully collected by shocked Tiger catcher Bill Freehan. Nettles explained that unbeknownst to him, an anonymous Yankee fan in Chicago had given him the loaded lumber. Long-time St. Louis manager Whitey Herzog once X-rayed Mets' bats the night before a game and found four corked models, and at one time the Cleveland Indians were accused of actually maintaining a woodworking machine dedicated to the art of hollowing and corking big league sticks.

Although corking a bat can take more than an ounce off its weight, the corking process is not the only way to make modifications, illegal or otherwise. Many players prefer the legal process of cupping. An M.I.T. professor once crafted a dimpled barrel design to help cut a bat through the air like a golf ball, an illegal manipulation of baseball physics, which may be what slugger Ted Kluszewski had in mind when on occasion he pounded nails into the end of his bats.

One of the most famous tampered-bat incidents of all time involved neither cork nor nails, but pine tar, and it provoked a near donnybrook. On July 24, 1983, Royals star George Brett clubbed a dramatic ninth-inning home run off Yankee stopper Goose Gossage to put Kansas City ahead 5-4. After Brett rounded the bases, umpire Tim McClelland (the same ump who tossed Sammy Sosa on June 3, 2003, for the cork incident) called Brett out and negated his home run because the bat was covered in sticky pine tar further up the barrel than the rules would allow. Brett was furious, his eyes popping as he exploded from the dugout and charged the umpire. He had to be physically restrained in full view of a huge television audience. The tar could not directly influence bat speed, but it could enhance a batter's grip, so it may have affected Brett's speed and control. But tar lower on the handle, including the grip, was and is legal. In any case, the whole episode became embedded in baseball lore as the great "pine tar incident"; country singer C.W. McCall recorded "Pine Tar Wars: The Ballad of George Brett." Eventually Brett's homer was reinstated by the baseball brass, and later the game was replayed from the pine tar point forward, the Royals managing to win 5-4.

Whether filled with cork or superballs, covered in pine tar, or studded with nails, big league bats continue to enjoy a special relationship with their owners. When Shoeless Joe Jackson took his bats home to the South in the off-season, he explained it was to protect them from the cold Chicago winters. One-time Yankee Bobby Mercer stored bats in the steam sauna to insulate them from the cold of Candlestick Park in San Francisco. Pete Rose used alcohol on his big league sticks, while Jim Frey preferred motor oil, borrowing the technique from many Negro League legends like the great "Double Duty" Radcliff. And for some reason now lost in the mist of history, the motor oil had to be dirty to achieve the best results.

Players are very sensitive to how their bats feel and respond, especially with the grip. Although he was about six-feet-two-inches tall and weighed over 250 pounds, Babe Ruth actually had small hands, so he would file down the handle (complimenting his egotistical habit of notching home runs *above* the handle). Old-time Cubs power hitter Hack Wilson, with big shoulders but oddly small feet and hands, did the same thing for the same reason. More recently, Albert Belle would often order special bats with exceedingly small handles. Over the past decade, the greatest drawback to the lighter, more fragile lumber has been their increased propensity to shatter in games, and shaving down the handle makes the problem worse. Almost all Major League bats are made entirely of ash, but some players—including Barry Bonds during his record seventy-three-jack season—are experimenting with maple as a harder, more effective wood. By contrast, in the old days the bats were largely hickory, a hard but heavy wood. Depending on size, some trees produce up to 250 big league bats. Willow was used very early on, but it was so pliable that its trampoline effect was ruled illegal at the end of the nineteenth century.

Although size, speed, feel and comfort are paramount, players are also particular about the bat's appearance, especially its color. Ash is a light-colored wood, and most players like its polished look. But lately players are leaning toward a more personalized appearance. During his home-run race with Mark McGwire in 1998, Sammy Sosa often relied upon completely black bats, and actually slugged homers sixty-four, sixty-five and sixty-six, with a black beauty specially crafted for Sosa by Hoosier Bat Company in Valparaiso, Indiana, a small business run by Dave Cook, a one-time Yankee scout. In 1975 Hillerich & Bradsby, makers of the "Louisville Slugger," produced a black bat for Pat Kelly of the Chicago White Sox, the first time a black bat had been used in about four decades. Black is becoming more popular, but players with less flair for the dramatic will stain their ash bats to achieve a deeper, richer look. Parenthetically, it is no secret that black hides defects better, though in today's game it is unlikely that black bats are also corked bats—most of the time, anyway.

Some hitters go a little further in the flashy-bat department, opting for the two-tone look. The Major League Rules Committee has approved black and brown, but some players have used an "inspired" brown tint that looks almost red. Pete Rose used a red bat in practice, though never in a regulation big league game. In the 1970s, eccentric Oakland A's owner Charles Finley deployed bats in his team's colors, green and gold, but only in exhibition games. Although the look of most unique bats is probably a fashion statement, some players prefer darker bats of any color, believing that it is harder for fielders to see the ball coming off a dark surface, especially at night.

So where does all this Major League lumber come from in the first place? Who makes these bats? There are several major companies and dozens of small shops, but the most famous brand worldwide remains the "Louisville Slugger." The most legendary bat manufacturer of all evolved in typical American fashion from the eccentricities of a pro slugger for the Louisville Eclipse back in 1884. According to one source, Pete "The Gladiator" Browning was himself known as the "Louisville Slugger" when he ordered a custom-made bat from a youngster named Bud Hillerich after visiting the woodworking shop of Hillerich's father. Browning loved the bat and kept ordering, as did his teammates, followed by numerous players on other teams, rapidly expanding what was becoming known as the Louisville Slugger brand. Soon Willie Keeler, John McGraw, Honus Wagner, and Ty Cobb were using the Hillerich bats.

Wagner and Hillerich were involved in another first in 1905 when the legendary Honus Wagner became the first player to have his autograph burned into the barrel of his Hillerich bat. The new bat company prospered, and Hillerich & Bradsby today is one of the premier baseball bat manufacturers, still turning out the famous Louisville Slugger. But their bats are becoming more sophisticated: Hillerich & Bradsby maintains over three hundred pro models of its Louisville Slugger, with over 20,000 individualized specifications on file.

Since the 1960s, aluminum bats have become popular among college, high school and Little League players because these bats are both light and produce a trampoline effect that propels balls faster and farther, suggesting an awkward oxymoron: "aluminum lumber." The aluminum bats are as light as twenty-eight ounces and they have a larger sweet spot to complement their durability. But pro ball prefers the mainstay, the wooden bat, a piece of Americana that has inspired players, sports writers, poets and fans including Thomas Wolfe, who spoke warmly of "the sound of the ball, the smell of dry wood." Pro scouts and coaches have great disdain for aluminum bats, which they believe distort a hitter's true abilities, making it more difficult to scout and find real hitting talent at the amateur level.

Aluminum notwithstanding, given Babe Ruth's powerful arms and natural home- run prowess, one can only wonder what his homer totals might have been with a lightning fast thirty-four-ounce bat designed with the true physics of baseball in mind. Thanks to Roger Maris and other modern players, we can hazard a guess—how about sixty-one, or maybe seventy-three—or even more? If Ruth had crammed a few superballs into the barrel, then juiced himself with a hefty dose of steroids, would triple digit seasons have been in reach? Maybe—but not if the infamous spitball had not been outlawed in 1920, the very year that Ruth first appeared in Yankee pinstripes.

In an obvious effort to manipulate the essence of the game and possibly to influence the emergence of the Murderers'-Row marketing machine of limitless home runs, the baseball lords dumped the spitter to help tip the balance from pitchers and spray hitters to the long ball sluggers of Ruth, Gehrig, Greenberg and beyond. But the wary pitchers were far from defeated, and went on throwing junk balls doctored by their own brands of baseball counter-fraud.

2
SCREWBALLS AND GREASEBALLS

*I don't feel a bit guilty. It was just a nice equalizer I
threw a spitter for five years and never got caught.*
—George Frazier, former Cubs pitcher

THE EARLY NINETEENTH CENTURY was the golden age of what
would become the modern game, boasting such near-mythical
stars as Honus Wagner, who led the National League in hitting
in 1903 and 1904; Napoleon Lajoie with a .426 league-leading
average for the 1901 Philadelphia Athletics; Ty Cobb, perhaps
the best pure hitter and also the nastiest Major Leaguer ever to
play the game; and the Cubs trio of Tinker-to-Evers-to-Chance.
It was also a time that ushered in a wicked but then-legal pitch
slung with heedless abandon and without remorse: the elusive
spitball.

On May 29, 1905, Elmer Stricklett, a journeyman Brooklyn pitcher now mostly forgotten, unloaded an errant moist-
ened missile that defied baseball physics. With a much nastier
break than a normal big league curve, the spitter was born. The
miscreant pitch may have been used as early as the late 1800s,
but it was reintroduced for real in 1902 by George Hildebrand,
who one day noticed the peculiar effect of outfield dew on a
hard throw. Hildebrand then developed the spitball and soon
taught the pitch to Stricklett, who seems to have introduced the

depraved missile at the Major League level. Stricklett proceeded to teach the spitter to at least two future Hall of Famers—Big Ed Walsh and Jack Chesbro—and once the spitball had emerged, it could really never be reined in again. It was declared illegal in 1920, but it went on through the twentieth century and into the new millennium. Post-1905 baseball was permanently altered by the spitter.

Cy Young was such a prodigious big league hurler that his name is still synonymous with masterful pitching. Young was an American League pitching czar, the achiever of lofty, unbreakable records in an era when sore arms did not count and complete games were expected. National Leaguer Christy Mathewson was cut from the same cloth, mowing down batters and leading his Giants with three World Series victories en route to the 1905 title. Both were consummate Hall of Famers and both pitched during the great spitball era, although they had mastered their craft long before the spitter emerged. Whether they also mastered, or even tested, the spitball is a matter of speculation, but it is interesting to note that Young managed to throw a no-hitter at the age of forty-one, not long after the spitter had debuted. There is no question that others did use the pitch—and continue to use it to this day.

The decades before the roaring twenties decidedly reflected Victorian attitudes, but baseball provided an escape that was bigger than life. Anything but prim and proper, the tobacco-spitting, sweaty, sometimes wayward ballplayers were a throwback to the roots of America itself, an industrious collection of misfits born of revolution and raised on fearless, no-holds-barred ingenuity. The American industrialists, adventurers, and entrepreneurs were risk-takers. Irreverent and self-willed, frequently willing to flout the law, and difficult to rein in, they left an often-romanticized American legacy of railroads, bridges, Wild West shows and circuses. Baseball, as it happens, began to offer an opportunity for the masses, both players and fans, to share in the excitement of flouting the rules, and not only get away with it, but win victories and even fame at the same time. As spitwads, spitballs, hidden balls, brush back pitches, stolen bases, pilfered signs, trash talk, and even brawls became commonplace, a new form of vicarious contumacy filled the baseball arena.

Unrestrained by lawsuits or civility, bench-clearing free-for-alls evolved as an early part of baseball and have remained an enigmatic part of an otherwise seemingly quixotic game. Romantic or not, these baseball donnybrooks are unique to the national pastime. Football, basketball, soccer and certainly hockey have their share of fighting, but baseball altercations are visibly different. Basketball incidents can be violent, but they are over in a flash. Hockey fights erupt regularly, but the two original combatants are usually the only fighters—the others grab each other and watch. Football fights, *per se*, do not even happen for the most part—in the era of helmets and pads, locking face guards is about as nasty as it usually gets. Moreover, in most sports, the fighting is generally limited to the players on the field—but not in baseball. Ty Cobb had a nasty habit of pummeling fans in the bleachers—a thing that seldom happened in other sporting events—until now of course. Much more recently a detail of Dodgers players charged the Wrigley Field stands after a fan reached over the wall and lifted a hat from a player in the visitors' bullpen. In baseball, fans return the favor, a few times each year invading the field in one condition or another, inviting still more altercations. The NBA Pistons-Pacers melee of 2004 notwithstanding, baseball brawls continue to spill in and out of the stands more than in any other American team sport.

Fights have been a peculiar feature of the game for over a hundred years. With few pads or equipment in the way, benches are emptied at the first sign of discord, almost always leading to a multi-player donnybrook. This was true in 1903 and 2003, including the American League Championship Series when the Yankees and Red Sox erupted into two fracases in the same game: Boston pitcher Pedro Martinez knocked down the charging seventy-two-year-old Yankees coach Don Zimmer, and a separate but no less bizarre fight broke out in the bullpen between two Yankee players and a Red Sox groundskeeper who was treated for cleat marks on his back.

Baseball is the only team sport built specifically around one-on-one confrontations. Certainly basketball, football and hockey are physical, and all sports have individual match-ups and even one-on-one play, but baseball necessarily has a personalized "here it comes, hit it if you can" attitude. With twenty-seven outs to each side in a game, there are more than fifty-four individual wars spotlighted between two proud, perhaps egotistical athletes—the pitcher and the batter. Because of the unique configuration of baseball, none of it gets lost in the action or flow of the game, so the pitcher-batter enmity is fueled by a relentless series of in-your-face, personalized match-ups. Each pitch is a singular event, a personal war between two fighters, so that the game seems closer to boxing than to a team sport. Emotions run high and are very personal, so when they are further ignited by the brush-back pitch, a hit batter, an errant curve or the boldfaced illegal spitball, the results are predictable.

With such perpetual one-on-one encounters, gaining a sliver of an advantage is at a high premium for both batter and pitcher. Just as the hitter uses everything from cork to superballs, to magic on his bats, the pitcher has an arsenal of his own brand of trickery and intimidation. Indeed, the entire art of pitching flows, in one form or another, from one common principle: deception. Changing speeds and location keeps a batter off balance, guessing, and sometimes second-guessing, himself. Even intimidation is a tool of deception, like brushing a hitter back to set up the outside pitch, but the best and most common deception stems from a pitcher's ability to alter the direction of a propelled ball in mid-flight.

The standard curveball is rooted in deceit, the whole purpose being to fool the batter. A longtime mainstay of baseball, the first in-game curve was probably thrown by under-hander Candy Cummins in the 1860s. Thrown slower than the fastball, the curve uses a spin applied to its seams in a manner that increases air resistance on one side of the ball, thus pushing the ball from its natural trajectory. The batter perceives a break in the flight of the ball as it approaches, sometimes downward, sometimes side-to-side, depending upon the pitcher's grip on the ball and type of release. The curve spins at a rate of about 1,500 revolutions per minute, roughly the same as a fastball, but it comes in slower and "bites" the air currents much differently.

Connecting on the curveball is a requirement of big league batters, but it is very difficult to do and is perhaps the most common impediment to an aspiring hitter making the Major Leagues. Remarkably, as much as the curveball bends and dips, it actually relies much more on a perceived deception than on actual physics, for tests show that even dramatic sweeping curves deviate from a normal path by at most about 3.5 inches.

How can this be? Hitters insist that some curves break a foot or more, leaving them swinging at nothing but air. The answer lies solely in the shell game of baseball and pitching—an illusion. Before a ball snaps 3.5 inches off-line somewhere around halfway to the plate, the batter's eye calculates where the ball would or should arrive. A small off-line deviation thirty or forty feet away presents an illusion that the ball will continue traveling in that same direction and perhaps miss the plate altogether. But then it snaps back, changing its flight direction so that the ball will catch the corner of the plate—or even the opposite corner. The batter's eyes and brain work together, erroneously believing the ball moved twelve to fourteen inches, but most of the change occurred only in the batter's mind, for the ball itself deviated only 3.5 inches from a direct path. The change in the angle of trajectory gives the impression that the ball will hit the outside of the plate, for example, but then a 3.5 inch deviation in mid-flight results in the ball actually traversing the inside corner. The batter, thus fooled, can manage to adjust and hit safely anyway, but he is more likely to swing and miss, fouling the pitch off, or to take offense at being brushed back or sometimes even hit by the errant pitch.

Deceptive as it may be, the curveball is legal under the rules. But it is a demanding pitch to throw and the greater the break the more difficult it is to execute. The appears to operate as a variation of the curveball, but in practice the spitball is also related to another tricky but legal pitch, the knuckleball.

The knuckler dips and jumps in dramatic and unpredictable ways because it depends upon a lack of spin. As the knuckleball makes its way to the hitter, the pattern of stitching on the baseball creates drag that causes the pitch to move significantly, due to an imbalance of forces across the seams on one side and a smooth surface on the other. The ball thus dances and flutters rather than following a predictable path. For that reason, the knuckleball confounds batters and catchers alike. However, it is difficult for a pitcher to master, so over the years only a handful of pitchers gained primary reputations as knuckleballers, including long time Major Leaguer Hoyt Wilhem, who was among the best, as were Phil Niekro and Wilbur Wood. But the pitch was so unpredictable that catchers had trouble controlling it and soon found themselves using oversized mitts, sometimes almost fifty inches in circumference, until the Major League rules were amended to limit the perimeter to thirty-eight inches.

The knuckle delivery is rough on the pitcher, too: it is impossible to control or even predict. It will move, to be sure, but where it goes is quite another thing. It is also difficult to master, because the pitcher must throw the ball off the knuckles with reasonable velocity but in a manner that exerts equal forces from all fingers almost perfectly so that the ball fails to spin upon release.

The illegal spitball is a tempting substitute: it also deploys a reduced air drag accomplished with the aid of saliva that causes the ball to slip from the pitcher's hand, sometimes with less rotation, but in any event with a smoother, wet surface sliding through the air. It can be thrown faster than the knuckleball, too, yet it still jumps and dips, sometimes dramatically. Although outlawed in 1920, the pitch is a seductive tool of deception and has been selectively used for decades.

George Frazier, a pitcher for the 1984 division-winning Cubs, threw the slimy pitch with abandon. Frazier says he learned it in 1983 when he was with the Yankees. He insists that Manager Billy Martin demanded he master the clandestine pitch in order to avoid being sent back to the minors. So Frazier obliged, learning the spitter from one of the best there ever was, Gaylord Perry. "I threw three in a row one day to [slugger] Dave Parker," Frazier says publicly. And when he found himself with the Cubs, pitching in Wrigley Field, a small park where Chicago winds often blow out, effective pitching was even more important—and tougher to do.

Frazier's mentor Gaylord Perry was the consummate magician on the mound, perfecting not only the delivery of illicit pitches, but the art of secretly doctoring the balls through deception and diversion, rendering him a virtual pitching Houdini. And he was a prodigious pitcher. In August of 1982, Perry fanned his hundredth batter of the year, the eighteenth time he had struck out at least that many in a single season, matching the record of Hall of Famers Walter Johnson and Cy Young. Highly effective and often intimidating, Perry was part pitcher, part showman, and part snake-oil salesman. He single-handedly embodied the brazen pioneer win-at-all-costs spirit, becoming the master not only of the spitball, but of the greaseball as well.

Spitting is only one way to moisten the baseball. Vaseline, hair gel, and other variations of grease would have the same—sometimes even better—effect on the trajectory of the ball. Perry not only hurled grease as well as anyone, but at one point his snake-oil side won out altogether as he capitalized on his well-earned reputation by marketing his brand of petroleum jelly to the general public. Adding to the Perry mystique, though, was a more subtle form of trickery: many of his antics may also have been part of a plan to get into a batter's head, if not under his skin.

Perry believed that his unsavory reputation was itself an edge, keeping batters off-balance, guessing what pitch might come next. Not only did Perry market the petroleum jelly, but his autobiography was audaciously titled *Me and the Spitter*. Perry milked his image on the mound, fidgeting incessantly, touching his face, mitt, cap, and uniform. It drove umpires and hitters to distraction, and probably helped to make his career a success. Whether Perry actually threw an illegal junk pitch at any given time, his tongue-in-cheek approach was itself a masterful slice of baseball gamesmanship. Indeed his junk reputation may have overshadowed his stellar overall career, for Perry pitched in the majors for twenty-two seasons, becoming the first pitcher to win the Cy Young Award in both leagues. Over that time he pitched 5351 innings, won 314 games with a career ERA of just 3.10, was a five-time All-Star and led the league in wins three times with records of 23-13 (1970), 24-16 (1972), and 21-6 (1978).

Notwithstanding Perry's antics on and off the mound, he expressly denied his spitball reputation. Although umpires often "undressed him" during games in a futile search for hardball contraband, Perry pitched in the majors for twenty years before being ejected for actually throwing a junked ball. But with or without jelly, grease, scuffs or saliva, Perry was a savvy pitcher with good-to-great stuff. In 1970 he threw four consecutive shutouts, capped a fifteen-game consecutive win streak in 1974, and no-hit Bob Gibson's Cardinals twice in separate years. But he always kept the hitters guessing.

As we have said, the spitball was officially banned in 1920. But on December 17, 1920, the American and National Leagues voted to grandfather in the existing spitball throwers. Any pitcher who threw the spitter in 1920 was allowed to continue to throw it for as long as he pitched in the leagues. Seventeen players stepped forward and continued to pitch the spitter for the rest of their careers. The last legal spitballer was Burleigh Grimes, a nineteen-year big leaguer who logged 4180 innings with 56 2/3 innings pitched in World Series games. Grimes hurled the spitball until he was finally released by the Pirates on October 11, 1934. Like Perry, he reveled in his image as a spitball thrower and, also like Perry, he often faked the spitter to keep the batters off balance. Both Perry and Grimes were elected to the Hall of Fame, although in Grimes's case it was all perfectly legal.

One result of the Grimes spitter was that Grimes had to grow a rather nasty beard. On days that he pitched, he chewed a special piece of slippery elm to generate extra saliva, but the stuff irritated his skin. The beard acted as a buffer, giving rise to his less than romantic nickname, "Ol' Stubblebeard." Another Grimes trait no doubt contributed to the effectiveness of his spitball and fake spitter. He was a headhunter. With a penchant for winging errant spitballs and an affinity for aiming at batters' heads, Grimes had an impressive one-two gimmick of intimidation and trickery good for 270 wins and a career ERA of 3.53.

The Grimes brush-back pitches were notorious, and he sometimes delivered them with abandon, if not venom. League scuttlebutt was that Grimes's notion of an intentional walk was to unleash four high and tight throws to the hitter's head. In one narrow victory over the Cubs in 1924, Grimes brushed back six batters in two innings, and on September 18, 1931, when batters did not yet wear helmets, he delivered a season-ending concussion to Mel Ott.

Two of Grimes's stranger encounters with baseball history involved the rare triple play—twice. In 1925 he lost a one-run, extra-inning game to the Cubs, due in part to his own hitting, or lack thereof, slamming into two double plays and an eleventh-inning triple play. Then, near the beginning of the 1929 season, Grimes switched roles, this time starting a triple play against the Braves.

Long after both Grimes and the spitball were officially retired in 1934, Browns pitcher Nelson Potter became, on July 20, 1944, the only pitcher in Major League history to be suspended for allegedly throwing the spitter—even though Potter denied throwing the pitch in the first place. Umpire Cal Hubbard, who had issued a warning, would have none of it. He tossed Potter after his second offense of the game, after which Potter was fined and suspended for ten more games.

Potter was hardly a one-pitch wonder; another delivery helped keep him in the Major Leagues for 1,686 innings: the screwball. A low-velocity pitch like the curve, the screwball released from a right-hander spins roughly top to bottom, but with a slight right-left bias along the axis. A curveball from the same pitcher would also spin downward, but with the opposite bias of left-right. Depending upon whether the pitcher and batter are respectively left-handed or right-handed, the screwball allows the pitcher's "curve" essentially to break away from the hitter in circumstances where the pitcher's natural curveball would break inward.

Although pitchers have evolved as a tricky lot, the ball itself has been known to play tricks on history, too. Allegedly the hardball has changed little under the rules. At the turn of the new millennium, the official Major League rules described a regulation baseball thusly:

> The ball shall be a sphere formed by yarn wound around a small core of cork, rubber or similar material, covered with two strips of white horsehide or cowhide, tightly stitched together. It shall weigh not less than five nor more than five and one quarter ounces . . . and measure not less than nine nor more than nine and one quarter inches in circumference.

Officially the ball is about five percent smaller than the 1861 rules allowed, as well as around nine percent lighter, and it can now have cork in the center—ironic, given the occasional penchant for corked bats—instead of just India rubber as in the distant past. Rules notwithstanding, however, the balls themselves are truly much different—so much so that the difference has certainly distorted baseball history in ways that may never be measured.

Until 1920, there was no rule or custom mandating fresh balls during the course of a game. Indeed, for nearly sixty years the practice was to utilize the same ball for the whole game, regardless of wear and tear on it or how mushy or lopsided it might become. The ball was replaced only when it was lost, and then only after the failure of a reasonable search in the stands or elsewhere. In 1920 the use of clean, new balls was mandated, and of course the spitball was outlawed. That was also the year Babe Ruth began his prodigious career with the Yankees, changing the game of baseball forever. Parenthetically, the ascension of Ruth and the concurrent alteration of those rules was no coincidence but, rather, a probable manipulation of the game by owners wanting to promote offensive firepower and excitement.

Other changes to the ball itself have also affected the game. The corked center was introduced in 1910 for the Cubs-Athletics World Series during which the combined teams batted .272, about twenty points higher than in the regular season. Even more dramatically, the following year, the first full season of the corked-center era, the number of American League players who batted .300 or better escalated from eight in 1910 to twenty-one, including Ty Cobb, who hit an astonishing .420.

Today the balls, including tightness of hide and elevation of stitching, benefit from superior technology.* Whether all the changes had measurable effects is difficult to say. For example, again in 1920, the yarn for the stitching was switched to Australian wool, causing some to speculate about whether that yarn change had an effect on the Ruthian blasts that were to come.

Nearly all baseball pundits acknowledge that the players themselves are much different today. As a group, the men are certainly

---

* The technology may have improved, but the method of sewing the balls is remarkably archaic. Rawlings supplies all the Major League baseballs from a cavernous sewing room in Costa Rica where 300 workers sit in high-backed chairs each stitching by hand, one at a time, as many as 35 balls per day.

bigger, stronger, quicker, faster. Nutrition and weight training are partly responsible, as steroids or other enhancers may have been, especially from the early 1990s. But pitchers still throw occasional junk, ranging from the legal knucklers and screwballs to spitters and scuffed balls, continuing the mischievous legacy of the game.

According to eccentric Red Sox pitcher Bill "Spaceman" Lee, who pitched in the great Boston-Cincinnati Series of 1975, Bill Singer of the Angels had a spitball "that could croon 'God Save the Queen' in forty different languages." Lee tells how in an All-Star game he saw Singer unleash a wicked spitter that broke dramatically as it passed batter Pete Rose, skipped by catcher Carlton Fisk, and dribbled all the way to the wall, inspiring Rose to remark to Fisk, "He surprised you more than me."

With ballplayers' history of spitting on and off the field, it is no wonder the spitter evolved, indeed it is remarkable it did not appear sooner. Baseball spitting—the unique chew-induced streams emitted throughout the course of a game—first appeared in the late 1800s when professionalism crept in, attracting more rough-edged players. Whether induced by tobacco, gum or sunflower seeds, spitting is unique to baseball. Experts suggest it is partly self-perpetuating as younger players emulate their heroes, but much of the phenomenon may be the product of the game itself, which is agonizing as well as entertaining. Tension builds slowly with each pitch, each swing, with each pitching change, and with each excruciating hit, walk, ground-out, or error. And since at any given time only three players in the park are actually doing anything—usually the pitcher, batter and catcher—there is no way for most of the others to work off the relentless tension as they sit on the bench or stand in the outfield—so spitting offers them a universal release. In this, too, baseball is uniquely American, a legacy of the gritty days of railroad men, cowboys, gangsters and the ballplayers themselves—from Cobb, Wagner, Young to the present.

Saliva breeds both spitballs and contempt, of course, but spitters are not the only means of stealing an out. Any well-thrown baseball will veer toward the side of the ball with the most physical resistance since this "drag" creates air resistance and currents of low pressure, both of which distort the flight of the ball. With spit, grease or jelly causing one side to slide through the air better, the natural drag of the seams and the dry covering on the other side intervenes, bending the trajectory. Just as the drag effect can be accomplished by smoothing one side, it can also be achieved by increasing the resistance on the other side with scuffmarks. Those marks occur naturally when pitches hit the dirt or are fouled off, causing umpires to replace over a hundred balls a game. But dexterous pitchers and catchers can skillfully scuff or mark the balls, too, albeit illegally. In his playing days, Leo Durocher was said to nick the balls on a belt buckle. Whitey Ford used a wedding ring for the same purpose.

There is at least one instance of a pitcher using a deformity to good, and perfectly legal, purpose. When he was seven, a farm accident left Cubs old-timer Mordecai "Three-Finger" Brown with three fingers (plus his thumb) on his throwing hand, one a useless pinky, the other a mangled index finger. The latter allowed him to grip and release the ball like no other pitcher, generating a strange spin on the ball that baffled hitters for fourteen seasons during the days of Ty Cobb and Christy Mathewson. Brown logged 239 wins and the third-best career ERA in the history of the game at 2.06.

Three Finger was a character on the mound, flinging bizarre pitches with abandon. Eccentricity is a common trait of pitchers, it seems, including the likes of Jim Bouton, Bill Lee, Randy Johnson, Phil Niekro and others, but they have no monopoly on baseball shenanigans. Batters, base runners, catchers and even stadium designers have all been known to behave strangely, often with mischievous intent.

3
Grass, Monsters and the Yankee Curtain

The unique size, shape, location and topography of every stadium has an impact on the game of baseball, sometimes intentionally, sometimes by accident, and often by mysterious acts of fate, if not of the supernatural.

As St. Louis Browns pitcher Ellis Kinder took the mound at Boston's famed Fenway Park on May 17, 1947, he was startled by a rude bolt from the baseball blue: a three-pound hapless smelt suddenly whizzed by his chin and thumped down abruptly at his feet.

Obviously, because Fenway is in a port city, Kinder's wayward missile had been dropped by a soaring seagull, probably with no allegiance to the Red Sox. The attack would be avenged in a manner of speaking thirty-seven years later when Detroit's Willie Horton launched a stove-pipe foul ball straight up from home plate, mortally wounding a Boston pigeon in mid-air, knocking it to the feet of surprised Red Sox catcher Bob Montgomery in the eighth inning of a Detroit shut-out win.

Although rarely influenced by such colorful interventions as dive-bombing smelts or plunging pigeons, the home-field ploys of Major League Baseball are nothing if not entertaining, cunning, and sometimes distinctly underhanded, including various fateful encounters with cats, squirrels, horses and, on at least two occasions, goats. Beginning with the development and subsequent manipulation of the field itself, mischief has evolved into an indelible part of the game.

To begin with, the playing area for baseball is called a "field" not by chance, but for particularly good reason. As the game emerged in the late 1800s, ball players roamed a hole-infested, root-marred, weed-plagued, rolling topography—indeed, a genuine, no-frills, in-the-middle-of-nowhere field that was anything but standardized, exposing baseball to creative play, gamesmanship and even mischief. The baseball fields of yesteryear were more likely to contain horse dung than fences, and in every case the base paths were just that: pathways. Dirt trails between the bases, as well as between home plate and the pitcher's mound, were not manicured as geometric base paths but, rather, were slowly worn into the infield by the feet of the players themselves. The outfields were by no means manicured, often rolling and dipping with the natural terrain.

Today the topography has been leveled—the exception being the bizzare thirty-degree slope in deep-center at Houston's Minute Maid Park—but modern baseball continues to shun uniformity more than any other major team sport. There are rules, of course, and a modicum of uniformity to render baseball a game rather than a free-for-all, but many of the rules invite contradiction and provide opportunity for endless shenanigans. For example, although today's regulation hardball is manufactured to a precise standard, the bats can be radically different within a much looser range of tolerance. In addition, the size and shape of every Major League outfield is intrinsically different, as is each and every foul territory, the location of bullpens, the size and location of outfield walls, upper decks, light standards, the length of infield grass—or even whether there is infield grass. These distinctions are reminiscent of a golf course rather than soccer or field hockey fields. Each golf course differs radically from every other golf course—yes, there are also uniform golf rules, of course, defining *ad infinitum* out-of-bounds markers, shape of clubs and size of holes, but the size and configuration of each golf course are left to the creative powers of its designer as with baseball's diverse parks.

Deceit is often a creature of opportunity, and few games offer opportunity like our national pastime. It all began innocently enough, because unpredictable events sometimes get in the way of the game, as when Charley Radbourn stepped to the plate on August 17, 1882. Charles "Old Hoss" Radbourn was a great pitcher, who went on to win thirty-one games that year for the Providence Grays and a legendary sixty games two years later in 1884, during his superhuman seventy-three complete game season. Although Charley sometimes played the outfield, he was a less than stellar hitter, so when he stepped up against Detroit that sultry August day, both fate and the Providence outfield played a notable role in his hitting career. So did the Detroit outfielders, who consisted that eventful afternoon of four players—three in Detroit uniforms and a fourth who wore only a bridle and four horseshoes.

Of the four, it was the wayward Providence horse that played the biggest role. When Old Hoss Radbourn picked up his bat, it was the eighteenth inning of a grueling tie-game, with the sky growing darker by the minute as the Providence sun slid slowly from sight. Charley Radbourn himself had never, ever, hit a home run. And the long ball seemed even less likely at Providence, a field with no outfield fence and enough long grass to choke a hay baling machine.

Tired and worn from virtually two games rolled into one, "Old Hoss" took his weary rip at destiny, connecting on a Stump Weidman pitch, smashing it to left field past Detroit's long ball king George Wood. The ball skipped its way to a wagon in the outfield where it rolled to the back hoof of a spirited black horse. As the desperate Wood dove to save the game, the horse kicked, and Wood came up empty. When Wood again reached for the wayward ball, the horse kicked again while a surprised "Old Hoss" Radbourn continued his gallop past first base and then around second.

The remaining crowd held its collective breath as the resource-ful outfielder Wood futilely tempted the beast with a clump of outfield grass. When the intractable horse snubbed Wood's offer-ing, the desperate outfielder clubbed the ball away with a stray stick and finally launched it back toward the infield. By then, of course, fate had successfully intervened as Radbourn streaked over home plate to wrest victory for the home team Grays.

The freedom to tailor fields and parks to unbridled home-team ingenuity is, however, a predictable recipe for mischief. In baseball, even home teams collectively win only about fifty-three percent of their games—a ratio that is far narrower than in foot-ball or basketball which, at the turn of the millennium, aggre-gated a home-win ratio closer to sixty percent. The 1927 Yan-kees, perhaps the most legendary professional team ever as-sembled, enjoyed a lofty .740 home record—a mammoth ac-complishment by baseball standards—but this still means they lost more than a fourth of their home games. By contrast, the great NBA teams often win nearly ninety percent of their home contests and even inept NBA clubs frequently have winning home records—the chameleon 2002 Chicago Bulls were a futile 3-38 on the road and a sparkling 27-14 at home. Michael Jordan's 1996 World Champion Bulls were 72-10 overall, win-ning 87.7 percent of their total games. Those Bulls were 39-2 in Chicago, a sizzling ninety-five percent home pace, and they won just over eighty percent on the road at 33-8. By contrast, the great 1927 Yankee team achieved a season record of 110-44, a 71.4 percent overall win ratio[*] with a stellar but more mortal road record of 68.8 percent.

Equality in sports breeds desperation. The extreme parity of baseball places a special premium on getting an edge at every opportunity, emphasizing the little things to distraction and re-

---

[*] A highly curious—but no doubt meaningless—coincidence is that the Mur-derers' Row .714 team winning percentage was precisely equal to Ruth's career record home runs: 714.

lying to an inordinate degree on manipulation, if not cheating—and therein lies the root of hardball skullduggery.

Every baseball field has a different effect on the game, often intentionally. In a brazen attempt to enhance the home-run prowess of its new left-handed slugger, New York constructed Yankee Stadium in 1923 especially for the Babe, featuring a grotesquely short right-field line at only 294.75 feet. By contrast, Chicago's Wrigley Field, known as a hitter's park and pitcher's nightmare, has a right field line of 355 feet. Yankee Stadium's right foul line was extended to 310 feet in 1976 and 314 feet in 1988, still short by big league standards. Consequently, New York historically sought to stack its lineup with left-handed sluggers from Babe Ruth and Lou Gehrig to Roger Maris and Reggie Jackson, not to mention switch hitters like Mickey Mantle. Although manipulative, such creative designs are by no means illegal or among the most outrageous big league acts, but the Yankees right-field foul line may have been one of the most effective machinations, contributing to the legendary seasons of Ruth, Gehrig, Mantle, Maris and Reggie Jackson.

The dynamic evolution of ballparks helped create baseball as a fluid, spontaneous game. But its unguarded, almost offhand character would open the door for rough-and-tumble behavior that both entertained and captivated the receptive public. As the nineteenth century neared its close, most ballparks were at least partially enclosed, but their differences were considerable. Lake Front Park in Chicago was thought to be a state- of-the-art facility, but it was cramped into inadequate space along Lake Michigan. Grotesquely small, Lake Front Park was only 180 feet to left field and just 300 feet to deep center—in some ways smaller than a contemporary Little League field. Its entire area would have been lost in Boston's expansive Huntington Avenue Grounds that would host the first World Series in 1903. Huntington sported a dead-center marker of 635 feet, about 230 feet longer than most modern Major League fields.

Constructed in 1913, Brooklyn's Ebbets Field suggested the configuration of parks to come, but still it seemed twisted, with left field a spacious 419 feet from home plate while right field was a near band-box distance of 301. The strangest shape, though, may have been that of the legendary Polo Grounds, built in 1911 and later reconfigured after a fire. The foul lines at the Grounds were a minuscule 260 feet while center field was a stunning five hundred feet, strongly suggesting a sort of elongated egg.

As baseball ingenuity and physics began to cross paths, so did the "inner game" of hardball. Just as Yankee Stadium's short right field invites lefty sluggers, Ebbets Field penalized right-handers. But manipulating outfield distances was by no means the only way to influence games. Though not even technically in the field of play, the size of foul territory has a significant impact upon hitting and runs scored. Although Wrigley Field's relatively modest dimensions are a challenge to pitchers, it is not grotesquely small—but its scant foul territory is another matter altogether. There was little foul ground behind the plate, and there is even less since the Cubs added two rows of new seats between the dugouts in 2004. The stands hug the foul lines in right and left fields, giving many a batter multiple second chances as fouled pitches easily find their way to the safety of a fan's mitt.

The snug, oft-manipulated confines of Wrigley can backfire, of course, and no greater example of that was the nationally televised fan interference during the Cubs' 2003 League Championship Series against the Marlins where, at a most crucial moment of a most critical game six, a Chicago fan robbed left fielder Moises Alou of a key second-out catch. That missive, along with a fading Mark Prior on the mound and a rare shortstop miscue, sent the Cubs back into their century-long tailspin. The fan, decked out with earphones, Cubs hat and a distinctive sweatshirt, inspired one of the most popular Halloween costumes in mortified Chicagoland.

As I have said, it is common baseball knowledge that some fields function as hitters' parks, while others are clearly pitcher friendly, and this is rarely a mere coincidence. Manipulating distance and foul territory is one thing, but what about fences and walls? Baseball physics plays tricks with the height and location of outfield barriers, but not in ways many fans would think about. It is logical to believe that high outfield walls and short distances cancel each other out, neutralizing the home-run effect—but they do not. Studies show that home runs are not the product of head-high line drives. They almost always drop into the stands as fly balls—even those that look like line drives have a significant natural arc over the course of their four hundred feet or so, dropping over the highest outfield walls.

But one wall that undeniably affects game results is the left field wall of Boston's Fenway Park. To opposing batters, the legendary "Green Monster" is an intimidating obstacle, but to Boston players it is a tool of the trade as they play the wall both at the plate and in left field. Oddly, although Fenway became a renowned hitters' park; when it was originally constructed in 1912 it was a home-run slugger's bad dream. Although the original foul lines were modest—324 feet to left and 313 to right—the outfield extended to 488 in center and a whopping 550 feet just to the right of center field. As originally constructed, Fenway discouraged home runs—total homers were fifty percent less compared to the remainder of the league—but its cavernous outfield invited singles and doubles so that overall run production was just five percent below the league average.

Fenway was reconfigured in 1934, complementing its short foul lines with more manageable outfield carries of 379 feet to left center, 389 to center, 420 just to the right of center, and then 380 in true right center. And of course the green monster wall in left field still looms. Estimates suggest that the redesigned Fenway increased home runs by twelve percent and runs scored by as much as fourteen percent over a typical neutral park. In the sixty-six seasons from the 1934 remodeling to the turn of the millennium, Red Sox batters led the league in hitting a stunning twenty-two times—exactly a third of all those years, showcasing such legendary players as Jimmie Foxx, Ted Williams, Carl Yastrzemski, Fred Lynn and Wade Boggs—not to mention the out-of-nowhere (out of the Cubs, actually) Bill Mueller of 2003.

Contributing most to the monster lore may have been Boston icons Williams and Yastrzemski. Both were left-handed power hitters, and both played left field in the shadow of the demon wall. Between them, Yaz and Williams roamed those left field shadows from 1939 to 1983, an impressive career of forty-four years, though twice interrupted for Williams' war service. The two Hall of Famers played very differently at Fenway, however. Ted Williams simply outshone everyone at Fenway. He won baseball's Triple Crown twice and was the last man to hit over .400 for the season. Although Williams excelled at home with career Fenway numbers including a .361 average, 248 homers and 965 RBIs, his aggregate road statistics would still translate to a career .328 average, 37 annualized long ball jacks, and 119 RBIs per season.

Yaz, however, may never have attained the Hall of Fame if it weren't for the dynamics of Fenway. He was a great hitter and the last American Leaguer to snare the Triple Crown, but away from Boston, Yastrzemski's cumulative numbers translate to those of a typical, near-journeyman season with a quality .264 average, twenty-one home runs, and seventy-eight RBIs.

Ted Williams, Yaz, and other Boston icons learned to play the monster wall both at the plate and in the field. And although visiting teams continue to find the monster intimidating, it is not, interestingly, its thirty-seven-foot height alone that gives batters fits—it is its distance. Fearfully close to the hitter, the wall is listed at 315 feet down the left-field line, but it is rumored to be even closer, knocking down countless line drives, often converting prodigious smashes into benign singles as the ball caroms back to fielders experienced at playing the wall.

Although overshadowed by the Green Monster, Fenway offers a myriad of other peculiar features, including its notable lack of symmetry and one extremely odd trait of baseball topography. Before 1934, Fenway Park sported a raised left field that sloped upward a full ten feet. Dubbed "Duffy's Cliff" in honor of Duffy Lewis, the Sox left fielder of the day, the vexing incline provided a dramatic reach advantage, but it must have confounded opposing outfielders navigating the uneven turf.

In baseball, size—or the lack thereof—certainly matters. The deepest portion of Fenway was 420 feet from the plate, but in 1940 the charismatic new slugger Ted Williams inspired the Red Sox to install bullpens in the same area, cutting the right-field power alley to a respectable 380 feet. It was a brazen effort to manipulate the park in order to pad Williams' home-run production, but there were no protests because, after all, that's baseball. A similar effort to raise a home-court basketball rim or to narrow one end of a football field would be deemed outrageous, laughable, and grotesquely contrary to league rules. But therein lies the essence of baseball the game and baseball the icon: it is different from other sports, and its potential for legend is thus multiplied geometrically, making the "art" of baseball a much more human—indeed, a much more American craft.

Both Yankee Stadium and Fenway Park were intentionally designed to gain advantages for their team superstars, but these were by no means isolated examples of shenanigans in the field. Wrigley grass has been known to grow a little longer in some eras, especially when the Cubs fielded a relatively slow team. The foul territory at Wrigley penalizes the pitchers, the outfield ivy confounds opposing fielders, and for nearly forty years the Cubs' perversely obstinate aversion to lights worked against them because they had to play so many day games, which tired them out.

Before the Wrigley ivy, which was the brainchild of baseball legend Bill Veeck as a young man in 1937, there was Chicago's

West Side Grounds where the Cubs played from 1893 to 1915, moving to Wrigley in 1916. Wrigley Field had been built two years before, in 1914, at a total cost of $250,000, but was originally named Weeghman Park after the owner of its first tenants, the Federal League's Chicago Whales. In the Cubs' early years at West Side, they were not called the Cubs but the Colts. For a time, West Side Park hosted not only the Colts/Cubs, but also the Cleveland Spiders who needed a home after their Cleveland stadium burned down in 1898.

The West Side Grounds did not offer ivy, but it did contribute to the quirky legend of the game in other ways. One afternoon in 1896 a then-staggering crowd of more than 17,000 inspired the umpire to rule that all balls hit into the throngs of fans would be a ground rule triple. Result? Nine triples by the Colts in a 16-7 thrashing of St. Louis. It was a notable ruling, because as we have said, at that time balls were customarily searched out, retrieved from the stands, and re-used in the game. West Side seems to have had a strange knack for provocative rulings. In May of 1892, the Giants' Christy Mathewson lost a game to the Cubs 4-0, but the defeat was erased the next day when the umpire ruled that Cubs pitcher Jack Taylor had been illegally pitching in front of the rubber, rendering the game a nullity and extinguishing all records, including Taylor's shutout and Mathewson's loss.

Not only did those fields sway umpires, but they also provided the language with one of contemporary culture's most enduring baseball idioms: "out of left field." The West Side Grounds were located just southwest of Chicago's Loop district. According to accounts of the day, visiting teams were impressed by a singular group of fans who watched the game not *in* the ballpark but from a mental facility looming over the left field fences *beyond* the park. The patients—in those days more commonly referred to as inmates—had a tendency to lean out the windows on hot summer days, observing the action in their own peculiar manner. Over time the visiting players noticed the

strange goings-on "in left field," and eventually ballplayers everywhere began referring to odd, quirky or dubious behavior
anywhere as emanating "from left field."

When the Cubs moved to Wrigley, a slice of baseball history was altered forever. It was at Wrigley Field that Babe Ruth
helped win a Cubs-Yankees World Series in 1932 and steal a
page of baseball history with his "called shot" gesture, followed
immediately by a smash home run off Cubs pitcher Charlie Root.
Whether the Babe actually called that shot by pointing his bat
to the stands is often the subject of debate. Surviving films suggest Ruth may have done so, but the legend has become more
important, inviting this line from the annals of Hollywood cin-
ema: "when the legend becomes fact, print the legend."

It was at Wrigley that Olympic legend Jim Thorpe broke up
the only nine-inning dual no-hitter in baseball history, the 1917
duel between pitchers Hippo Vaughn against Fred Toney of the
Reds. Pete Rose caught up to Ty Cobb on the all-time list with
his 4,191st Major League hit at Wrigley; Ernie Banks blasted
homer number five hundred there; and during the 2003 playoffs Sammy Sosa nearly became the first player ever to hit the
classic scoreboard in dead center field, Sosa's mammoth shot
landing just to the left before a national television audience.

One thing that has never happened at Wrigley is an assault
on its classic manual scoreboard looming well up over the stands
in deep center. In 1926, Hack Wilson hit the previous scoreboard that was located at ground level, but the current version,
installed in 1937, has been hit only by Sam Snead, who bounced
a golf ball off its green face during a 1951 pre-game exhibition.
Roberto Clemente once came close with a shot that landed near
Sammy Sosa's playoff smash, and in 1948, Bill Nicholson skied
a moon shot that sailed past the scoreboard, exited the park
altogether, bounced off a building and eventually clunked the
hood of a moving car.

The three oldest stadiums in use today are rich in baseball
legends. While Fenway Park (1912), Wrigley Field (1914) and

Yankee Stadium (1923) may have the most colorful history, reflecting both glory and skullduggery, they certainly do not stand alone.

The Pittsburgh Pirates played at Forbes Field from 1909 to 1970, a sixty-two-season span without any no-hitter at any time—and that was no accident. Named after the general who founded Pittsburgh, Forbes did have an enormous foul territory behind home plate that favored pitchers, but the field itself was cavernous, inviting bloop hits and line drives of every variety. It also deployed left-field bullpens to create favorable hitting targets to its star sluggers Ralph Kiner and Hank Greenberg, providing a shorter left-field landing area, eventually known as "Greenberg Gardens."

Interestingly, although Babe Ruth played in the American League during most of his career, he ended in the National League with the Boston Braves and there contributed mightily to Forbes Field history. The last three home runs of Ruth's illustrious career came at Forbes Field—all on the same day, May 25, 1935, making Ruth the first to log triple dinger games in both leagues, just once in each league. Ruth had blasted 708 home runs in the American League, but only once in all those years did he club three in one game. Suddenly, on one spring day in 1935, the forty-year-old slugger erupted once again at Forbes.

Whether the aging Ruth was mystically endowed that fateful day, or whether he simply surprised a pair of National League pitchers who were not prepared for the Bambino, or if someone grooved the slugger a pitch or two—it didn't and doesn't matter. Ruth achieved one of the two most magical walk-off home runs in history. The more recent was the Ted Williams career walk-off blast on September 28, 1960, when "The Kid," at age forty-two, launched the last-ever long ball shot in the eighth inning at Fenway, then walked away, took a seat in the dugout, and never emerged again. But the most extraordinary career-ending blast was appropriately clubbed by Ruth himself at Pittsburgh.

Babe Ruth's third home run on May 25, 1935, off Pirates pitcher Guy Bush, made history three ways at once. It was a thunderous, true Ruthian blast that rocketed six hundred feet, the very first ball to clear the park over the Forbes Field right-field grandstand. The awesome blast was not lost on Bush, a veteran hurler with years on the mound, who later reflected, "I never saw a ball hit so hard before or since . . . It's probably still going."

Forbes Field is no more, but its home plate is on display in the University of Pittsburgh library on the field site. Interestingly, Boston's Northeastern University also pays homage to a baseball legend. A life-size statue of Cy Young stands in the middle of the campus at the precise location of the pitchers mound from the old Huntington Avenue Grounds that once occupied that site.

Because of the nature of baseball, every stadium is unique in one way or another, each leaving a special imprint on the game. Although many of the memorable early shenanigans started in Boston, New York and Chicago, two stadiums built in the 1960s and 1980s may have affected the game in radically different ways.

When the Houston Astrodome opened in 1965, it was hailed as the Eighth Wonder of the World. That may have been an overstatement, but the facility was really dramatic in size and scope. Its colossal roof spanned 660 feet and the field quickly became a pitcher's park. The cavernous original dimensions of 420 feet to center and 360 down the lines were eventually reduced to 400 and 325, but the ball never carried well in the vast air-conditioned atmosphere, which penalized hitters and caused many pitchers to miss being named to the Hall of Fame, including some, like Nolan Ryan, who were later inducted.

Surprisingly, when the dome opened, there was real grass on the field, but the fielders had fits coping with the clear sunlit dome. When the roof was painted to reduce glare, the natural grass died and the turf was painted green. Monsanto Chemical saved the day with a new breed of artificial grass and turf immediately christened "Astro Turf," changing not only baseball but soon NFL football as well.

Domes today are more sophisticated, of course, even featuring retractable roofs, but the early versions, though impressive, had many quirks that influenced the evolution of baseball. Normal fly balls and even home runs were not impeded by the Astrodome structure, but skyward line drives and monster pop-ups were quite another thing. Powerful Phillies slugger Mike Schmidt once rocketed a skyward rope that clunked a public address speaker suspended from the Astrodome roof three hundred feet from home plate. The ball rebounded to the field for an impressive single. Astro Turf, hanging debris, cavernous dimensions and dead air are some of the elements that penalized hitters and rewarded pitchers. Furthermore, once, on June 15, 1976, torrential Houston rains prevented the visiting team, umpires and most fans from entering the stadium, and the game had to be cancelled.

Taking a page from Houston was the Hubert H. Humphrey Metrodome that opened in downtown Minneapolis for the 1982 Twins season. Some quickly called it the "Hump Dome," recalling the 1960s "dump the hump" chant during Senator Humphrey's vice presidency. Others labeled it the "Homer Dome" when 191 balls were tagged for home runs in its first baseball season. Soon air conditioning was added and the left-field fences raised to thirteen feet, cooling off the long ball but still leaving the dome with one of the hardest, quickest surfaces in the majors.

The Metrodome's most notable influence on the game may have been the crowds: the dome acoustics produce a deafening clamor that still disrupts, and even intimidates, visiting teams. Like the Houston dome, the Metrodome had its own quirks that went down in baseball history. In 1984, Dave "King Kong" Kingman skied a prodigious infield pop-up that simply never came down—ever. The ball, as it happens, was not in orbit but had lodged in a dome ceiling drainage hole. It surely would have been caught by a fielder anywhere else, but with little down-to-earth explanation at the time, the umpires improvised a ground-rule (or was it a "sky-rule"?): a double. Kingman fared much better than Detroit's Rob Deer, who in consecutive at-bats during a May 1992 game in the Metrodome, caromed two pop-ups off the roof, both of which were caught for outs.

When Yankee Stadium was built with a short right field to accommodate the home-run power of Babe Ruth; and then, when for years the Yankee team was stocked with left-hand power to perpetuate the ruse, nary an eyebrow was ever raised. More recently, a green curtain in Yankee Stadium was designed to shade the blur of center-field shirts in the batter's line of sight, a practice not much different from the creation by many teams of a favorable background for hitters. But then the curtain became fluid, sometimes raised or lowered almost like a window shade, depending upon which team was batting. That, too, is a ruse, but it is open for all to see. Sure, it's a mischievous, even juvenile trick. But that's baseball.

Although the fields, stadiums and stands can be, and often are, manipulated for devious purposes, they are no match for the antics on the field and in the stands by players, managers, fans—and even by animals. But one thing we know for sure—you cannot steal first. Or can you?

4

STEALING FIRST

IT IS BLACK-LETTER BASEBALL law that a player cannot steal first base. Yet Germany Schaefer did just that while playing for the Washington Senators.

The Senators had traveled to Chicago to play a struggling White Sox team. It was a tie game in the bottom of the ninth on August 4, 1911, a particularly torrid summer day in the Windy City, when Schaefer was suddenly inspired to swipe first. He began by laying down a good sacrifice bunt, moving teammate Clyde Milan from second to third. The play was at third base where Milan beat the throw, allowing Schaefer to reach first. With Kid Elberfeld at the plate, Schaefer stole second. Elberfeld popped out, leaving runners on second (Schaefer) and third (Milan). When Doc Gessler struck out, both runners failed to advance, remaining respectively at second and third with two outs.

With veteran Sox pitcher Doc White on the mound, Schaefer took a lead off second—toward *first* base. No one noticed the mischievous lean, but everyone was soon mortified when Schaefer bolted for first base, which he made easily. The surprised Sox manager Hugh Duffy exploded from the dugout, hurling profanities at the umpire—one might wonder why, since having Schaefer on first was beneficial to Chicago. During Duffy's colorful fit of rage, Schaefer was impishly inspired to take off again, this time full throttle back to second base, drawing a precise throw from the catcher Freddy Payne that beat Schaefer and stranded him between first and second.

With all the ensuing excitement erupting among the catcher, second and first base, the man on third, Clyde Milan, suddenly broke for the plate. His attempt to steal a run failed when the Sox first baseman shot a rocket to home where Milan was tagged for the third out, ending the inning on a dramatic note. The Senators protested en masse, insisting that the White Sox had ten men on the field during the whole fiasco, which they did, counting manager Hugh Duffy, who was still on the field arguing about the first transgression. The umpire ruled against these new protestations, citing the Senators for causing the ruckus in the first place. Eventually, Milan did finally score to win the game, but not until a failed double play attempt had allowed him to cross the plate in the eleventh inning.

The inverted base-stealing scheme was by no means Germany Schaefer's only dramatic display: he was an eccentric ballplayer for more reasons than one, contributing to baseball lore and reflecting the American spirit of resourceful mischief. During one game-shortened downpour in 1906, Schaefer mocked the umpires by playing the last innings in a raincoat. On another occasion in Chicago, Schaefer jacked a pinch home run and then slid into all four bases en route to home. After he retired from baseball, the charismatic Schaefer remained a showman, partnering with former teammate Charley O'Leary in a baseball-based vaudeville act that was the inspiration for the Gene Kelly/Frank Sinatra hit film, *Take Me Out to the Ballgame*.

Schaefer was hardly the only entertainer in a game filled with charismatic stars. One was the impulsive Jimmy Piersall. Ripping a page from Schaefer's base-running antics, Piersall banged his hundredth home run with a blast at Shea Stadium off pitcher Dallas Green, the future Phillies and Cubs manager, on June 23, 1963, and promptly celebrated with a trot around the bases—running backward the whole way. Piersall had broken into the majors eleven years before with the Red Sox where he soon suffered a nervous breakdown that he describes in his autobiography, *Fear Strikes Out*. But he came back with energy and style.

Outspoken, brash, funny and knowledgeable, Piersall knew the game cold and played it with gusto, never quite taking it seriously, playing baseball for what it was and is: a game. Piersall's playful personality recognized few limits. He was actually ejected in 1960 when, in an obnoxiously playful attempt to distract the great hitter Ted Williams, who was once his teammate, Piersall broke into a war dance in the outfield while playing for the Indians. But that was no more outrageous than another antic that found Piersall brashly hiding behind the venerable player monuments guarding the outfield at Yankee Stadium. Piersall's eventual motto embodied a refreshing approach to baseball as entertainment: "Give 'em their money's worth." That he did over a span of 1,734 colorful games during which he was a two-time All-Star, winning the Gold Glove twice before his post-retirement stint as a brash White Sox broadcaster and eventually a part-time Cubs coach.

Piersall and Schaefer notwithstanding, the most notorious miscue in baseball history was committed with such indelible verve that it altered the course of a pennant and haunted at least one life forever. It all began and ended with a single unforgettable gaffe on the bases by one Fred Merkle, a gaffe that would always be known as "Merkle's Boner."

The Cubs' Three-Finger Brown met Christy Mathewson, the immortal Giants pitcher, in what amounted to a one-game playoff for the 1908 pennant that some regard as one of the most controversial baseball contests ever played. The tight pennant race was going to the wire, and the Giants were barely in first by a scant percentage over the second-place Cubs on September 23, 1908. The game was tied with two outs in the ninth with the Giants threatening. It was the first start of the year for nineteen-year-old Merkle who was filling in for veteran Fred

Tenney and about to make baseball history. The Giants had two men on base, Merkle himself at first and Harry McCormick on third, when Al Bridwell singled to score McCormick for an apparent Giants victory. But the win never happened. When he saw McCormick score from third, Merkle turned away, walked off the base path and headed for the clubhouse past center field.

Meanwhile, the alert center fielder retrieved the ball, throwing it back to the infield to Joe Tinker. Giants' first base coach Joe McGinnity saw the dangerous play developing and took immediate action, fighting Tinker for the ball and then throwing it into the surging crowd. Rube Kroh, a Cubs pitcher not officially in the game at the time, insisted he saw which fan grabbed the ball. Kroh chased the fan down and lunged for the ball. When the fan stubbornly refused to relinquish control, Kroh responded the American way and punched the fan out, wrested the ball from him, forged through the crowd, and handed it to Johnny Evers at second base. Evers stepped on the bag for the force out on Merkle—the third out, which the umpire eventually ruled valid. The game was declared a tie, because by that time the crowd had completely overrun the field and darkness was falling. The next day, the Giants went on to defeat the Cubs in the next scheduled game of the series but, alas, when the last day of the season finally arrived, the Cubs and Giants found themselves at 98-55 each, with the Merkle Boner game still lingering in a tie.

On October 8, the two teams met each other one last time to play the protracted make-up game at the Polo Grounds. Over a quarter-million rabid fans showed up and stormed the gate, forcing firemen to subdue them with high-pressure hoses. Eventually 35,000 spectators were allowed entry and 40,000 more found alternate vantage points from atop everything from telephone poles to Coogan's Bluff.

As fate would have it, pitchers Mathewson and Brown faced each other again, the latter in long relief. Three-Finger bested

Mathewson for a 4-2 Cubs win, Brown's twenty-ninth of the season, propelled largely by a key triple from Joe Tinker. Fred Merkle's play, therefore, had doomed the Giants, and he lived with that error for the rest of his life, stuck with the colorful moniker "Bonehead Merkle."

Merkle always maintained he had received confirmation from the umpire that the game was over and McCormick's run had scored. The true boner, then, may have been committed by the umpire, but that version of the facts was overruled and the Cubs eventually ended up with the pennant, which they may actually have stolen, notwithstanding the Merkle Boner play. Not only had the ball been delivered to second base by a player not even in the game, but there was also considerable disagreement about whether the official ball had found its way to Johnny Evers at all. Some accounts suggest it was a bogus plant and not the game ball that was mugged from a fan, and if so, Merkle would not have been officially out under the rules. No matter. The Cubs ended up with the pennant, defeating the Tigers in five games to snare the World Series victory behind the .421 hitting of Frank Chance. That's baseball. That's history.

At the end of the day, then, it appears that fate had intervened to steal both the Boner game and the pennant for the Cubs, but as it happens, Rube Kroh or may have helped fate by scrounging up a phony ball for the alleged fateful out on Merkle. It was not the first or last time, however, that deceit would intervene through a fateful game ball—not by a long shot.

The great hidden ball trick has been around for over a century and was deployed for the first and only time in World Series history in 1907 when the Tigers met the Cubs for the title. Not surprisingly, it was effected by none other than the perpetual miscreant Germany Schaefer, who stole an out at the expense of Detroit's Bill Coughlin en route to a Chicago Series sweep. The hidden ball stratagem is deployed when an infielder pretends to throw the ball back to the pitcher, but keeps it instead, luring a base runner to take his normal lead, exposing himself to a sudden pick-off. It has been successfully accomplished fewer than 150 times in all, nailing journeymen and stars alike, as when the Mets nailed Houston's Jimmy Winn in 1963.

Sometimes a variation of the hidden ball is improvised on the spot, as happened with the gutter ball fake-out at Wrigley Field on July 1, 1958, that stole an inside-the-park home run. Batting for the Cubs, Tony Taylor jerked a ball past third base as Giants left-fielder Leon Wagner gave chase. The ball landed in fair territory and rolled its way into a rain gutter past the Cubs bullpen. Sensing an opportunity, the Cubs pitchers in the pen began staring under the bench together, misdirecting Wagner, who could not find the ball resting fifty feet down the line, while Taylor circled the bases home.

As tricky as the hidden ball ploy may be, it certainly has nothing on the hidden potato trick instigated just once, so far as we know, by Dave Bresnahan, an anemic hitter for the Class AA Williamsport Bills. As described by Greg Couch of the *Chicago Tribune*, the stealthy play "didn't start with a windup and a pitch, but with Dave Bresnahan going to the grocery store to buy some potatoes." Bresnahan, a catcher, peeled a number of the contraband spuds, drew fake laces with a red marker to disguise them as baseballs, and then hid one in his spare glove, leaving it on the bench as he took his place on the field.

In the fifth inning, with two outs and an opposing player on third base, Bresnahan called time and switched gloves. He caught the next pitch, but then fired the red-seamed potato down to third, intentionally missing everyone as it sailed into left field. Sensing an obvious opportunity, the base runner on third bolted for home where he met up with Bresnahan and, to his great surprise, the game ball, promptly notching the third out of the inning. The trick worked for the moment—except that it cost Bresnahan his job, the "out" was reversed and the aborted run scored after all. But it had an aftermath worthy of master showman Bill Veeck himself: the next night you could get into the fame for a buck, if you brought a potato with you and, what's more, Bresnahan was there signing autographs.

Those kinds of in-your-face surprises on the base paths can cause hard feelings, and there is no shortage of player altercations at all levels, including the big leagues. On July 2, 1939, for example, the Dodgers' Leo "Nice Guys Finish Last" Durocher grounded into a double play and took it out on the Giants' Zeke Bonura, spiking the first baseman as Durocher crossed the bag. Bonura took great offense and ran Durocher down, throwing his mitt at Leo, then engaging him in an all-out wrestling match, earning an ejection for both players. And just two weeks later, those same Giants sparked an on-field battle themselves when Billy Jurges and umpire George Magerkurth disputed a fly ball by spitting on each other, earning a double ten-day suspension.

One day in 1960, superstars Frank Robinson and Eddie Mathews actually got into a fistfight at third base after Robinson had slid in hard—too hard in the opinion of Mathews, who quickly retaliated, giving Robinson a swollen eye, a bloody nose and a jammed thumb. Sometimes these wayward altercations don't reach a physical level, but start and finish with little more than trash talk on the bases. One of the more colorful such incidents was the 1962 exchange between the Giants' Orlando Cepeda and a Reds pitcher. Cepeda, who frequently spoke Spanish to teammates Juan Marichal and two of the Alou brothers, was perched on second when the pitcher barked, "Don't you know how to speak English?" The entire infield was treated to Cepeda's succinct, articulate reply, "Kiss my ass, you cock-sucker—is that English enough for you?"

As nasty as on-field altercations may be, from Ty Cobb to Roger Clemens and others, they are overshadowed by acrimonious encounters between players and the stadium crowds. There have been legions of these encounters—like Rube Kroh slugging a fan in the midst of the Merkle Boner melee, and Cobb invading the stands to bludgeon a disabled fan who, as it turned out, had no hands. As volatile as Cobb may have been, he was hardly the only explosive player in the majors. Even the admired but fiercely competitive Ted Williams, on one September day in 1958, angrily threw his bat, not only into the stands but squarely into the face of one very surprised Gladys Heffernan. Williams, immediately apologetic, was further stunned to find he had just clubbed the housekeeper of Red Sox General Manager Joe Cronin. To make matters worse, Cronin had fined Williams two years before after a Williams spitting fit when the slugger had launched a series of wads at both the hated Yankees and a section of jeering Boston fans. Gladys Heffernan was not seriously injured, but she has not been forgotten.

Not known to be passive, Boston fans have participated in many a controversy over the years, including a relentless roar of abuse against the Giants' Fred Snodgrass at Fenway Park in 1914. The Boston Braves were playing a double header, when Snodgrass took a pitch on the arm and then thumbed his nose at Braves pitcher Lefty Tyler. When Snodgrass next took the outfield, the crowd grew so uncontrollably hostile that the mayor of Boston left his seat in the stands, rushed to the field and demanded that the umpires remove Snodgrass, which, remarkably, the umpires did, accomplishing what was perhaps the first player ejection by the mayor of an opposing town.

Obnoxious fan behavior—which sometimes occurs against their own team—is not a thing of the distant past. On September 28, 1995, the Cubs became the first team in history to win after six deficits in a single game, finally overcoming the Astros 12-11. Perhaps because the contest was so grueling and emotionally charged, a frustrated Chicago fan jumped the stands and bolted for Randy Myers when the Cubs pitcher yielded an eighth inning two-run blast. Myers was not a pushover target. A 230-pound martial arts expert, Myers flattened the oncoming fan with an elbow, then pinned the hapless intruder on the ground until help arrived.

An incident on May 16, 2000, also at Wrigley Field, set the record for the number of suspensions resulting from one baseball brawl. A fan had reached over the right field wall to snatch a cap off the head of Chad Kreuter, a Dodger player in the bullpen, who took immediate offense. Several Dodgers spontaneously jumped the wall in pursuit of the fan, sparking a melee in the seats that gave new definition to the expression "hat day." Both players and coaches were suspended eight days later for a total of eighty-four games.

Whether throwing potatoes, laying eggs by committing Merkle Boners, or attacking umpires as the St. Louis fans did on July 8, 1908, baseball shenanigans on, around, and near the base paths have left an indelible, sometimes disastrous, imprint on the game.

But with all the antics, fighting, trickery, intimidation and retaliation, baseball still manages to "come home again," finding itself and reaffirming its sentimental roots. Nowhere was that more evident than when two of the most legendary competitors of the early twentieth century decided to call it quits— together. Partly to help draw a huge Labor Day turnout in 1916, rivals Christy Mathewson and Three-Finger Brown decided to manipulate history a little on their own by playing the last games of their careers against each other.

At the time, Mathewson was the manager of the Reds, but he agreed to pitch one more game to mark the occasion, the only game he ever pitched not wearing a Giants uniform. Brown, meanwhile, had moved over to the Federal League Chicago Whales, a short-lived sojourn before being bought back by the Cubs earlier in 1916. The two warriors had faced off against each other a total of twenty-five times throughout their careers. Brown had won thirteen of those games and lost ten, but victory would not be his on that last day, as Mathewson prevailed 10-8 for career win number 373.

5

THE GIANTS STEAL THE PENNANT!
THE GIANTS STEAL THE PENNANT!

THERE ARE MOMENTS IN sports history that transcend the games themselves, entering the world of pop culture to become an unforgettable part of Americana. Sometimes, perhaps once in a career or even in an era, those great sports episodes influence who we are as a nation, as did Jesse Owens' memorable defiance of Hitler and racism at the 1936 Berlin Olympics. Some explode into history with one defining instant: there are Muhammed Ali's first defeat of the unbeatable Sonny Liston; the Dempsey-Tunney long count at Soldier Field in Chicago; the final Roger Maris home run of the 1961 campaign—and certainly the 1951 Bobby Thomson blast that rocked Ralph Branca and baseball history. And certainly with Ruth, Gehrig, Mantle, Mays, Clemente, Robinson, Aaron, Williams, DiMaggio and all the rest, baseball has served up more of those defining moments than any other sport.

In the real world, though, all is not always as it seems, and so it goes with our threshold moments of historical sports glory. There are many such cloudy instances in the world of sport, as when officials manipulated three game-ending chances for the Russians to win the 1972 Olympic gold in basketball or when sprinter Ben Johnson lost his brief Olympic medal as a result of a positive steroids test. Naturally, those kinds of situations crop up in the course of baseball history, but in baseball, mischief has somehow become a part of the game itself, in the context of its implied rules of gentlemanly, or not so gentlemanly, conduct. The tobacco-spitting, chip-on-the-shoulder legacy of the game can award a free pass to those transgressions that fit the character and the spirit of the game as it has evolved, regardless of the letter of its rules.

Certainly not every baseball transgression is forgiven, especially not those that slip over the line of tolerated mischief toward something more malevolent. But in many ways, baseball is different from the other major sports. For example, although the use of instant replay is occasionally considered, baseball has always disdained it, preferring to risk errors slipping by. The game's avoidance of replay is not necessarily intended to encourage cheating, but reflects the innate understanding that the feel and flow of the game takes precedent over the replay of any isolated event. Thus, in baseball, sometimes the facts do get in the way of the truth, depending, of course, on how the "truth" is defined. By embracing the esoteric in its own strangely transcendental manner, baseball operates perpetually on the edge, inviting controversy but at the same time preserving the singular, spontaneous essence of the game and its history.

Just ask the 1951 Dodgers. One of the most memorable flashes of baseball glory erupted with Bobby Thomson's "shot heard 'round the world," a defining blast that still rings down through the decades. And it was probably—almost certainly—stolen. Yet somehow the theft of the 1951 pennant is overlooked, given a pass, even dismissed, in favor of the bigger picture—the sweeping portrait of baseball rather than just one detail of grand larceny.

Although the entire Thomson episode could not have taken more than about ten seconds, the tale of Thomson's assault on both American baseball and culture does not simply begin with Ralph Branca's last pitch of the ninth inning on October 3, 1951. And it does not end with Thomson rocketing that famous throw into the seats, capping perhaps the greatest walk-off home run in big league history as the Giants took the cross-town pennant from Brooklyn with one fateful swing of big league lumber.

Indeed, the Thomson-Branca tale has never ended. But its beginning can be traced to one moment certain: June 28, 1911. On that date, a full half-century before Thomson's momentous blast, a 16,000-seat, concrete-and-steel structure opened in Manhattan on 159th Street between Coogan's Bluff and the Harlem River. The innovative Polo Grounds stadium replaced an antiquated version that had burned down only months before. The new arena was not even finished at the time, and would not be completed for another year when 18,000 more seats and a double-decker grandstand would be added, but on that June day in 1911 a baseball shrine was born.

The refashioned Polo Grounds would be home to the New York Giants from 1911 to the team's unfortunate exodus to San Francisco after the 1957 season. It also hosted the New York Yankees from 1913 until 1923, when Yankee Stadium, the House that Ruth Built, opened for business. More recently, the Polo Grounds were home to the hapless Mets teams in 1962-63 before they settled into the new Shea Stadium.

Those Polo Grounds had an amazing knack for creating history, helped along by the dynamics of the times, the first truly golden age of baseball: the era of Ty Cobb, followed by seasons with Ruth, Mays, Durocher, Gil Hodges and others. The grand old stadium's history was also influenced by its location in rough and tumble turn-of-the-century Brooklyn, as well as its own peculiarities, especially its unique elongated shape. The Polo Grounds have been compared to a bathtub with a square at the end—the center-field bleachers at the far end, as well as the deep center clubhouse behind the pitcher in distant view of the catcher—a significant location that would contribute to the theft of opposing signs and the 1951 pennant.

For the ball players of the day, deep center field was defined by a huge wall that cut off the entire length of the outfield. Not only was the wall's sixty-foot height extraordinary, its 500-foot distance from home plate rendered the outfield a vast cavern. Not only did no ball ever clear the gigantic wall in center, not one ball ever hit it on the fly. In front of that wall once stood a five-foot statue of Eddie Grant, a Major Leaguer killed during World War I, and even though it was actually *in* the field of play, the statue was never an impediment in the distant, nearly boundless outfield.

Compensating for the grotesquely deep outfield wall, and contributing to its bathtub look, were the old park's shallow foul lines. They ran only 279 feet to left and even shorter to right at 258 feet—short by any standard, especially those of the big leagues. The outfield fences swept abruptly from the foul lines, creating very deep left-center and right-center dimensions of 450 feet. No home runs cleared the sixty-foot dead center wall, few made it to left or right center, but many were pulled into the stands near the foul lines, rendering the stadium a baseball enigma with pitchers' dimensions in deep center and yet a batter's dream for pull hitters.

Ruth loved the short foul lines, especially the tempting right field where the left-hander could easily pull home-run jacks in bunches. Ruth was the first player to club a long ball over the right field roof altogether, and in 1921 the Babe smacked thirty-two dingers at the home-field Polo Grounds alone, an extraordinary total for any era. It took four decades for someone other than Ruth to reach the right field stands. Remarkably, two players did it on consecutive days in June of 1962, with Lou Brock becoming the second player ever to reach those bleachers in right-center with a 470 foot shot. The very next day Hank Aaron became the third such player when he blasted a missile into the same seats. And of course the Grounds offered its share of great defensive play, too, including one of the most famous catches in the history of any outfield, the Willie Mays over-the-shoulder grab in the 1954 World Series.

Mays and Ruth notwithstanding, the most significant single baseball feat at the Polo Grounds was the Bobby Thomson shot that closed that remarkable 1951 season. The Giants were down 4-2 in the bottom of the ninth. The Dodgers smelled victory even though the pesky Giants threatened with two men on, Thompson up, and the pennant on the line.

Bobby Thomson played from 1946 to 1960 and had a career batting average of .270 over a respectable 1779 games during which he clubbed 264 career home runs with 1026 RBIs. Thomson was with the Giants for seven seasons, and in six of those he smashed at least twenty-four homers. He was the regular Giants center fielder until 1951, when he accepted a reassignment to first base so that a talented new kid could take over in center: Willie Mays. The move worked, and the Giants narrowly outlasted the Dodgers for the pennant, thanks to the memorable Thomson smash and a hint of baseball mischief.

Enter Ralph Branca, who was first brought up to the big leagues by the Dodgers in 1944 when the pitcher was only eighteen years old. By 1947, Branca was logging a twenty-one-win season for the Dodgers, in the same year that he turned twenty-one himself. Branca capped that outstanding year with a game six World Series win over the Yankees, but fate had much more in store for the journeyman Dodgers pitcher.

The portentous season of 1951 would see a marathon struggle between the New York Giants and their rival the Brooklyn Dodgers. Although it would end with the Thomson shot heard 'round the world, the struggle began with the Dodgers exploding from the gates, building an eleven-and-a-half game lead on the Giants by August 7. Four days later, the lead would swell to thirteen-and-a-half games, a seemingly insurmountable margin with September fast approaching. Enter Willie Mays. And a little Thomson larceny.

Even as the Dodgers were building their early lead, it may have been the beginning of the end when, on May 25, 1951,

Willie Mays first stepped to the plate in a Giants uniform. Mays struck out in his first trip, and actually went hitless in his first twelve at-bats for manager Leo Durocher. But the "Say, Hey" kid came out of it with a vengeance three days later at the expense of legendary pitcher Warren Spahn. When asked about the pitch Mays rocketed into the stands at the Polo Grounds for his first career home run, Spahn casually observed, "For the first sixty feet it was a helluva pitch."

Durocher was much more emphatic. "I never saw a fucking ball get out of a fucking ball park so fucking fast in my fucking life."

Mays' rookie-of-the-year season contributed mightily to the historic Giants comeback. So did a matching pair of twenty-three-win seasons by Giants pitchers Larry Jansen and Sal Maglie, both totals leading the league. And of course there was Bobby Thomson, who hit .293 with thirty-two homers and 101 RBIs as the Giants compiled an impressive 98-59 mark.

Thirteen-game leads do not evaporate by accident. On September 7, Thomson had a five-for-five day as the Giants prevailed over the Braves. Two days later, Sal Maglie would win his twentieth of the year in a close 2-1 victory over the leading Dodgers. That win, powered by Monte Irvin's two-run jack launched off Ralph Branca, cut the fading Dodgers' lead to just five-and-a-half games. By the end of September, the Giants had caught up, but the Dodgers were hardly finished. On September 30, Jackie Robinson all but willed an extra-inning win to tie the Giants and force a National League playoff, but it would not be enough to stem the tides of fate, misfortune, and malfeasance. Was the ensuing Giants charge propelled by luck or sheer talent? Certainly it was both of those, plus an incendiary dash of larcenous ingenuity that only a baseball fan could fully appreciate.

As already pointed out, the unique shape of the Polo Grounds somehow affected every game. Sometimes it was the cavernous outfield, sometimes it was the short left field line or the inviting right foul line; often it was Willie Mays making an impossible catch in the outfield. But in 1951 the significant factor was the distant clubhouse tucked far, far away in center field, but with a dead-on view of the opposing catcher.

The clubhouse was positioned perfectly for mischief, if not for grand theft. It now appears that Giants' players used a telescope to steal signs from the opposing catcher during much of the 1951 season. The Giants' incredible come-from-behind season was punctuated by the greatest walk-off home run ever. Fifty years later, three Giants players confessed that they had had a sign-stealing system throughout the 1951 season, and one of them, Sal Yvars, admitted that it had been operational during the Giants-Dodgers playoff itself.

As the dramatic 1951 campaign drew to its fairytale close, the Giants found themselves clocking home runs against the Dodgers in bunches, including off pitcher Ralph Branca. With the Giants stealing signs at will, Branca must have begun to doubt his own "stuff" as he watched long balls leave the park like flocks of migrating birds. If the beginning of the end had begun with Willie Mays at the plate, it was well on its way by August 15, 1951, when Mays ran down a drive from the Dodgers' Carl Furillo and then gunned a throw to the plate to nail Billy Cox at home, preserving a 1-1 tie in the third. The play stunned Dodgers manager Charlie Dressen who then carelessly challenged the baseball gods: "When he does it again I'll believe it."

The August 15 game was still tied in the eighth inning when Wes Westrum struck a Ralph Branca pitch to blast a game-winning two-run jack, trimming the Dodgers' lead to a still hefty ten-and-a-half game margin. The crucial homer was at the Polo Grounds and could easily have been stolen by use of the clubhouse telescope. Whether it was is only a matter for speculation, but since the use of the center field telescope is a known fact, it certainly was possible if not probable—considering the extent to which the Giants' home runs began to pile up near the season's end.

On September 1, the Giants' Don Mueller clubbed three home runs himself for an 8-1 Giants victory over the Dodgers.

The first Mueller blast was at the expense of none other than the seemingly stunned Ralph Branca, who had pitched two straight shutouts prior to that game. With that, the Dodgers' lead was down to six. Eight days later, on September 9, Monte Irvin's two-run shot for a 2-1 victory over the Dodgers came also at the expense of Branca. The lead was cut to five-and-a-half games.

By September 30, the charging Giants had caught up altogether, forcing a three-game playoff with the struggling Dodgers. It was Ralph Branca who took the mound in game one, the first Major League game telecast live coast-to-coast. With much of America watching, Branca promptly gave up home-run smashes to both Monte Irvin and Bobby Thomson, losing to the Giants 3-1. Since that first game was played in Brooklyn and not at the Polo Grounds, we can't be sure signs were stolen on that occasion. But, in any case, the Dodgers, having won the coin toss, tempted fate by opting to play the first playoff game at home, thus placing the next two games at the Polo Grounds. Spyglass notwithstanding, the Dodgers actually prevailed in game two of the short series, thumping the Giants 10-0 in their own yard, setting up the final Thomson climax at the Polo Grounds on October 3, 1951.

Don Newcombe took the pitching rubber for the Dodgers to start the third and final contest, while Sal Maglie started for the home team Giants. The game was all Dodgers into the bottom of the ninth inning when singles by Alvin Dark and Don Mueller put two on for the Giants. Dark was then doubled home, cutting the four-run Dodgers lead to 4-1. Mueller took third on the play but severely injured his ankle sliding into the base and was replaced by a pinch runner. The score was 4-2 with Bobby Thomson on deck and two runners on base. The Giants went to the bullpen, fatefully choosing usual starter Ralph Branca over teammate Carl Erskine when the pen coach pronounced Erskine's warm-ups "too wild."

All New York was on edge, while nearly all of America watched or heard Bobby Thomson step to the plate. The Polo Grounds were alive with adrenaline, the crowd rocking from heart-pounding excitement as Branca took the signs and unleashed a snake-bit big league hardball into Major League history. It is now believed that those signs may have been stolen and telegraphed to Thomson who in turn preyed on Branca, thrusting a deep three-run, historic 5-4 dagger into the still palpitating Brooklyn hearts. Giants' play-by-play man Russ Hodges capped the Thomson shot with his exuberant call that quickly became momentous histrionics as he shouted over and over, "The Giants win the pennant! The Giants win the pennant! The Giants win the pennant!"

Just how extraordinary, how unbelievable was Thomson's season-ending smash? Red Smith of the *New York Herald Tribune* may not have been fully in command of himself when he wrote: "The art of fiction is dead. Reality has strangled invention. Only the utterly impossible, the inexpressibly fantastic, can ever be plausible again." Maybe, though, fiction was not dead, but very much alive, especially in the shadows of the Polo Grounds clubhouse. Branca was devastated, confiding in Fordham University priest Frank Rowley just after the game, "Why me? I don't smoke. I don't drink. I don't fool around. Baseball is my whole life. Why me?"

6
Breaking the Midget Barrier

When Eddie [Gaedel] went into that crouch . . .
his strike zone was 1 1/2 inches. Marvelous.
—Bill Veeck

ENIGMATIC BASEBALL ICON Bill Veeck had an uncanny ability to be both affable and cantankerous at the same time. Even his autobiography *Veeck—As in Wreck*, written with Ed Linn, was a work of mischief, poking fun at himself with the title, a veiled reference to both his outside-the-box behavior and his physical appearance, the result of smoking, drinking, and a trademark wooden leg from World War II wounds suffered in the South Pacific.

Creating baseball history would soon become his specialty, but Veeck especially enjoyed tweaking the owners, commissioners and others along the way. He could push all the right buttons because there was little about baseball that Veeck did not know, little he had not experienced first hand. Bill's father, William Veeck, Sr., was a baseball writer who had caught the attention of chewing-gum mogul William Wrigley in the early days of Wrigley's involvement with baseball through a big team with a diminutive name, the Cubs.

Wrigley Field had been constructed in 1914 as Weeghman Park by Charles Weeghman, owner of the short-lived Chicago Whales of the Federal League. In 1916 Weeghman and nine investors bought the Cubs and moved them to Weeghman Park. Then in 1920, after Wrigley bought out Weeghman's share of the club, the stadium became known as Cubs Park and in February 1926 the name was changed to Wrigley Field. One day in those early years, reporter William Veeck, Sr., wrote an insightful series in the *Chicago American* spelling out how he would run the Cubs, if given the chance. The piece impressed Wrigley so much that Veeck was actually named president of the club in 1917—and the rest, as they say, is history.

Bill Veeck was only three years old when his father joined the Cubs, so he literally grew up in a ballpark—and not just any park, of course, but in the future shrine of Wrigley Field where the youngster did much more than just watch. As a pre-teen, Veeck worked the grounds, sold soft drinks, mailed tickets, and soaked it all in. He even sat in the president's box with an endless parade of dignitaries, including Chicago's Kenesaw Mountain Landis, the federal judge who soon would become the most powerful commissioner in baseball history.

It was not long before the precocious young Veeck was giving advice as well as taking it. When his father died in 1933, Veeck quit college at the age of nineteen and went to work for the Cubs. He soon made an impact: it was his idea to plant the ivy along Wrigley's brick outfield walls in 1937. A stadium beautification project had run aground when an attempt to place potted plants in the aisles was ridiculed, so Veeck came up with the notion of moving the plants from the steps to the walls where they would be less intrusive to the fans.

Even though young Veeck eventually became treasurer of the Cubs, he was still restless and ambitious. At twenty-seven, he left Chicago and bought a struggling, nearly bankrupt American Association franchise in Milwaukee, arriving at the beer capital with only eleven dollars to his name.

Veeck admitted he had an affinity for mischief. "Since baseball rules are ridiculously and ineptly written, I have always read the rule book with an eye toward loopholes." That observation was not lost on the American Association, which passed nine new rules, all directed at Veeck's new franchise. No wonder: Veeck may have been the best ever at conjuring up tricks to adapt the field to the strengths and weaknesses of his own teams.

The first problem he encountered in Milwaukee was the woeful quality of the Brewers team itself. The players could neither run nor hit, a notable drawback. They were so slow that the manager didn't even bother to implement steal signs for the coaches. Veeck couldn't make his team run faster, so he did the next best thing: he slowed all the players down. In the "interests of closer competition," as Veeck put it, he introduced a loose mixture of sand and dirt to bog down the base paths "in such abundant quantity that the runners would sink up to their ankles . . . like kids running on the beach."

Of course the players could still not hit, a particularly odd deficiency since the park's right field wall was only 265 feet from home plate. Unfortunately, Milwaukee had no left-handed power hitters so, close or not, they seldom reached the right field wall. Instead they watched lefty sluggers on the opposing team launch missiles over that inviting wall, game in and game out. Until Veeck could find some left-hitting sluggers, he had to deal with that inviting, vexing wall, an entrenched structure that couldn't easily be moved. Undaunted, he built a sixty-foot wire fence on top of that stubborn wall, immediately converting enemy home runs to impressive singles as they clunked back into the field of play. Eventually the fence was even rigged to a motor so it could be raised or retracted for each game, depending upon the quality of the opposition's power hitters.

Veeck believed that gamesmanship was an integral part of baseball itself. Indeed it was, and perhaps it should always be, distinguishing baseball from any other team sport. In Milwaukee, Veeck extended that gamesmanship into marketing and entertainment, giving away live pigs, beer, even cases of food. He invented baseball fireworks, allowed weddings at home plate, and moved up starting times to accommodate swing-shift laborers with demanding war-time work schedules. If nothing else, Veeck clearly knew that he was in the entertainment business. He sold the team four years later, in 1945, for $275,000, and learned along the way about business, marketing, people—and, not least of all—showmanship.

In 1946, Veeck had taken center stage with the purchase of the Cleveland Indians by a syndicate under his control. In the next year, the Indians had doubled their season attendance to 1.5 million spectators. Just a year later, Cleveland was in the World Series, almost doubling attendance again with a then-American League record 2.62 million fans. And Veeck's lessons in Milwaukee had accelerated the marketing process, including a new round of fence manipulations—Cleveland style.

Cleveland Stadium had a vast outfield, so large that it discouraged Veeck's players, whose 450-foot missiles were easily caught by a waiting outfielder. In "fixing" the problem, Veeck may have learned more about people than about baseball. When he constructed shorter fences around the field, cutting the foul lines to 320 feet and dead center to a distant but manageable 410 feet, Veeck not only increased his players' home runs, but boosted their confidence as well. Soon they were launching balls not just over the short fence, but even past the original far-away walls as well.

Somehow, those Cleveland fences also found a way to move around the stadium, albeit stealthily under the cover of darkness. When the Yankees came to town, the Cleveland outfield grew mysteriously larger, and when weaker teams like the Browns visited, the fences could be safely moved closer to better suit the Indians' own weak hitters.

Walls, fences, fireworks and marketing aside, Veeck's biggest contribution to the game of baseball, if not to ethics, was his embrace of black ballplayers. He did not break the race barrier with Jackie Robinson, of course, but he was the first to sign a black player, Larry Doby, to an American League team, followed by the ageless wonder Satchel Paige and many who came later.

That Series-bound team was stocked with talent: player-manager Lou Boudreau, Larry Doby, Bob Lemon, Bob Feller and of course Satchel, who, at possibly forty-nine years old, would become the first black pitcher in the World Series. Satchel gave his age as forty-two, but Veeck believed he was born in 1899 and had shaved seven years off his age.

Veeck continued to reinvent the game, and to reinvent himself as well. In so doing, he would soon sell off the Indians franchise and take over the moribund St. Louis Browns. His new team was so bad that St. Louis, already known for its breweries, was also saddled with this colorful tag: "First in booze, first in shoes and last in the American League." One-time Browns second baseman Don Gutteridge observed years later, "Sometimes the players outnumbered the fans." He was not kidding. One day in 1933 only thirty-four fans attended the game. "Some days," Gutteridge said, "I knew everybody in the ballpark on a first-name basis. You could fire a shotgun into the stands and not hit anyone."

Veeck didn't fire any guns, but he did make numerous memorable public relations shots, including the mischievous legend of Eddie Gaedel.

Willie Mays and Eddie Gaedel had two things in common: they had both worn a big league uniform at least once, and both debuted in 1951. As it happens, Eddie actually fared better than Mays during his first trip to the plate, drawing a famous walk on four pitches while Mays struck out. Gaedel's superiority clearly began and ended right there, however, for Mays would launch 660 home runs during his Hall of Fame career and Gaedel would just get launched—period.

At three feet seven inches, Gaedel provided his infinitesimal strike zone to the Browns on August 19, 1951, when he popped out of a giant birthday cake as part of a double header celebration at home against the Tigers. The cake was intended to celebrate the dual fiftieth anniversaries of the American League and the Browns' long-time radio sponsor, Falstaff Brewing, but it ended up as a footnote to history.

After emerging from the cake, Gaedel took a seat on the bench. The Browns started Frank Saucier in the field in place of Jim Delsing, the usual starter, and then promptly pulled Saucier for pinch hitter Gaedel in the bottom of the first inning. Wearing elfin slippers with upturned toes and the number 1/8, Eddie crouched into his batting stance to reveal his one-and-a-half-inch top-to-bottom strike zone. Facing a nearly invisible target, Detroit pitcher Bob Cain fired two fastballs but was laughing so hard that he nearly fell off the mound. Needless to say, the pitcher failed to find the Gaedel's strike zone, walking the pinch hitter with four straight balls. A well-known photograph taken that day clearly shows one of those pitches sailing more than a foot over the stooping Gaedel's head and being easily caught by the catcher whose knees never leave the ground.

The Sportsman's Park home crowd of 18,000 went wild as Gaedel took first, and gave him a standing ovation as he yielded to pinch runner Jim Delsing and exited for the dugout. Opposing manager Red Rolfe went wild, too, objecting to Gaedel's legitimacy in the line-up. But Veeck had had the foresight to sign Gaedel to a legitimate big league contract well before the game, and Gaedel was officially listed on the active list. Browns' Manager Zack Taylor produced the contract for the umpire's inspection, so Gaedel's appearance was allowed—although the Browns lost the game to the Tigers anyway, 6-2.

Still, the Eddie Gaedel saga was not over. The following day, American League president Will Harridge disallowed the Gaedel contract, invoking the league's "conduct detrimental to baseball" clause. With that, the midget's plate appearance was stricken from the record books, an action Gaedel protested as discrimination. Notwithstanding these league machinations, the Baseball Encyclopedia continues to list Gaedel with one official at-bat in the Major Leagues, and he remains more than just a footnote in the annals of baseball.

One of the more remarkable aspects of that memorable day is often overlooked: the respectable Sportsman's Park attendance of 18,000. The Browns had been a terrible draw, but Veeck's antics sparked St. Louis with renewed vigor and temporarily reversed the trend. The fans loved Veeck's no-holds-barred approach to the game and appreciated his showman's approach to baseball as entertainment. Even when Veeck didn't break the rules outright, he was so good at bending them beyond recognition that new rules were continually written to keep him at bay. In this way, Veeck personified the game, enhancing its spirit with a kind of good-natured disrespect and ultimately honoring it with his ingenuity.

In fact, the deployment of a midget was not even Veeck's own idea. Responding to charges that he stole the idea from a James Thurber story, "You Could Look It Up," Veeck says in his autobiography, "I didn't steal the idea from Thurber—I stole it from John McGraw." Thus the indefatigable Bill Veeck stole a base on balls, and created a slice of Major League history.

Five days after the Gaedel walk, Veeck was at it again, supplying 1,115 fans with flash cards, so they could all help to manage a home game against the Athletics. In fact, the fans did a credible job, benching the catcher, putting Sherman Lollar and Hank Arft into the game, and instinctively leaving pitcher Ned Garver in the contest despite a rocky episode that allowed two runs to score. The Browns, and the fans, won the game 5-3.

In baseball as in life, intent can sometimes be everything. A close friend's apparently insulting remark, for example, can be interpreted and accepted as mere playfulness, while the same remark from a stranger could provoke an immediate physical response. And so it went with Bill Veeck: his genuine love for the game seemed to bubble to the surface with every trick. With his legendary wooden leg, love for beer and baseball sunshine, Veeck identified with the working-class fan, bringing a lunch-bucket character to the game. His affection for baseball may have been exceeded only by his love for humanity, and the game often benefited from both—as when he insisted upon signing black ballplayers to the American League. Eddie Gaedel and the cake may have been Veeck's greatest stunt, but Veeck's greatest single moment was probably his launching of the Jackie Robinson legacy.

It is no surprise, then, that Veeck himself took up the discrimination cause of the so-called "little people." The importance of this was unfortunately lost on league president Will Harridge. Veeck publicly chided Harridge, pointing to examples of "small people" in the game, like Phil Rizzuto, the slightly built teenager from Brooklyn originally dismissed by Casey Stengel as too small and frail for the Dodgers. All Rizzuto did was win the American League MVP as a New York Yankee in 1950, only months before Gaedel's debut. On June 20, 1980, Fred Patek smashed a double and a three-run shot to the bleachers for the Angels in a 20-2 thrashing of Boston—despite being the smallest player of his era at just five feet four inches. In 1952, manager Eddie Stanky labeled his new pitcher, Stu Miller, "the stenographer" when he saw how thin Miller was at 165 pounds. Nine years later, Miller was pitching in the All-Star game—even though he was literally blown off the mound that day by a stiff Candlestick Park wind.

Although Veeck planted ivy at Wrigley, perfected the art of special promotions, and invented baseball fireworks and the exploding scoreboard, his most impressive accomplishment was championing the downtrodden, the underdog. More touching than Gaedel's highly publicized appearance, for example, was that of outfielder Pete Gray, called up to play for the Browns in that same 1951 season. Veeck believed in his new outfielder despite the fact that Gray had lost his right arm in a childhood accident. As a thirty-year-old rookie, Gray struck out in his first at-bat on April 18, but he also stroked a single that day, going a serviceable one for four. Even though in the field Gray had to catch the ball, drop his mitt, flip the ball and catch it again before throwing to the infield, he maintained a remarkable .983 fielding percentage his prior year as a minor leaguer for the Memphis Chicks where he also hit an astounding .333. Gray soon made an impact for the Browns, as well. In a double header against the vaunted Yankees on May 20, the one-hander went four for eight, made ten outfield putouts, and even scored the winning run in game two as the Browns swept New York, 10-1 and 5-2.

Bill Veeck died in Chicago just after New Year's Day, 1986, at the age of seventy-one. He surely must have smiled from wherever he was three years later when Angels' manager Doug Rader was accused of engineering a publicity stunt by signing lefty pitcher Jim Abbott to a Major League contract straight from the University of Michigan. Despite being born without a right hand, Abbott had found a way to field and catch using a right-handed mitt on his left hand, complementing his big league left arm. Despite doubts and even ridicule, Abbott won twelve games as a rookie starter, the most big league games won by any pitcher in his first professional year since 1925. All Abbott did after that was pitch a career total of 1674 innings over eleven seasons with the Angels, Yankees, White Sox and Brewers. Not only did Jim Abbott win an impressive eighteen games with a 2.89 ERA for the Angels in 1991, but as a Yankee he pitched a 4-0 no-hitter against the Indians in 1992. Moreover, he managed officially to go two for twenty-three as a one-armed batter in a Major League uniform, not to mention slugging a 400-foot triple in a 1991 spring training game against the Giants' Rick Reuschel.

Jim Abbott, Stu Miller, Phil Rizzuto, Fred Patek, and many others contributed to the singular character of the game. Pete Gray, Eddie Gaedel, Larry Doby and Satchel Paige all made baseball history along with their venerable mentor William Veeck, Jr.—master showman, magician, and mischievous champion of the "little people."

7
GOATS, GODS AND CURSES

THERE IS SOMETHING ABOUT the game of baseball that invites the occult as no other sport does, despite football's Raiders' "Immaculate Reception" and the Daryle Lamonica curse of the Buffalo Bills. Baseball is in a perpetually delicate balance between success and failure, between a stovepipe foul ball and the towering home run, between a wicked curve and a pitcher's nightmare hanging curve. And it is from such minute nuances that generations of rampant baseball superstition is spawned.

The game is famous for its idiosyncrasies, like players believing they should never change socks or underwear in a hitting streak, never mention a no-hitter in progress, or that it would help their game if they fidget endlessly at the plate à la Sammy Sosa or Nomar Garciaparra. It is also a game of streaks, where a hitter can suddenly get hot as balls drop magically between, in front of and behind bewildered outfielders. Most of all, there is the belief in the perpetual power of the curse.

Technically, curses are the most dreaded form of magic— black magic—and are invoked for one of only two reasons: protection or revenge. The Mummy's Curse protected the tomb of King Tutankhamen, discovered in 1922 supposedly with a clay tablet bearing the ominous inscription: "Death will slay with its wings whoever disturbs the peace of the pharaoh."

Anyone can call down a curse, of course, but whether the curse "has legs" depends on what happens later. When do several coincidences reach a point where they appear to be more than coincidence? Within six months after they entered Tutankhamen's chambers, six of the seven leaders of the excavation team died from bizarre causes. Coincidence?

Revenge is the usual motive for curses, and nothing spawns a desire for revenge like the game of baseball. The revenge itself could be benign, like the Wrigley Field tradition of tossing visitor home runs from the stands back onto the field of play. It could also be absurd, like the great Colonel Sanders curse that haunts the Japanese Hanshin Tigers baseball team. At one time, the Tigers were the top team in Japan, and when they won the league championship in 1985, the fans were so ecstatic that they hijacked a train in Tokyo and began to throw themselves into the polluted river in Osaka's Dotonbori entertainment district. As the crowd called out the names of each player, someone who resembled that player jumped into the river. Not surprisingly, nobody looked like the team's bearded American star, Randy Bass, so the fans stormed across the town in search of a Bass look-alike. They found him—sort of—in the form of a life-sized statue of Colonel Sanders at the local Kentucky Fried Chicken outlet. The hysterical mob ripped down the statue, hauled it back to the river and dumped it in.

The graven image of the Colonel, or Randy Bass, is somewhere at the bottom of the river, and it is believed that the Hanshin Tigers will never win another series until it is found. Divers have been sent down to look for it, but to no avail, and the Tigers have never since won the Japanese Series, at least not till now. Apparently Colonel Sanders has taken his revenge.

But there are more profound, more sweeping vengeful hexes like the curse of the great Bambino. This, the grandfather of all baseball curses in both scope and chronology, emerged from the grassy confines of the early Fenway Park.

Babe Ruth, the Bambino, was the icon who changed baseball and possibly all professional sports. As even casual fans know, Ruth first began his career as a productive member of the Boston Red Sox, pitching and hitting his way into Bean Town headlines, and then emerging nationally as a Boston superstar. Few realize that Ruth actually began his professional career on March 6, 1914, as a teenage member of the International League's Baltimore Orioles. On April 22 of that year, Ruth was fast making his mark as he pitched a shutout victory against the Buffalo Bisons, going two for four at the plate. Some trace Ruth's nickname back to his stint with the Orioles when he was called "one of [owner] Jack Dunn's babes" by a Baltimore scout.

Less than three months later, the Red Sox bought the Babe and two other players from the Orioles. Two days after that, on July 11, 1914, Babe Ruth first took the mound in Fenway, striking out Cleveland's Jack Graney, the first batter he faced in a big league uniform. Ruth's lasting impact on baseball remains unsurpassed, but it should be pointed out that he achieved most of his legendary feats in his 2,084 games when he was wearing New York Yankees pinstripes.

To the chagrin of the Red Sox faithful, the true story of Babe Ruth began the day after Christmas, 1919, when Boston owner Harry Frazee inked a clandestine deal with New York, sending Ruth to the Yankees for a combination of cash and loans. There are conflicting versions of the sale, especially over the price paid for Ruth, but it seems likely that Frazee received $25,000 in cash, another $100,000 over four years at six percent interest, plus a guarantee of a $300,000 Frazee loan backed by Fenway Park itself. Those were staggering numbers for the day—Ruth's entire 1918 salary with the Red Sox, for example, was $7,000—but they were virtually nothing compared to the New York windfall that was about to follow.

On January 3, 1920, the Ruth transaction was made public. Prior to that, the Red Sox had won fifteen American League pennants and six World Series. Although the team managed to capture a few pennants in the ensuing decades, they didn't win the World Series for eighty-three straight years, until, miracle of miracles, they finally beat the Yankees in 2004 for the pennant, followed by a World Series sweep over the Cardinals.

It was believed for those eighty-three years that Ruth had cursed the Red Sox, or that the team's own fans had done it. One immediate effect was that because of Ruth, and then Lou Gehrig and others, the Yankees would be the better team for years to come.

Ruth was very upset by the sale at the time, but he was more angry personally at Frazee than he was over the move to New York, per se. When Ruth heard of the sale and learned about the price, he approached Frazee in an attempt to wrest $15,000 of the Boston sale price for himself. That attempt got nowhere fast, summed up by Ruth's colorful observation about Frazee afterward: "The son of a bitch wouldn't even see me." So did Ruth really retaliate by putting a curse on the Red Sox? Maybe he did. Or maybe this episode aroused the wrath of the gods of baseball. Was there one grand curse or an eighty-three-season coincidence? You decide.

One thing is for certain: the Yankees became the team of the century while the Red Sox languished. But a number of other memorable events occurred in those formative baseball years: there was the discovery in May 1920 of seventeen-year-old New Yorker Lou Gehrig, when he launched a ninth inning grand slam home run before 10,000 Chicago fans at a high school match-up with Chicago's Lane Tech, the ball clearing the right field fences of what would be called Wrigley Field. Another noteworthy event occurred on February 9, 1920, when Major League Baseball banned the spitball, as well as other special deliveries, tipping the balance of power to the batters—just in time for the arrival of Ruth and Gehrig.

Ruth's emergence as a Yankee long-ball hitter was no coincidence. Eventually Yankee Stadium would be built with a short right field line to accommodate Ruth's left-handed power. On

September 20, as the 1919 season neared its close, Babe Ruth had already tied the Major League home run record, blasting number twenty-seven against the Chicago White Sox. Just four days later, still with the Red Sox, Ruth broke his own record as he launched a moon shot over the roof at the Polo Grounds. Undoubtedly the Yankees watched that missile sail into big league destiny—carrying their future with it.

The Red Sox would suffer many disappointments in the ensuing years. Ted Williams would become one of the greatest hitters in history, but he would not help the team win a Series; and the Sox may have played in the greatest World Series ever, when Boston lost to Cincinnati's Big Red Machine of 1975, leaving only the image of Carlton Fisk willing a sixth game home run over the left field foul pole. Three years later, the Sox would knock at the Series door again, building a big lead over New York, then sinking fast as a spate of injuries allowed the Yankees to pull ahead. Unwavering, Boston caught fire once more, winning their last eight games to catch New York and force a one-game playoff to decide the 1978 AL East championship on October 2.

The Yankees threw ace pitcher Ron Guidry at the Sox, but Boston hung tough, taking a 2-0 lead into the seventh. With two outs in that fateful seventh inning, Bucky Dent stepped to the plate with two runners on base. Dent may have been a speedy, defensive infielder, but a power hitter he was not. By the end of the 1978 season, he had been such a weak hitter he was relegated to the ninth spot in the line-up. He had hit only forty home runs in twelve years, and if the Yankees had not already depleted their bench he might have been replaced by a pinch hitter, with the Yankees down by two.

When Dent dug in at the plate, he was blessed by fate and perhaps the ghost of Babe Ruth. He fought off several pitches and even fouled one off his foot, which required some attention from the trainer. He then returned to the batters box using teammate Mickey Rivers' bat. The very next swing was a liner to left that ordinarily would have been a long single or a double off the loom-

ing Green Monster wall. But the line drive never descended into
the park, disappearing instead into the sun and just barely over the
top of the Monster, a three-run shot for the Yankee lead, the pennant, and, eventually, the World Series. When the great Carl Yastrzemski popped out in the ninth, the game was officially over.

Actually, the Dent homer may have been the doing—as well
as the undoing—of the Red Sox themselves. The Sox for years
insisted the Green Monster was perched 315 feet from home
plate. If it had been that far away, Dent's ball would not have
cleared the left field façade. Three years earlier, during the 1975
Series, aerial photography and computer calculations determined
the actual distance to be precisely 304.779 feet, just short enough
to accommodate Dent's historic dinger.

In 2003 also, the Red Sox were doomed, needing just one
more win to clinch the pennant. They had the Yankees on the
ropes and the specter of Ruth was waning before a national
television audience but, alas, the wheels came off and New York
again prevailed. The 2003 Yankees went on to lose the Series to
a pesky team, but that was small consolation for the residents
of Bean Town. It was a great letdown for Boston, and for the
national television audience.

But there may have been no curse to begin with; if there were,
there may be a time limit on curses or perhaps the Babe relented,
or maybe the rare lunar eclipse on the very night of the Series
victory had a mysterious hand in the outcome, because in the
2004 championship games against the Yankees, the Red Sox won
four of the last seven games and then went on to defeat the Cardinals at Busch Stadium in the World Series 4-0. They were the
only team to come back from a 3-0 deficit. It was a phenomenal
win, not only because it laid the Bambino's Curse to rest once
and for all, but also because the Red Sox had accomplished the
jaw-dropping feat of winning eight games in a row in a championship season . . . a season that now belongs to the ages.

The up-and-down 2003 Cubs came together at the end of
the regular season, clinching the division with a dramatic double-

header sweep over the Pirates. It was a Cubs team of deep starting pitchers, including dual aces in Kerry Wood and Mark Prior, streaky but suspect hitting, and a manager who had seen it all before—Dusty Baker—all jelling at the right time to defeat the formidable Braves and face the never-say-never Marlins for a trip to the Series. The Cubs squandered, then quickly regained, home field advantage, and ultimately had Florida on the ropes three games to one. The Marlins kept fighting, but the Cubs still had two home games in which to win just one more, and had both Wood and Prior in their arsenal.

Again, no matter. The Cubs of Prior, Wood, Sosa, Alou, Lofton, and Karros had the World Series in their sights—and a goat on their back named Murphy. They also had a date with destiny and with one fateful, perhaps goat-inspired, foul ball.

It had all begun on an energized October day in 1945. It was game four of the World Series at Wrigley Field as the Cubs faced Hank Greenberg's Tigers with a two games to one lead and a chance at home to go up 3-1. Baseball in Chicago could not have been better; it could—and did—get a lot worse.

On October 6, tavern owner William "Billy Goat" Sianis, owner of the Billy Goat Tavern,* clutched two game four tickets on his way to Wrigley Field. It was a magnificent time in Chicago: World War II had just ended, the Cubs had won the pennant, and Wrigley was hosting the Series. Sianis was also hosting his goat Murphy.

Cubs ushers were happy to welcome Mr. Sianis, but they rudely rejected the goat, even though the four-legged fan had

---

* At the time of the curse, the Billy Goat Tavern was located across the street from the original Chicago Stadium, now the United Center. The tavern has since moved to lower Michigan Avenue, directly under the Magnificent Mile. Because it was squarely between the headquarters for both the *Chicago Tribune* and *Chicago Sun-Times* buildings, it became a haven for Chicago celebrities like Studs Terkel and Mike Royko, sportscaster Tim Weigel, Roger Ebert and Gene Siskel, Richard Roeper, Rick Kogan and many more. The tavern is owned by the same family with Sam Sianis at the helm, and achieved its own celebrity with a John Belushi routine on "Saturday Night Live."

come prepared with its own ticket to the Series. Frustrated, Sianis appealed to Cubs owner P.K. Wrigley, asking why the goat wouldn't be admitted. Wrigley replied, "Because the goat stinks." According to legend, Sianis raised his fist, shouting "The Cubs ain't gonna win no more. The Cubs will never win a World Series so long as the goat is not allowed in Wrigley Field." The Billy Goat Curse was swiftly and duly invoked; Detroit won game four and took the Series in game seven when Detroit erupted for five runs in the first and never looked back. Sianis promptly sent a telegram to Wrigley, asking, "Who stinks now?" So far the Cubs have never made it back to the Series, falling apart in 1969, 1984, and 2003. They had a shot in 1989, but were heavily outmatched and had no realistic hopes of winning the pennant.

But 1969 was another matter. An All-Star line-up of Cubs built a nine-and-a-half game September lead behind Ferguson Jenkins, Ernie Banks, Billy Williams, Ron Santo, and others, only to collapse into a hopeless muddle as the Mets caught and blew past the shell-shocked Chicago team. Some blamed the relentless summer heat and humidity of Wrigley day games—no lights would be installed in Chicago until 1988. But others blame the Billy Goat Curse for yanking the Wrigley carpet from under a power-ful Cubs line-up. Punctuating, or perhaps telegraphing the curse of 1969 was the untimely appearance of a black cat that walked across the path of third base slugger Ron Santo.

As in 2003, a 1984 Cubs powerhouse also had three games to play but needed to win just one as they battered a San Diego club in the early going. Nothing to it. Except that the Padres won the next three in a row, largely on the strength of a ground ball between the legs of hapless first baseman Leon Durham. That opened the floodgates and drowned the Cubs, despite the fact that the team included 1984 Cy Young winner Rick Sutcliffe, league MVP Ryne Sandberg and manager of the year Jim Frey. The curse was not overcome.

But it seemed that nothing short of black magic could have stopped the 2003 Cubs. Even though the team sometimes struggled at the plate, it strode back to Wrigley with a two-game lead and two unstoppable horses on the mound ready to go back-to-back. So what happened had to have been the result of black magic. It was game six of the NLCS, the Cubs had a 3-0 lead and ace Mark Prior on the mound. Then the proverbial wheels came off again, wresting the title from Chicago partly because of the antics of a devoted Cubs fan, who wore a Cubs hat and who still insists, no doubt sincerely, that he bleeds Cubby blue. When this fan blindly reached for a right field foul pop-up batted by the Marlins' Luis Castillo, he deflected it from the waiting glove of Cubs left fielder Moises Alou, who had timed his leap perfectly to make the out at the Wrigley left field wall. After the fan, Steve Bartman, knocked the ball out of Alou's mitt, the Marlins scored no less than eight runs that inning, bouncing them off the shortstop's glove, off the "left field fan," into the bleachers—everywhere, it seemed, but into a waiting Cubs mitt. Even though Chicago built a 5-3 lead in game seven, the curse of the goat had unnerved them, and they lost the anti-climactic final game 9-6.

There was a general feeling that Steve Bartman had been manipulated by the Curse of the Billy Goat. On October 16, the *Chicago Tribune* ran a story headlined "The Bleat Goes On, Goat curse lives: Cubs' pennant drought reaches 58 years." A Cubs pennant in 2005 and beyond would have to require a little more than pitching and hitting—like, say, an exorcism. Harry Caray's restaurant bought the famed Bartman ball and ceremoniously blew it up, yet that has not helped Chicago to reverse the curse.

Baseball curses may be real, temporal, or illusory, existing only in the minds of fans, players, pundits or charlatans—but it is in those minds that curses do the most damage. Whatever the truth, the curses of baseball live on, feeding off the game's superstitious roots, burrowing into the heads of managers, fans and players alike. Of course, any sport can be manipulated by mind games, trash talk, and psychological warfare. The Bulls'

Michael Jordan reveled in wearing down the opposition with mental distractions. Muhammad Ali relied on the psych job as part of his game, a nice complement to his strength, his iron will, quick moves and lightning jabs. And when baseball curses creep into the psyche of the players at the plate, on the mound or in the field, do those curses really exist? Surely they do, spawning their own psych job on baseball history as in no other sport.

Weak pitching, clutch hitting, bad weather and cold bats can all be explained, but the one factor that cannot be disproved, it appears, is the impact of curses on the larcenous, in-your-face legacy of Major League Baseball. The Red Sox may have softened that impact.

> *You can look it up.*
> —Casey Stengel

PART II
ALL THE BABE'S MEN

8

THE DECADE THAT ROARED

Who the hell is Johnny Sylvester?
—Babe Ruth

ONE THING ABOUT CURSES—there has to be a flip side. One city's curse is another's blessing, which is what happened to New York City or, more specifically, to the Bronx, at Boston's expense.

With the advent of Ruth in 1920, Yankees attendance surged. The team immediately began to outdraw the Giants, its co-tenants at the Polo Grounds, but an ensuing fit of economic and theatrical jealousy forced the Yankees out, a process completed by Opening Day, 1923. Manipulative schemes often backfire, of course, and it was short-sighted to push the emerging Ruth-led Yankees from the Polo Grounds—a blunder that sent the Yankees to the Bronx sooner rather than later. In any case, with all that was to come, a new Yankees stadium was inevitable.

From 1903, the Yankees' first official year in New York, through 1919, the year before Ruth arrived, team attendance averaged less than 400,000 spectators annually. The team was woefully bad during most of that stretch, never finishing first in any of those seventeen years, and frequently finishing well behind the American League leaders, and twice, in 1908 and 1912, losing over 100 games. For five consecutive years, from 1911 to 1915, the Yankees finished behind the league leader by twenty-five-and-a-half, fifty-five, thirty-eight, thirty and thirty-two-and-a-half games in a staggering display of ineptitude. The mean average in that stretch computes to thirty-six games back each year, and in 1912, the year they finished fifty-five games out, the Yankees drew only 242,000 fans for the whole season.

Boston's Harry Frazee struggled to explain the exodus of Ruth after the 1919 season, calling the Babe selfish and inconsiderate, while even the sports writers in town loudly denounced the twenty-five-year-old slugger as being past his prime. Frazee had publicly expressed the fear that the Red Sox were fast becoming a one-man team; he undoubtedly had reservations about the growing popularity and consequent power of Ruth. He may also have been impelled by the monetary value of selling Ruth after a very good year; Frazee's penchant for dabbling in Broadway shows is well documented.

When Babe Ruth, the "one-man-team," stepped onto the field in a Yankees uniform, he almost immediately revitalized a mediocre but rapidly building franchise. The Yankees' record had already improved from 71-82 in 1917 to 60-63 in 1918, followed by a jump to 80-59 in 1919 when the team finished just seven-and-a-half games back. Attendance had remained weak in 1917 and 1918 at 330,000 and 282,000 respectively, but in 1919 it almost doubled to a pre-Ruth record 619,000 in response to the team's much improved performance. This spurt probably funded the purchase of Ruth from Boston, no doubt inspired by Ruth's record home-run season punctuated, as 1919 drew to a close, by his cannon shot record-setter over the Polo Grounds roof against, of course, the awestruck—and opportunistic—Yankees.

In 1920, the Cleveland Indians won the pennant and took the World Series in seven games against the Dodgers. But just the same, it was the beginning of the Yankee dynasty, with the surging New Yorkers finishing a close second at 95-59, just three games out of first. Perhaps more importantly, Yankees attendance exploded to almost 1.3 million, more than doubling the prior year's record 619,000 as fans became excited by their first legitimate taste of winning.

New York fans came to life in 1920, when the times were rough and tumble: there was the rise of Al Capone in Chicago, baseball gambling, and raucous, even violent fans and players. One day in June, angry Cincinnati fans pummeled umpire Bill Klem with bottles. Another attack on Klem followed when Reds pitcher Dolf Luque punched him in the head. That was by no means the only such incident, and even Ruth later attacked fans and umpires. But Babe Ruth was a big part of the Yankees' rise that year, hitting a staggering fifty-four homers. His revolutionary long ball total was well over three times the leading total hit by his National League counterpart, Cy William of the Cubs, who hit a then-respectable fifteen.

Overshadowed by the acquisition of Ruth, another effective raid on Boston occurred on October 29, 1920, when the Yankees quietly signed baseball sage Ed Barrow, the Red Sox manager who had led the team to an impressive World Series title in 1918. Still reeling from the sale of Ruth, Barrow eagerly took over as Yankees general manager just as both baseball and the Yankees were about to take a quantum leap forward.

In 1921, a new controversy emerged: the lively ball scandal. A baseball centered with unforgiving cork had been implemented in 1910, but the league insisted that no other changes had been made since that time. Still, the ball seemed literally to jump off bats, a perception no doubt reinforced by Ruth's stunning long ball total of the year before. The controversy was odd inasmuch as the ball *had* been altered, and it was official Major League policy that had changed it. At the beginning of 1920, new standards were set for the big league hardball. The spitball had been outlawed, as were scuffed and nicked junk balls, diluting the pitcher's arsenal. No wonder the batters perked up right away, while many people protested the rules changes. Existing spitballers who had been grandfathered in so they could continue to throw the ball until they retired, gradually disappeared. Pitchers were also immediately banned from tossing scuffed-up junk balls.

While the pundits argued the lively ball issue, the Yankees played ball with abandon, winning ninety-eight games and the American League pennant in 1921. Attendance held strong at 1.2 million for the year, and would remain over one million annually for four years, a period that saw three Yankees pennants and three Subway Series including, finally, a Yankees World Series title in 1923 over the Giants.

The Yankees would become the greatest sports dynasty over the course of the twentieth century, but the roaring twenties belonged most of all to Ruth. The Babe exploded with a vengeance in 1921 and continued his one-man assault on the league until the last day of the season. On May 7, he had smashed the longest home run ever hit in Washington, and on May 25 he hit the longest ball in the history of Sportsman's Park in St. Louis. By June 6, 1921, Ruth had hit the most home runs of any player in the twentieth century, and had barely gotten started. As September drew to a close, Ruth had already hit fifty-eight home runs on the year, but he was not finished, blasting long ball number fifty-nine on October 2 in a season finale over the reeling Red Sox. Ruth had stunned the baseball world, finishing the year with a .378 average and 171 RBIs to go with his record fifty-nine homers.

But even with this impressive record and the invincible Ruth, the Yankees lost the first Subway Series in 1921 to the Giants. After the season, the news got still worse as three Yankees— Ruth, Bob Meusel, and Bill Piercy—were all suspended by newly appointed Baseball Commissioner Kenesaw Mountain Landis because of a post-season barnstorming tour. Baseball rules prohibited World Series players from playing exhibition games during the off-season, but Ruth chose to ignore the rules; he and his two teammates earned a lot of money on their usual barnstorming tour. Commissioner Landis ruled that all three players must miss the first six weeks of the 1922 season. When he came back, the Yankees named Ruth their first on-field captain. However, he lost that position five days later on May 25 when he was ejected for arguing an umpire's call at third and made everything worse by climbing into the seats to challenge a hostile fan. Ruth was suspended three more times in 1922 for objecting to umpires' decisions. Despite all this, the Yankees took the pennant for a second straight year, losing to the Giants again in the less-important Subway Series.

The 1922 season saw Ruth become the highest-paid player in the game at $50,000 per year, even with his suspensions. That year, ground was broken on the Yankees' new Bronx stadium. The "House that Ruth Built" would take less than a year to complete, a year consumed by suspensions and skirmishes with the fans. Just five days after beginning the season, Ruth was ejected and then suspended for throwing dirt at an umpire and attacking a fan. He was suspended again in June, a sentence raised to three games when he continued relentlessly to criticize umpire Bill Dineen.

As the year wore on, New York raided Boston yet again, stealing Joe Dugan and Elmer Smith. Dugan, a third baseman, would be a mainstay of the great 1927 "Murderers' Row" Yankees juggernaut. By August 30, Ruth had been suspended once more, this time for three days after another umpire and fan altercation. It was Ruth's fifth suspension of the year, but also his last as a professional baseball player, to be followed by a productive 1923—and beyond.

However, the suspensions and related distractions took their toll. It was not Ruth, but Ken Williams of the St. Louis Browns who won the 1922 home run title with thirty-nine. The Browns' George Sisler led the league in hitting with a stunning .420 average, while Ty Cobb finished second despite his own .401 pace. In the National League, Rogers Hornsby collected three hits on the last day and finished also at .401 to lead the league, winning the triple crown in the process with forty-two home runs and 152 RBIs.

In 1923, Babe Ruth behaved himself and the Yankees took the pennant for the third year in a row. Bob Meusel scored with a .313 batting average and Wally Pipp, whose name would one day be synonymous with bad luck, hit .304. The 1923 Yanks won ninety-eight games and drew 1,007,000 fans, finally beating the Giants to take the Series in six games. Ruth was the league MVP, and the Yankees were on a roll—almost. New York slipped ever so slightly in 1924, winning a healthy eighty-nine contests, but still finishing two games behind the Senators, who had been propelled by pitcher Walter Johnson's MVP year of twenty-three wins and 158 strikeouts. But Ruth himself was clearly back, leading the league in both homers (forty-six) and average (.378).

As the 1925 campaign approached, two changes in the rules were subtly injected into the game. First, the minimum distance for home runs was increased from 235 to 250 feet, a change that may not have affected the game itself as much as it made a statement about the condition of the game, for neither distance was much of a challenge to sluggers and would even eventually be treated as a joke. But the second modification may have had an immediate impact on offensive baseball: the introduction of balls with cushioned cork centers.

Corked balls and some bandbox home-run fences notwithstanding, Ruth was again diverted by off-the-field distractions such as a feud with the Yankees manager and a string of health issues, including an intestinal abscess which required surgery. Limited to just ninety-eight games for the season, Ruth would have one of his worst records right in the middle of his prime, notching only twenty-five home runs and a "mere" .290 average. Ruth and the Yankee distractions of 1925 dragged the whole team down as they finished a staggering twenty-eight-and-a-half games out of first place.

Although the Yankees did not win a pennant in 1925, the year was replete with baseball landmarks, beginning immediately on a chilly April Opening Day in Chicago, when the Cubs' winning game over the Pirates was broadcast live, the first regular season broadcast of a Major League game. Radio would make a lasting imprint on baseball, of course, but on June 2 another historic event took place when a likeable first baseman with a chiseled face and affable smile stepped to the plate as a Yankees starter, replacing the failed Wally Pipp. Lou Gehrig would get three hits that day, giving the world a first-hand look at what the Ruth-Gehrig dynamo would mean to baseball. Unfortunately, however, the 1925 team would sink precipitously behind the league-leading Washington Senators. Attendance took a beating, too, falling by almost fifty percent to 697,000. The decade was more than half over, and while the Yankees had shown flashes of greatness, they could not sustain it, capturing only one World Series in six years.

The New York Yankees revived in 1926. Possibly spurred by what to him would have been an embarrassing 1925 season, the Babe began the year with a bang and ended it as a legend in his own time.

On June 8, 1926, Ruth hit a 602-foot blast in Detroit that may have ushered in the most legendary of all Yankee eras, the three historic years from 1926 through 1928 and the home-run barrage that exemplified them. New York would again capture the 1926 pennant behind a ninety-one-win campaign and almost took the Series, too, pushing St. Louis to seven games before succumbing to the Cardinals with players Rogers Hornsby and Grover Cleveland Alexander. No matter—few fans remember the St. Louis title that year, a championship overshadowed by a legend of baseball magic that still lives today.

There are at least three lasting images of Ruth dominating baseball history. One is the Babe's legendary sixty-home-run season of 1927; another is the flickering image of Ruth's called-shot home run at Wrigley Field in 1932. The third is the fabled chronicle of Johnny Sylvester. The tale goes that on the eve of the 1926 World Series, Ruth heard about a youngster who was in a hospital dying of blood poisoning. Johnny Sylvester was an avid baseball fan—nearly everyone was a baseball fan then, especially in New York. With the Series set to begin the next day, Ruth visited the boy in the hospital and promised a World Series home run just for him.

Ruth's home-run promise became a heart-warming sideshow to the Series, but tensions mounted as game one came and went without Ruth fulfilling his promise, even though Gehrig won the game for New York with a single in the sixth. The Yankees lost game two, still without Ruth's home run. The Yankees left New York without that homer, then sank further with a game-three loss in St. Louis as the Sylvester promise hung in the balance. And then there was game four.

Johnny, the story goes, lay in his hospital bed hanging onto radio reports of the game. Ruth stepped to the plate in Sportsman's Park to face pitcher Flint Rhem in the first inning. The nervous crowd watched as Ruth swung, connecting on a Rhem pitch that took off and sailed over the roof in right field. The Babe's pledge had been fulfilled, but history wasn't finished yet. Two innings later, a determined Ruth faced Rhem again, this time clearing the roof in right center field. With two plate appearances and two balls over the roof, the legend of Babe Ruth had been established forever.

Burned by Ruth's power, the Cardinals also walked the Babe twice that day, but they took a chance in the sixth inning. Ruth hung tough, taking Hi Bell to a full count with a runner on, then connected yet again, sending a smash to deep center where it found the bleachers for the third "Sylvester" homer of the game. It was the first time anyone had ever slugged three home runs in one World Series game as the Yanks tied the Series at two games each.* As reported by none other than the *New York Times*, Johnny Sylvester's fever broke just as word of the record three jacks reached his hospital bed in New Jersey. Although

---

* Accounts of the home runs conflict, but one of them was perhaps the longest ball hit in St. Louis history, breaking the window of a car dealer across the street from Sportsman's Park.

the Yankees won again, making it three games to two, the Cardinals returned to New York and grabbed the final two contests for a seven-game Series title. This disappointed New York fans, but the Sylvester magic was not quashed and the stage was set for bigger things to come.

Did Ruth really cure Johnny Sylvester? It seems unlikely, but the facts are what they are, though some have subsequently been distorted. Did the *New York Times* embellish those facts? Perhaps. But those were different times, when legends were revered, made, lost, and sometimes made up in the interest of a greater calling. Ruth did hit those three home runs, two leaving the ballpark altogether, and Johnny did recover. But did Ruth just luck out? That seems unlikely, too. Was the whole thing somehow set up? It is possible but not likely. In those days, college football was bigger than the NFL is now. Boxing was big also, with fighters like Jack Dempsey dominating the ring, and the NBA did not exist. Baseball was king, the national sport, indeed the pinnacle of all sports, and Ruth and the Yankees were at that pinnacle.

In retrospect, it is clear that baseball or history—or both—embellished the Sylvester legend, and when some of the facts got in the way of the legend, the myth won. A review of the *New York Times* articles from October 1926 reveals that the *Times* itself helped to perpetuate the legend. To begin with, Ruth could not have gone to see young Johnny in the hospital, because Johnny was bedridden at home in New Jersey. And Ruth did not visit him there either, to promise him a home run: by the time Ruth made his visit, the games were over. In fact, Ruth visited Sylvester on October 11, 1926, the day *after* the Yankees had lost the World Series to the Cardinals.

The real story is interesting, but of course it lacks drama. It was not Ruth alone who contacted the boy: both the Yankees and the Cardinals had learned about Johnny's illness, and both teams sent him baseballs signed by most of the players. It's unclear how that happened in the first place, but since the boy's father was vice president of a bank, perhaps his influence was behind all this activity. The truth is that the Yankees' baseballs were sent along with a letter from Ruth—not a visit or a phone call—promising a home run, and it was that letter that caught the attention of the press.

The *Times* said that it was the delivery of the signed baseballs *before* the Series that had already been the "catalyst" for the boy's recovery—a conclusion steeped more in sentiment than fact: "The baseballs buoyed the spirit of the failing lad and gave him a new lease on life."

Game six took place on October 9 with New York leading the Series three games to two. In the October 8 article, the *Times* reported that Johnny remained confined to his bed on doctor's orders and was not allowed to go downstairs to listen to the radio—and, also, the boy ". . . was so far recovered today that his parents went to the big game so they could tell Johnny all about it." So the question arises, how sick was Johnny Sylvester? And on that same day, football star Red Grange suddenly got into the act, sending the boy an autographed football with his own letter promising a touchdown in his upcoming game at Yankee Stadium after the Series. Four days later, tennis star Bill Tilden sent over a racket—by then, it appears, the Sylvester legend had become something of a bandwagon.

Red Grange was the "Galloping Ghost" halfback out of Illinois who helped put the Chicago Bears and the NFL on the map. At that time, though, he was playing for a pro team called the "Yankees" which was scheduled to play the Wilson Wildcats. A rain-soaked crowd of 20,000 saw Grange's Yankees win 6-0, but Grange did not keep his touchdown promise to Johnny—teammate Eddie Tyron scored the only touchdown of the game. In that small, almost insignificant slice of sports lore may lie the symbolic essence of baseball through much of the twentieth century: Ruth delivered in the grand style that only the Babe himself could create, while Grange—and football—came up empty. The success of baseball's symbolic legends may have less to do with the entertainment value of the game than the deep-rooted American love of baseball, but at the end of the day, there had to be a driving reason for the "national pastime" label.

Perhaps Ruth was annoyed by Grange's attempt at one-upmanship. In any case, just two days after the Grange football made the papers, Ruth showed up in person at young Sylvester's doorstep. The *Times* allowed itself to be further carried away by the story:

> This afternoon Johnny was lying in bed listening to his brother and some friends kick a football just outside. He sighed deeply and clasped his cherished baseballs. The doorbell rang and Johnny could hear his mother greeting some one in a subdued tone. . . .
>
> [It was Ruth at the door, of course.] "Glad to meet you, Johnny," said the apparition. "How are you feeling?" . . . Mrs. Sylvester took the visitor to the door, thanked him for coming, and then returned to her son's bedside, where Johnny was on the verge of both laughter and tears. "Gee, I'm Lucky," he says.

It was reported that in the spring of the following year Johnny Sylvester's uncle met the Babe and told him that the boy was doing fine. A perplexed Ruth later asked nearby reporters, "Who the hell is Johnny Sylvester?"

But it no longer mattered. With Ruth back with a vengeance, Gehrig on board, and the legend of Johnny Sylvester inscribed firmly in the books, New York was poised for its pending date with sports history. The murderous Yankees of 1927 were so successful, so legendary, so invincible that the name of the '27 Yankees to this day represents the pinnacle of successes on and off the field. Ruth had led the league in 1926 slugging percentage, home runs and RBIs, but history had seen nothing yet. On April 15, 1927, Babe Ruth hit his first home run of the year, and on September 30 he clocked his last, capping the famous sixtieth home run season with a shot to the right field bleach-ers. Ruth had broken his own record of fifty-nine homers, which had broken Ruth's prior record of fifty-four, which had already broken Ruth's record before that.

Still, it was not Ruth alone who made it the Murderers' Row. There was also Lou Gehrig, the young first baseman who would hit his prime in the same legendary year of 1927. On May 7, Gehrig launched a grand slam as the Yankees beat the White Sox 8-0. It was the first ball hit into the right-field pavilion at Comis-key Park, one of many firsts of Gehrig's stellar career. On July 4, no fewer than 74,000 spectators showed up for the holiday double header against the Senators. The swollen Yankee Stadium crowd saw Ruth go five for seven on the day as Gehrig blasted two more homers, one of them another grand slam. In all, Gehrig would slam forty-seven homers that year, enough to lead either league most of the time. New York annihilated Washington on that Fourth of July, sweeping both contests 12-1 and 21-1 for a first place lead of eleven-and-a-half games.

The Yankees would win a staggering 110 games that year, a total made more remarkable by the shorter 154-game season, meaning they had lost only forty-four times all year for a strato-spheric .714 winning percentage. But even Ruth and Gehrig could not, and did not, carry the team by themselves. Although Gehrig led the team in batting with .373, Ruth's .356 was tied for second with Earle Combs, who himself led the league in hits with 231. Overall, five of the nine key starters hit over .300 in 1927, with Tony Lazzeri hitting .309 with 102 RBIs and Bob Meusel at .337 with 103 RBI's. Remarkably, Lazzeri's lofty 102 runs batted in were only *fourth* best on the team behind Gehrig (175), Ruth (164), and Meusel.

True to form, the Yankees went on to demolish the Pirates with a four-game sweep of the World Series, and the 1927 jug-gernaut was in the record books. That magical season may have belonged to Ruth with his stunning sixty home runs, but it was Gehrig who led the league with his 175 RBIs, garnering the

MVP ahead of teammate Ruth. The Yankees would win it all again in 1928, besting the Cardinals in a second consecutive World Series sweep after winning 101 regular season games, confirming Murderers' Row as a landmark lineup for all time. As of 2004, Ruth and Gehrig still held every major career batting record for the Yankees, including all-time runs scored (Ruth, 1959), hits (Gehrig, 2721), doubles (Gehrig, 534), triples (Gehrig, 163), home runs (Ruth, 659—as a Yankee), RBIs (Gehrig, 1995), walks (Ruth, 1852), average (Ruth, .349), on-base percentage (Ruth, .479), and slugging (Ruth, .711).

The milestone year of 1927 had not been just a great season for baseball generally—it was a time when legends were born, propelling the game to an Olympian status that it enjoyed until the Mantle and Maris year of 1961. And all the rules, the myths, and the on-field heroics of Ruth and Gehrig combined in one fateful season to make it happen in the midst of the chip-on-the-shoulder decade called the Roaring Twenties. Ruth had been acquired from the Red Sox, the spitball had been outlawed, Yankee Stadium had been built with a short right field to help propel the home run pops of Ruth and other lefties, the legend of Johnny Sylvester was elevated to an eternal myth, the 1927 Murderers' Row was born, and baseball became king in America for generations to come.

9

STEALING RADIO

Like Carl Sandburg's fog, radio sneaked in on "little cat feet"
before baseball owners and fans realized what was going on.
—Ford Frick, former baseball commissioner

WHEN YOUNG JOHNNY SYLVESTER was yearning to share Ruth's World Series through the magical new radio box, few realized at the time the power of this new broadcast medium. Those few did not include many of the baseball pundits and owners, most of whom should have realized it. Their lack of vision led them even to try to quash the new medium altogether. Remarkably, the first reaction of many early owners was not to nurture radio at all, but to steal it.

Symbolized by the Sylvester-Ruth saga, there were lonely people, isolated from the high-energy pulse of the roaring 1920s—the sick, the elderly, the shut-ins, the poor, the disenfranchised. But their isolation was about to be abrogated by a friendly electronic voice at the very time that Ruth was king and the boys of baseball had become seasoned men. People all over the country would be united by a single voice that provided comfort to the forgotten, and exalted baseball as the national sport.

There had already been hints of the vast potential the new medium held for baseball. The last game of the 1908 season, played at Chicago's West Side Grounds, decided the pennant, but the biggest crowd was not at the game. With the Pirates in it to the end, a throng of fifty thousand in Pittsburgh followed the Cubs game by "watching" reports of the game on a large manual scoreboard.

The fans of yesteryear loved their game of baseball, in ways that would seem foreign to the modern game. Their heroes on the diamond in the 1920s had been hardened by driving horse-drawn plows in the cold spring-planting seasons, or hammering on a blacksmith's anvil; they had lost family members to the scourges of pneumonia, polio or tuberculosis. Their fans, subject to the same Dickensian hard times, were often adrift in a sea of loneliness, sickness or despair.

Those 1920s ballplayers would be the first to reach an entire nation in its parlors through the magic of radio, a talking box that was about to change baseball, the world of sports—and the world altogether.

The Chicago Cubs opened at home on April 14, 1925, a typical Chicago spring day. There was a swirling wind, but the chill in the air was warmed by the anticipation of a Major League ballgame. Opening Day was always special—indeed, a near-national holiday in those days—but the first 1925 pitch thrown in Chicago was different, an important leap for all of baseball, the first time a regular season Major League game would be broadcast live on radio. This was not the first baseball broadcast, but it would be the most significant, ultimately proving the power of the medium not just for the World Series, but for the whole regular baseball season.

The very first baseball broadcast, as mentioned, had taken place on August 25, 1921, when on America's first commercial radio station, KDKA of Pittsburgh, an announcer described a game in progress between the Pirates and Philadelphia from inning to inning, a Pirates 8-5 victory that lasted one hour and fifty-seven minutes. In 1924, a game between the Giants and Senators was actually carried live, but it was only an exhibition game, not a regulation contest.

Although baseball was at the cutting edge on radio, it was not the first sporting event sent over the air waves. A Jack Dempsey prizefight was re-created over New York's WJZ on July 2, 1921, only about a month before the historic KDKA delayed baseball broadcast. First operational on November 2, 1920, KDKA was to pioneer a series of sports firsts, starting with tennis on August 6, 1921, followed by the first football broadcast nine weeks later when Pitt met West Virginia. When the first World Series game was broadcast on October 5, 1921, narrated by legendary sportswriter Grantland Rice, the Yankees defeated the Giants at the Polo Grounds 3-0 in a game carried by WJZ and WBZ of Springfield, Massachusetts, both stations linked to KDKA. By 1922, the World Series was playing to an impressive audience of five million. Fan interest grew rapidly: in 1949 the Series radio audience reached twenty-six million, and in 1968 eighty-eight million.

But before 1925, no regular season Major League baseball game had yet been broadcast live. None of the owners had ventured to try systematic live broadcasts of regular season games until Cubs owner William Wrigley endorsed the idea. Despite some success up to then, including the limited but popular World Series broadcasts, baseball owners had actually *feared* the radio medium. They were willing to chance the World Series broadcasts, because no amount of radio interest could hold down attendance at the fall championship spectacle. The owners were comfortable—complacent—with newspaper accounts that offered a convenient time delay that did not compete with the actual games.

Baseball has been covered in print since at least May 1, 1853, when the *New York Sunday Tribune* described a short barnstorming tour by a team from Washington. The game eventually developed a strong bond with the press, helping build the careers of famous sportswriters like Grantland Rice, Damon Runyon, Heywood Broun, and many more. But newspapers reported only *past* events, clearly not competing with attendance at the game itself. The owners were afraid that live radio might be a direct competitor, causing the public to stay home, weakening gate receipts and hurting the owners' pocketbooks. This was a possibility not lost on the National Football League decades later when it instituted home blackout rules where the games failed to sell out. But radio would soon prove itself a powerful tool for baseball, not only carrying the game to millions, but actually publicizing it, creating far more fans than may have been lost at the gate.

William Wrigley had first been approached by Judith Waller, managing director of Chicago's WMAQ Radio, who encouraged Wrigley to embrace baseball broadcasts. Wrigley was an astute businessman who already controlled a worldwide chewing gum empire; he also had a distinct advantage over all the other owners, in the person of William Veeck, Sr. When Waller pitched WMAQ to carry the regular Cubs games, Wrigley consulted the elder Veeck, the father of the budding showman, who saw radio as an asset, not an impediment, believing it would introduce baseball to legions of fans, especially the young, generating even more interest, followed by greater attendance.

Wrigley bought into the vision and decided to broadcast a limited number of Cubs games, starting in 1925. It was a time when young Bill Veeck hung out at the ballpark daily, soaking up everything and even participating with his own contributions along the way, including his suggestions about the famed Wrigley Field vines. His ultimate flair for baseball marketing can no doubt be traced to those early days when radio was about to reinvent the national pastime, and Veeck was wide-eyed and eager.

Remarkably, the other owners would not concede the attendance issue quietly. In fact, they actually vetoed Wrigley's radio broadcasts, challenging the Cubs and the formidable Wrigley influence. It proved to be no contest when Wrigley vowed to proceed anyway, and the other lords of the game failed to muster the means or even the fortitude to block the popular Cubs in their powerful home market.

Originally, the radio rights to baseball games were literally given away, first by Wrigley, then by other owners, once they recognized the true economic potential of radio, a commercial dynamo in waiting.

That Opening Day, April 14, 1925, 38,000 spectators were packed into the ballpark. Seven years had passed since the Cubs last played in the World Series, losing in six games to Boston. The Red Sox Series had been remarkable, with a youthful Babe Ruth, still in Bean Town, pitching a six-hit shout-out win to claim game one. In game four Ruth prevailed again, winning 3-2 at home, setting a World Series record of twenty-nine-and-two-thirds consecutive scoreless innings in the process. In a notable precursor of things to come, the entire Red Sox team that season had hit fifteen total home runs—with the pitcher Ruth smashing eleven of them.

In the six intervening years, the Cubs had struggled to regain the dominance of their 1918 team that had finished ten-and-a-half games ahead of the Giants on the strength of twenty-two wins from legendary pitcher Hippo Vaughn. By 1920, Ruth had left the Red Sox, having been sold to the Yankees by Harry Frazee for cash and loans, but he would by no means be gone for long from the World Series. The Cubs and Red Sox would eventually become two of baseball history's most enduring bridesmaids, while the Yankees and Ruth went on to achieve baseball immortality. The 1919 Series did feature Chicago, but it proved to be the dubious Chicago team from the south side, the White Sox, remembered mostly for throwing the Series to the Reds in eight games (out of a possible nine in those days). After Cleveland beat the Dodgers in 1920, the next three Series, from 1921 through 1923, were decidedly New York affairs, with every single Series game played entirely in New York City by the Giants against the Yankees, the Giants winning the first two Series, the Yankees taking the third.

By 1925, Cubs fans had little hope of regaining the dominance of recent years, but they came in droves on Opening Day as WGN radio occupied the stadium roof.* Aging Cubs fireballer Grover Cleveland Alexander took the mound to face the Pittsburgh Pirates, and if ever there had been an unlikely major leaguer, it was Alexander. He had been in France with an artillery corps in World War I where he was partially deafened by the thunder of battle at the same time that he developed epilepsy. Eventually he became an alcoholic. When he was in the minor leagues in Galesburg, Illinois, Alexander took a hard throw to second directly on the head, knocking him unconscious for two days, after which he awoke with double vision. Yet this wounded warrior kept coming back to post staggering numbers from the mound, including three thirty-win seasons in a row and a Major League record sixteen shutouts in 1916 alone. After all that, Alexander was traded from Philadelphia to the Chicago Cubs, landing on the mound for another Chicago Opening Day.

With the Cubs going nowhere again in 1925, Wrigley was both shocked and pleased when radio broadcasting suddenly flexed its fledgling muscles. Letters of appreciation began first to trickle, and then to pour, in from grateful invalids, shut-ins, hospital patients and even prisoners. Then, especially on weekends, fans from neighboring Midwestern states began streaming through the turnstiles, even though the Cubs kept sliding until the team hit bottom. From 1925 to 1931 a very poor Cubs team saw attendance explode by 117 percent. Wrigley had discovered the true entertainment value of radio baseball, and the Cubs have profited from it ever since, seldom on top but draw-

---

* Most sources agree that the first live broadcast of a Major League regular season game was on April 14, 1925, by announcer Quin Ryan on Chicago's WGN radio, but Chicago's now-defunct WMAQ radio takes credit for Cubs radio coverage as early as 1924. Although WMAQ did broadcast Cubs games regularly in the early years, it appears WGN pioneered the first live broadcast.

ing throngs of tourists from Des Moines, Dubuque, Peoria, Rockford, Springfield, South Bend and beyond.

Radio was pulling America closer, baseball was the glue that held it together, and legendary Cardinals broadcaster Joe Buck explained why: "Turn the radio on, and you'll hear a friend. . . . Turn the radio on in your car, in prison . . . in a nursing home, and you will not be alone, you will not be lonely. . . . Radio remains the trusted common denominator in this nation."

A 1925 editorial in *The Sporting News* was a bit less enthusiastic: "Broadcasting stories of games as the games go along is the equivalent of a succotash party with neither corn nor beans." In his 1973 retrospective on baseball, former baseball commissioner Ford Frick sounded a romantic chord as he reflected on the influence of early broadcasting: "Like Carl Sandburg's fog, radio sneaked in on 'little cat feet' before baseball owners and fans realized what was going on."

The impact on Wrigley and the shooting-from-the-hip entrepreneurs of radio broadcasting was anything but subtle. By 1929, virtually all the Cincinnati Reds games were being broadcast, and by the early 1930s Chicago's WMAQ was carrying all the home games of the Cubs and the White Sox. The marriage of baseball and radio was permanent, but it would not continue without significant turmoil.

At first there was disagreement about the role of the broadcaster. Would he just report the events, would he editorialize, or would he even provide commentary and stories between and during the action? Today the radio and television booths are the source of deliberate banter between reporters and colorful commentators, not just in baseball, but in football, basketball, and most other sports, too. When the St. Louis Browns began their broadcasts in 1930, they limited announcers to factual reporting with no commentary. *The Sporting News* approved: "This should be mutually satisfactory to both the fans and the magnates, for there are some announcers who prove to wander far from the actual occurrences on the field."

In time, of course, commentary became the lifeblood of the radio broadcast. Some announcers, like Harry Caray, not only provided opinionated commentary, but also spiced each game with romantic legends and lore, helping to make stars of themselves as they defined the true role—and power—of the medium.

Still, not everyone caught on quickly. In 1926, the year following the Cubs broadcast breakthrough, American League president Byron Bancroft "Ban" Johnson banned regular season baseball broadcasting for the entire league. He changed his mind at year's end, though, when broadcasts of the 1926 World Series became a smash hit as the Cardinals decked the Yankees in a seven-game barnburner. The league office could fight history, but it couldn't win.

Nevertheless, several teams continued to fear that radio would hinder the live gate. The Browns, the Cardinals, the Pirates and some others continued to ban broadcasting on Sundays and holidays—an act that today seems like an exercise in sports heresy. Then when the Great Depression hit hard and attendance dipped, the lords of baseball thought that radio might be responsible. They considered cutting out broadcasts entirely, but team by team the medium waned anyway, as the Depression wore on. By 1934 only three cities continued to broadcast games on a regular basis: Boston, Chicago, and Cincinnati. But then, in the heart of the Depression, the pendulum began to swing, and the following year, as clubs aggressively reached out to boost interest, no fewer than thirteen teams were broadcasting their games. Ironically, New York was one of the last to catch on.

By the 1940s and '50s New York City would become the broadcasting Mecca, but in the 1930s all three of its teams stubbornly fought the radio medium, in 1934 executing a five-year mutual agreement to keep all baseball broadcasts out of the city. So for five straight years New York fans were denied the right to hear the exploits of Jimmie Foxx, Hank Greenberg, Carl Hubbell, Mel Ott, and of course many of the great Yankees teams led by Gehrig and DiMaggio. It was Larry MacPhail who broke the cabal when he took the helm at Brooklyn, refusing to renew the agreement and opting to sell the rights to his Dodgers broadcasts. Common sense—and money—finally won out. The Giants immediately followed suit but, interestingly, the Yankees were the last holdouts in all of baseball, most ironic given the modern broadcasting talents of owner George Steinbrenner.

In the present world of law and sports, the three-way New York agreement to keep baseball off the radio and out of the parlors of millions of fans would be a blatant antitrust violation. But in 1934 it was just a legal means of stealing the game from the fans—ironically to the detriment of the very perpetrators who denied their teams the exposure—and eventual revenue—of radio. That same year the face of sports marketing changed forever when Henry Ford became the first major sports sponsor, shelling out $400,000 for the rights to four years of World Series broadcasts. Gillette soon joined in, paying $14 million for the exclusive sponsorship of ten years of World Series and All-Star games beginning in 1946. Gillette kept the World Series rights for twenty years, wielding great power and even participating in the choice of World Series radio announcers.

Everywhere—except in New York—Major League baseball, radio and America were united in a three-way marriage as the 1930s unfolded. Baseball featured bigger-than-life stars in Ruth, Gehrig, Greenberg, and DiMaggio, and it combined spurts of fast action with pauses suitable for reflection on the history of the game. In other words, the pace was right for verbal description, lending itself almost poetically to the future celebrated commentary of Red Barber, Jack Buck, and the rest. America listened from the living room and the kitchen and in machine shops, stores, filling stations and even automobiles, the car radio having been invented as early as 1923.

Just as radio took hold, baseball began a magic age in 1925. It was the year that a young Babe Ruth was hitting his stride and a long-in-the-tooth Ty Cobb was extending his records as he launched three home runs in one game against the Browns at age thirty-eight. It proved to be a staggering year for hitters everywhere, a season when Rogers Hornsby batted .403, Ty Cobb hit .378 for the Tigers, Cobb's teammate Harry Heilmann slugged .393, and the entire pennant-winning Pirates team batted .307. Moreover, pitcher Walter Johnson not only won twenty games for the twelfth time, he hit for a .433 average, a record for pitchers with at least seventy-five at-bats. Indeed, there was so much hitting that a juiced "rabbit ball" controversy surfaced, but tests failed to reveal anything unusual except better stitching—and great hitting.

While radio took over baseball, baseball was taking over America, the broadcasts propelling the game to its permanent hold on pop culture, if not on history itself.

10

THE LUCKIEST GAME ALIVE

WHEN JOE DIMAGGIO BROKE into the Major Leagues as a rookie in 1936, he assured a continuum of Yankees greats that had begun with the Ruth explosion of 1920. In between there was Lou Gehrig, the epitome of sports figures on and off the field, the glue between generations of the Yankees dynasty.

Radio, Ruth and the Yankees had converged in the 1920s to propel baseball to unprecedented popularity, but none of it would have been the same without Gehrig. Gehrig was actually discovered in 1920, the same year that Ruth debuted as a Yankees slugger, but Gehrig was only a high school junior at the New York City School of Commerce at the time. An exhibition high school championship game was held in Chicago with the School of Commerce meeting Chicago's Lane Tech high school at the baseball shrine soon to be called Wrigley. Not only did New York win the game 12-8, but scouts and fans alike were stunned by a Gehrig grand slam home run, a prodigious smash that sailed out of the ballpark.

Ruth had been hitting home runs in a Yankees uniform for almost four years when the Gehrig kid was brought up from Hartford near the end of the season. Gehrig would eventually launch 493 career home runs, the first on September 27, 1923, at Fenway Park in an 8-3 Yankees victory over Bill Piercy. Even though he played during much of Ruth's reign, Gehrig's glow was not to be overshadowed since he would lead the league in home runs three times (1931, '34, and '36) and RBIs five times. Many still call Gehrig the greatest first baseman who ever played, and with a career .340 average, thirty-four World Series games, and one of the greatest of all records, the 2,130 consecutive games streak, few could argue the point.

Gehrig began playing ball as a sophomore at Columbia University, where he broke a host of Columbia records, including a season best batting average of .444. Gehrig's consecutive-games streak began somewhat by accident, first with a pinch-hitting appearance on May 31, 1925, followed by a start the next game when he substituted for regular Yankees first baseman Wally Pipp, who had been hit in the head during batting practice and had to be hospitalized for a time, thus opening the door to the Gehrig legend.*

Gehrig was not always infallible. He batted sixth and hit three-for-five in his first start but sometimes struggled, as rookies often do, and he was yanked for a pinch hitter more times than he would have liked. Remarkably, Gehrig played for over three years as a Yankee before earning his cleanup slot in the lineup. With Ruth batting third, Gehrig was ultimately inserted in the fourth spot, followed by slugger Bob Meusel. Essentially, Gehrig protected Ruth in the lineup, assuring the Babe of decent pitches, while Meusel did the same thing for Gehrig, establishing the heart of the most famous offensive lineup in Major League history, Murderers' Row.

---

* The standard story about Wally Pipp is that Lou Gehrig took Pipp's job as first baseman for the Yankees when Pipp sat out a game with a headache. Apparently this story is apocryphal: there is evidence that Yankee manager Miller Huggins benched Pipp that day not because of a headache, but because the team was doing poorly and Huggins intended to replace many of the players. Pipp was hospitalized with a concussion when he was hit with a fastball, but that was on July 2, a month after Gehrig had taken his place. See Barbara and David Mikkelson, "Wally Pipp," Urban Legends Reference Pages: Sports, 12/18/04. www.snopes.com/sports/baseball/pipp.asp.

Ruth's persona was bigger than all of baseball, but Gehrig's place in history as the consummate ballplayer is indisputable. Ruth, of course, held legions of records, including career homers and the season standard of sixty long ball jacks, but when the smoke of the 1920s and '30s cleared, it was Gehrig who owned the American League season mark with 184 RBIs and the lifetime grand slam record of twenty-three. He became one of only two American leaguers to clock four home runs in one nine-inning game, a feat never accomplished by Ruth. An outstanding athlete, Gehrig hit for the cycle not just once, but twice, something Ruth failed to do throughout his storied career. For thirteen straight years, Gehrig had over 100 RBIs and 100 runs scored, and he exceeded 150 RBIs seven times in his career, an all-time record.

Years later, the 1962 New York Mets would become synonymous with baseball failure, inspiring Casey Stengel's widely quoted, "Can't anybody here play this game?" But at the opposite end of the baseball spectrum are "the 1927 Yankees," still a standard for greatness not only in baseball, but in any sports endeavor. Those Yankees slumped, however, when the Athletics won the American League pennant three years in a row beginning in 1929, followed by another Yankees title in 1932. By then, though, Ruth was aging and the Ruth-Gehrig dynamo was losing some of its luster. The last year those two icons would play together was 1934, when Gehrig shone, winning baseball's triple crown with a .363 average, forty-nine homers and a lofty 165 RBIs.

Gehrig emerged as the reigning Yankees star in the heart of the Great Depression, and he proved a worthy distraction in those brutally tough times, for he was not only a genuine gentleman, devoted to his mother, he was a fierce competitor with remarkable determination, who inspired a nation. During his famous consecutive-games streak, Gehrig played with back problems and a broken thumb and broken toe, establishing himself as the consummate competitor, team player and genuine baseball hero. In the depths of the Depression, the nation yearned for heroes. By the time he retired from the game, Gehrig had become the poster boy for underdogs, a bigger-than-life tragic figure that still symbolizes the game.

Nineteen-thirty was a memorable year, a time when baseball offense suddenly erupted in inexplicably record proportions. The Cubs' Hack Wilson set an amazing fifty-six home run National League record, one that would survive assaults by legions of stars to come from Willie Mays to Stan Musial, Ralph Kiner and Hank Aaron. Furthermore, Hack Wilson set the all-time record for RBIs at a staggering 190, the Giants' Bill Terry hit .401, and the entire National League hit a collective .303. Indeed, no fewer than six teams slugged at a pace greater than .300, led by the New York Giants team average of .319, and three of the four highest team batting averages of the twentieth century occurred in that one year alone. All eight starters of the St. Louis Cardinals batted over .300, and the Cubs boasted a fearsome lineup in Woody English (.335), Kiki Cuyler (.355 and 134 RBIs), Hack Wilson (.309, fifty-six homers, 190 RBIs), and Gabby Hartnett (.339, thirty-seven homers, 122 RBIs).[*]

The American League also featured three teams that hit over .300: the Yankees, Senators and Indians. A disparity of talent at the lower-level teams dragged down many of the American League averages, but the top teams were nothing short of awesome. The 1930 Yankees, with four Hall of Famers,[**] scored an amazing 1062 runs, averaging just under seven per game, but that impressive lineup finished only third in the American League. The best team from 1929 to 1931 was the Philadelphia Athletics of Al Simmons, Jimmie Foxx and Mickey Cochrane,

---

[*] Hartnett is rated by many as the second best catcher of the Twentieth century, just behind Johnny Bench and ahead of such legends as Mickey Cochrane, Yogi Berra, and Roy Campanella. His 1930 campaign was one of the best performances by a catcher in Major League history.

[**] Earle Combs in center; Tony Lazzeri at second; Babe Ruth in right; and Lou Gehrig at first.

all Hall of Famers who benefited from superior Athletics pitching from Lefty Grove and George Earnshaw.***

Two other American League teams also excelled in 1930, the Washington Senators and Cleveland Indians. With hefty averages from Joe Cronin (.346), Sam Rice (.349) and Heinie Manush (.362), the Senators were a prodigious force, but the Indians may have been even better behind Eddie Morgan (.349, 26 homers, and 136 RBIs), Johnny Hodapp (.354, including 225 hits), and Dick Porter (.350).

What happened in 1930—was it fate, a conspiracy, an aberration? The only unusual thing about that year was a national heat wave that may have warmed batters earlier in the year and fatigued pitchers as the season wore on. There is no evidence of a conspiracy to explain the grotesque hitter's year. But the same cannot be said for 1931 when baseball openly changed the ball in favor of the pitcher.

The new ball had both a thicker cover than the old one and the seams were raised rather than recessed. The ball carried less well than the old one, and pitchers loved the new firm grip. As a result, runs scored per game plummeted, as did earned run averages. Interestingly, the fact that both leagues did not adopt the new ball at the same time provides a unique historical study on the effects of ball manipulation. Both leagues introduced a new ball with raised seams just after the 1930 season, although the American League didn't adopt the new cover until 1934. With the new seams in each league for 1931 the league batting averages dropped dramatically. The National League average fell from .303 to just .277 with runs per game sinking from 5.68 to just 4.48, a full 1.2 runs fewer per game. Without the new cover, the American League differences were real but not as precipitous, with league averages falling from .288 to .278 while runs per game were reduced from 5.41 to 5.14.

*** Even though 1930 was the year of the hitter, Lefty Grove logged one of the greatest pitching seasons ever, leading the league in every major category: wins (28), strikeouts (209), ERA (2.54), winning percentage (.848), and even saves (9).

Even more dramatic was the fall in home runs, especially in the National League where the heavier ball was used right away. League home run totals fell by 44.7 percent, and certain individual performances were even more radically affected, such as the record home-run total of Hack Wilson. The Cubs slugger went from fifty-six home runs in 1930 to just thirteen only one year later!

Beginning in 1931, baseball was manipulated to favor the pitcher. Although legendary, the impressive feats of Ruth and Gehrig are tempered a bit by the changes in the ball of their era, while the efforts of hitters between 1934 and 1968 seem to merit more appreciation. In 1968, the pitcher's pendulum had finally swung too far as failures at the plate soared to all-time highs. More than twenty percent of all games that year included a shutout, including the season opener when the Senators lost to the Twins 2-0. It was the year Don Drysdale broke Walter Johnson's consecutive scoreless inning streak with fifty-nine straight shutout innings. The 1968 Cubs were shut out in four straight games including a yawn-inspiring eleventh inning 1-0 loss to the Braves. It was the year the Cardinals' Bob Gibson mowed down National Leaguers with an astonishing 1.12 ERA while Detroit's Denny McLain owned the American League with thirty-one wins. Juan Marichal of the Giants won twenty-six, Gibson struck out 268, and Luis Tiant of the Indians struck out a whopping 283 en route to a 1.60 ERA.

Only one American Leaguer eked out a .300 season in all of 1968: Carl Yastrzemski at .301. The league batting averages had slipped to a dismal .243 in the American League while the Nationals could muster only a paltry .230, both far cries from the lofty 1930 levels. Perhaps the 1968 All-Star game symbolized the league-wide failures as much as any other statistic, when the best hitters of both leagues combined for just eight total hits and one solitary run for the entire boring game.

What happened? It all began with that new ball in 1931. Night baseball emerged in the 1930s and '40s, favoring the pitcher because the hitters' vision was affected by twilight. New stadiums proliferated, and they tended to be bigger to accommodate larger crowds. Fielders' gloves were much improved by the use of better leather: the fielders became more sure-handed and had slightly better range, so that National and American League errors dropped by about thirty percent per game from 1930.

Adding to the hitters' woes was the rise of yet another new phenomenon—the relief pitcher. In 1930 Herman Bell of the Cardinals led the league with eight saves, while Lefty Grove topped the American League with nine. By 1968, the league leaders were up to eighteen and twenty-five, as managers trotted out more and more fresh players. The latter phenomenon continued to accelerate, with relief pitchers becoming stars in their own right. A decade later, in 1978, New York's Goose Gossage logged twenty-seven saves and Rollie Fingers logged thirty-seven for the Padres. By the 1980s, Dennis Eckersley and Bruce Sutter were reinventing relief pitching with save totals in the mid-forties each.

With runs and batting averages sinking fast in the 1960s, managers struggled for ways to score. Hitters intentionally slugged for the fences, and base stealers proliferated. The 1961 home-run duel between Mantle and Maris was reminiscent of the Ruth-Gehrig days, even though league hitting was dropping. And that same year, 1961, Maury Wills broke Ty Cobb's 1915 steals record to lead the majors with an astounding 104. As the '60s wore on, the Cardinals' Lou Brock emerged, stealing seventy-four in 1966, another fifty-two in 1967, and sixty-two in the pennant-winning year of 1968.

In the end, the 1930s had a profound and continuing effect on the game, directly influencing the record books with .300 league averages, the Hack Wilson RBIs and others, and indirectly affecting the game with relief pitchers, wide-ranging fielders, home run totals, and perhaps most of all, '30s legends. Beginning in 1936, with Ruth gone from the Yankees, Joe DiMaggio, one of the game's greatest hitters, emerged to complement

Gehrig, the superstar. It was no coincidence that 1936 was an MVP year for Gehrig and was the year that the Yankees won first of four straight World Series titles. A career year for DiMaggio followed in 1937, when the new Yankees star jacked forty-six home runs with 167 RBIs and a lofty .346 average.

But then fate intervened. Lou Gehrig was fatally stricken with ALS, amyotrophic lateral sclerosis, now widely known as Lou Gehrig's Disease. On July 4, 1939, Gehrig gave a brief but unforgettable speech before 61,808 people in Yankee Stadium. He never played again. Less than two years later, on June 2, 1941, exactly sixteen years to the day that he first started in the Yankee lineup, the Iron Horse was gone.

Fans, for the past two weeks, you have been reading about a bad break I got. Yet today I consider myself the luckiest man on the face of the earth.

... When everybody down to the groundskeepers and those boys in white coats remember you with trophies, that's something. When you have a wonderful mother-in-law who takes sides with you in squabbles against her own daughter, that's something. When you have a father and mother who work all their lives so that you can have an education and build your body, it's a blessing. When you have a wife who has been a tower of strength and shown more courage than you dreamed existed, that's the finest I know.

—Lou Gehrig, July 4, 1939

PART III
STEALING HISTORY

11

THE EVIL GAME?

Baseball is one of the evils of the day.
—Judge J.W.F. White, Pittsburgh, 1887

IT IS WIDELY ACCEPTED that the 1919 Black Sox World Series games were rigged, but few are aware that 1919 may not have been an aberration. It is possible that even the very first World Series had been corrupted by greed, that the fall classic was tarnished from its inception.

By the turn of the nineteenth century, baseball may have been so corrupt that the game was in danger of slipping into little more than a slimy vaudeville show, a century-old version of professional wrestling where games were not true contests, but were staged exhibitions. When the Black Sox Series blew up in America's face, the corrupt gamblers could no longer hide from public scrutiny. Baseball was forced onto a sometimes unsettling anti-gambling path, partly by the strong personality of the virtual despot Kenesaw Landis. Before that, virtually all big league games were subject to gambling, with even the players and the owners placing bets on the outcome.

Betting on baseball probably began soon after the game was invented some time in the middle 1800s, and was surely commonplace by 1871, when Boston papers had begun printing the odds for local Red Stockings games. Not only fans openly bet in the grandstands—wagers were regularly placed by players, managers and owners, including early star Cap Anson, who unabashedly bet on the White Sox thirty years before the 1919 Sox scandal and a full century before the shenanigans of Pete Rose. Grandstand betting was so common that it developed its own traditions, one being the placing of bets down the third base line where eager gamblers regularly congregated. Baseball thus earned a dubious reputation: in 1887, J.W.F. White, a criminal court judge in Pittsburgh, lectured a convicted thief: "You should never go to a ball game. A majority of the persons connected with the baseball bet on the results of the games, and all betting is gambling. Baseball is one of the evils of the day."

Even team managers wagered on games in those days, sometimes with team brass—as when John Montgomery Ward won a piece of the Giants from betting with Giants club director Edward Talcott. With time on their hands and money to burn, the owners were notorious gamblers, placing bets indiscriminately, with and against their own players.

Trouble was certainly brewing with the low wages paid to early players for their work on the field. Low wages and open gambling combined to foment the scourge of betting off the diamond—or maybe even on it in some cases. Certainly, with high stakes and plenty of opportunities, fixing the outcome of games was inevitable. The original term for throwing games to win bets or earn bribes was an odd one: hippodroming. By 1920, a string of other descriptive terms emerged as players and gamblers fixed, dumped, rigged and threw games for profit.

Gamblers impacted the game almost from the inception of the big leagues. The original league of organized baseball, the National Association, succumbed to gamblers and folded altogether in 1875, although its rules had expressly prohibited betting by players, umpires and official scorers. The National League, set up the following season, faced a similar crisis a year later when the first-place Louisville team curiously lost eight

straight games at the end of that season. An investigation un-
covered a gambling conspiracy that led to four lifetime suspensions, although the league itself managed to survive the ordeal.

The winners of the National League and old American Association played unofficial games against each other for a decade
beginning in 1882, but it was not until 1903 that the idea of an
official "world series" championship became a reality. The prospect of such a "winner take all" extravaganza must have caused
great excitement in the gambling world. During a two-day meeting in January, 1903, the owners negotiated the ultimate makeup
of the two leagues, including territories, players, scheduling, and
the almighty reserve clause designed to prevent teams from raiding each other's on-field personnel. They also agreed upon an
official post-season world championship series between the two
league pennant winners, tossing the season-finale World Series
into the deal as part of the overall armistice between the leagues.

The first World Series was a best-of-nine affair between the
Boston Pilgrims and the Pittsburgh Pirates, but it was born on
the run with the final details not resolved until two weeks before the Series opener. The stakes were high, including bragging
rights, to be sure, but the viability and the economic futures of
the respective leagues were notably at risk. The upstart American League was especially eager to prove itself, and even league
president Ban Johnson reportedly pressured Boston owner Henry
Killilea to win one for the league. Given the animosity between
the owners of those respective leagues, it is remarkable that the
Series managed to hold itself together long enough to play the
first game—and even when that game was finally played, the
owners could hardly control their petty jabs and insults, as when
Boston's Killilea forced Pittsburgh's owner Barney Dreyfuss to
pay his own way into game one at Boston's Huntington Avenue
Grounds, a move that earned Killilea a full fifty cents, the price
for the best seats in the house.

Despite its disorganization, the petty squabbling and gambling associated with it, the first World Series generated tre-

mendous excitement. Both Pittsburgh and Boston had won
ninety-one games that year, each building a sizeable lead over
the respective second-place clubs. Pittsburgh had two prodigious storied hitters in Honus Wagner, who batted .355 during
the season, and Fred Clarke, who hit .351, while Boston enjoyed relentless top pitching from its three twenty-game winners, one of whom was the immortal Cy Young.

Fittingly, the first pitch of the first World Series game ever played
was thrown by that same Cy Young, one of the best pitchers in
baseball history. Remarkably, though, Pittsburgh beat Young that
autumn day on October 1, 1903, before a crowd of 16,242. Such
a crowd seems small by modern standards, but the attendance was
really quite good for those very early days of baseball, two decades
before the time of Babe Ruth and other famous players.

Boston fared better the following day. Down one game to
the Pirates, Pilgrims pitcher Bill Dinneen tossed a three-hit shutout, tying the young series at one game each. Apparently the
initial curiosity of the fans waned, though—only 9,415 were on
hand for the first Boston win.

Attendance picked up, with over 18,000 witnessing game
three, a Pirates road victory at Boston. Again interest diminished, when the smallest crowd of the first four games, just 7,600
fans, watched the Pirates win again, this time in Pittsburgh.
Game five took place the next day with Cy Young again on the
mound tossing a six-hitter that benefited from an impressive
eleven-run Boston attack, and Boston won also the following
day in Pittsburgh, tying the Series at three games each. The teams
remained in Pittsburgh for game seven. When cold weather delayed play an extra day, Cy Young was able to pitch yet again
before 17,000 eager fans, winning the game for Boston 7-3.

Back in Boston for game eight, Bill Dinneen got the nod
again for the Pilgrims, throwing a shutout to seal the historic
Series victory at home. Oddly, only 7,455 Boston fans, the smallest crowd of the entire series, were on hand for what proved to
be the final game.

Each winning player earned a series bonus of $1,182, good money for that time, but perhaps not enough to keep the gamblers at bay. The Pittsburgh management waived its losing share, in order to increase each losing player's bonus to $1,316. This may have been a simple act of generosity, but rumors of gambling on the first World Series began to surface soon after the Black Sox scandal.

It is undisputed that before the Boston-Pittsburgh Series, gamblers had approached Lou Criger, the Boston catcher, to try to bribe him and the Series starting pitcher Cy Young. Two decades later, Criger signed a sworn statement that he had been offered and rejected $12,000 to throw the World Series to Pittsburgh, that he did not take the offer to Young, but reported it straight to league president Ban Johnson. Still, Criger committed three errors in the Series, two in the first game alone—the game one loss in which Cy Young gave up seven runs for a 7-3 Pittsburgh victory. In surprised delight, a Pittsburgh reporter observed, "It's not often that [Cy Young] fails to land the money, even if he is a bit fat."

Certainly, Young could have lost because he was out of shape, or because Pittsburgh had an especially good day, or because catcher Criger had a bad day. Many baseball writers agree with these possibilities, pointing out that Young followed up with two outstanding performances that helped Boston to win the series anyway.

Still, it is a fact that $50,000 was wagered on the outcome of game one alone, much of it by Boston fanatics, one of whom was Joseph "Sport" Sullivan, a member of the "Royal Rooters," who was emotionally tied to the game and was close to the team and its players. His nickname, "Sport," was in those days a synonym for "gambler." In 1919, Sullivan participated in the Black Sox fix with funds backed by the notorious Arnold Rothstein. Sullivan's connection to Rothstein and the Black Sox scandal does raise questions about his wagers in 1903. His open betting on Boston was no secret at the time, so the only issue becomes whether his gambling efforts affected the series itself in any way. Given the rough and tumble times of baseball gambling, the visibility of the World Series showcase, and the obvious proclivities of Sullivan, it would be naïve to assume there was no gambling influence. Especially since in 1924, American League President Ban Johnson discussed the possibility of a 1903 Series fix. In 1923 Lou Criger, the Boston catcher, seriously ill and thinking he was dying, confessed the offer to rig the Series.[*]

Those who continue to support the integrity of the 1903 classic argue, logically, that if Criger's revelations were a deathbed confession, he would certainly have also confessed that he had thrown the series if he had done that. They also note that Boston won the Series anyway, that Cy Young was not the type to take bribes, and that although Criger committed three errors, Pittsburgh star Honus Wagner butchered the field even more badly with six of his own.

But maybe Boston was not the targeted team. Given Wagner's errors, and Pittsburgh's eventual loss even after whipping Cy Young in the opener, the gamblers may have shifted their focus to the Pirates players. If Criger told the truth—that he and Young had spurned the offers—the gamblers may have approached the opposing team.

There is still another possibility: that only the first game— the one that Cy Young lost—had been rigged. The gamblers may have thought that interfering with the first game was sufficient for their purposes, because initially World Series money flowed heavily for Boston, leaving little action on the other side. Gamblers were reportedly nervous about betting on the games since the Series was new and the two teams had not faced each other in regulation play. If nothing else, potential Pittsburgh betters may have been intimidated by Cy Young's reputation. By that logic, a game-one fix makes sense—especially since it was in that game alone that Criger made two of his three errors

---

[*] Criger did not die, however; he recovered and lived another eleven years.

and where Cy Young failed. Moreover, Dreyfuss, the Pittsburgh owner, was known to be a gambler, hardly unusual in those days, who frequently bet on horseraces and on baseball games, including those played by his own team.

As the first Series progressed, the Boston rooters began to heckle the Pittsburgh team, singling out star Honus Wagner, who committed six errors. The Boston gamblers took a bath in the early going, but they recovered, possibly because confidence and money started flowing to Pittsburgh—undoubtedly aided by the crucial game-one Pittsburgh win over Cy Young. The Boston press reported that Sullivan alone netted $8000, although others speculate that his take may have been as high as $20,000.

Gamblers certainly bet heavily on the first World Series. And Cy Young lost game one at home while his catcher was committing two errors. That same catcher admitted years later that he had been approached by gamblers to throw games in the series. And the big winner in 1903—Sport Sullivan—is known to have fixed games with Arnold Rothstein in 1919.

I think we can conclude that the first World Series—or at least game one of the series—was probably influenced by gamblers in some manner. The legacy of open gambling extended back at least to 1871; it is not surprising that this legacy would lead to scandal.

I have played a crooked game and I have lost.
—Eddie Cicotte, Chicago White Sox, 1920

12
THE COBB CONSPIRACY

THE 1910 AMERICAN LEAGUE batting title was stolen at least three times. The crown was eventually won by Ty Cobb, who sported the best lifetime average in history (.367), but not before an open St. Louis Browns plot to wrest the title for Napoleon Lajoie fell just one hit—and two schemes—short.

Cobb, one of the most narcissistic players in baseball history, was the all-time hits leader before Pete Rose, holding ninety Major League records at his retirement. He was a fierce competitor who was not afraid to charge opposing second basemen with his spiked shoes, and engaged in more than a few head games of intimidation by publicly sharpening his spikes. A favorite, possibly apocryphal, story about Cobb is that when he was asked in the 1950s how he might hit against contemporary pitching, Cobb, who sometimes hit over .400 in his playing days, gave a surprisingly modest answer, saying he could hit between .310 and .315. When the interviewer asked why he offered an estimate of only .315, Cobb explained, "Well, you have to remember. I'm seventy-two years old now."

In 1937, "Nap" Lajoie was the first second baseman elected to the Hall of Fame. He was both talented and likeable; hitting .363 in 1896, the first year he became a regular player. In 1901 he jumped from the Phillies to the fledgling American League, for more money, joining Connie Mack's new Philadelphia Athletics team and helping to establish the American League as a baseball force. The National League team sued in Philadelphia to prevent Lajoie from joining the Athletics, and obtained an injunction which was upheld by the Pennsylvania Supreme Court. But Lajoie was able to get around that by being traded to the Broncos, the American League franchise in Cleveland, where the Ohio courts refused to implement the Pennsylvania decision. Lajoie could never again play in Pennsylvania. His .426 average still reigns as the American League record.[*]

Ty Cobb played his last game, his 3034th in two decades, on September 11, 1928. Not only did Cobb set the all-time record with a total of 4191 hits—the last coming on a pinch-hit double against the Senators on September 3, 1928—he did it with only 357 career strikeouts, an astonishing mean average of only about fifteen per year during his whole career. When the very first Hall of Fame vote took place on February 2, 1936, five players were admitted on that first ballot: Ruth, Honus Wagner, Christy Mathewson, Walter Johnson, and Cobb. Lajoie was elected the following year.

Although Cobb, the "Georgia Peach," was a spectacular competitor, his contemporaries despised him. When he died in Atlanta on July 17, 1961, only four baseball people attended his funeral—one of them the director of the Hall of Fame. Cobb was one of the nastiest players ever to don a baseball uniform. In 1921 he was suspended for a bloody fist fight with umpire Billy Evans who had accepted Cobb's challenge to a fight; in 1909 he spiked third baseman Frank Baker, and on another occasion he reportedly bludgeoned a heckling fan, even though the fan was disabled and had no hands.

One of the most colorful and intriguing stories about Cobb centers on an event that occurred in 1910 when Cobb and rival Nap Lajoie were locked in the throws of a tight race for the league batting title. Given the huge egos of both players—Nap

---

[*] Some sources suggest a .422 average, but Major League Baseball lists Lajoie on top at .426.

played for the Cleveland Broncos, the predecessor to the Cleveland Indians whose name was changed after only one year to the Cleveland Naps in Lajoie's honor—the competition was intense. Add to the stakes a new Chalmers automobile to be awarded to the champion, and the contention grew white hot. Both players were among the all-time great hitters, each having on occasion batted over .400, and both were future locks to the Hall of Fame. But the irascible Cobb was so hated that on October 9, 1910, the St. Louis Browns hatched a plot to steal the title from him. It was the final day of the 1910 season with Cobb ahead of Lajoie by a narrow fraction. Cobb's Tigers were playing the White Sox, and Cobb opted to sit on his lead by benching himself for the final two games of the season. Lajoie was behind, needing an unlikely eight hits to surpass the ill-tempered Georgia Peach, so he was forced to play a finale double header against the Browns.

St. Louis manager Jack O'Connor apparently ordered his rookie third baseman Red Corrigan to play inordinately deep at the outfield grass behind third base, obviously inviting Lajoie to bunt. Lajoie failed to notice this at first but lashed a triple anyway, a fly ball that was allegedly "lost in the sun." On his next tip to the plate, Nap caught on and bunted for a single, which he did virtually all day. The other fielders, and the scorer, helped as well. Bobby Wallace uncorked a wild throw to first that was scored a hit for Lajoie. Later, at Lajoie's last at-bat, he was safe at third on an error call. By the end of the day, Lajoie had garnered eight hits in the double header for an apparent statistical tie with Cobb. Lajoie was congratulated by many, receiving, remarkably, letters written by no fewer than eight of Cobb's own Detroit teammates.

Lajoie's apparent success was short-lived, however. The American League was embarrassed about the episode, and the St. Louis papers called it "a deplorable spectacle conceived in stupidity." The Browns denied any skullduggery, insisting that Lajoie simply outguessed their new strategy of "cheating deep."

The league held hearings on the matter, and ultimately the Browns manager Jack O'Connor was fired. The final season statistics, taken to the fifth decimal by a very annoyed league president Ban Johnson, were ultimately computed to .38415 for Cobb to Lajoie's .38411. Disgruntled Browns' manager Jack O'Connor had even offered the scorer a new suit of clothes to change Lajoie's last error to a hit, but the official record books were finalized, crediting Cobb with the league title. The Chalmers Company, out of embarrassment or perhaps sympathy for Lajoie, eventually awarded new cars to both players.

Decades later, in 1981, *The Sporting News* made a stunning discovery. When Cobb's average was calculated, one of his two-for-three games had been counted twice, overstating his 1910 average by approximately .002. In actual fact, Cobb's official average should have been .382, giving Lajoie the championship in the first place. However, Lajoie's average remained tainted by the eight bunts fiasco, and Commissioner Bowie Kuhn refused to change the record books, thus effectively stealing the title back again, and completing a baseball hat-trick of skullduggery that covered more than seven decades

Months later, in April, 1911, the Chalmers auto company offered the award of a new car to the winners of a more subjective honor: the Most Valuable Player of each league as voted by a select committee of baseball writers. The "Chalmers Award" was one of the first major corporate sponsorships in the world of sports. (Cobb himself had also achieved something of a sports marketing first by endorsing Coca-Cola in 1907.) At the close of the 1911 season, the writers voted Cobb the American League MVP winner, earning him a second Chalmers car. Frank Schulte of the Cubs was the first National League winner.

Loved or not, the volatile Cobb was a relentless player. Counting the 1910 episode with Lajoie, Cobb won a record total of twelve batting titles. Explosive and emotional, his chip-on-the-shoulder style also got him into more fights than heavyweight champ Jack Dempsey, including a high-profile altercation with Honus

Wagner during the 1909 World Series. Cobb was notorious for stealing bases, and he held the all-time season record of 96 until Maury Wills broke it in 1962. During the 1909 Series, Cobb, leading off first base in the second game, shouted down to Honus Wagner playing second, "Watch out Krauthead, I'm comin' down on the next pitch." Cobb did, barreling into second base where the unimpressed Wagner tagged him out squarely in the mouth.

The beginning of Cobb's professional life was overshadowed by a tragic event: in August, 1905, the month of his Major League debut, Cobb's mother shot and killed his father, apparently by mistake. In 1948, after he retired, Cobb became a philanthropist and donated a then staggering sum of $100,000 to his hometown hospital. Between those years, Cobb's career was a roller coaster of awards, honors and controversy.

In a 1911 game against the Yankees, Cobb literally stole a run after doubling in two runs that provoked an all-out argument at the plate. With a vehement crowd of distracted players debating the call, Cobb ambled from second base to third, then stealthily wandered down the line toward home, through the agitated crowd, and then finally slid in with the lead run. In all the frenzy, the contentious players had forgotten to call time out. That same year Cobb managed a forty-game hitting streak, a record at the time, and then won the first Chalmers MVP award after that season.

After attacking a crippled fan in 1912, Cobb was unceremoniously suspended by league president Ban Johnson, which, in turn, caused a mini-strike by his Detroit teammates. The league threatened the Tigers with a major fine unless they fielded a team for a scheduled game against the Athletics, so Detroit recruited a band of locals who, along with two of the Tigers coaches, managed to lose to those Athletics 24-2. The whole affair eventually led to the formation of one of the first players' associations three months later.

In a 1914 game against Boston, Dutch Leonard drilled Cobb with a pitch that fractured one of Cobb's ribs. Cobb stayed in the game and later bunted down the first base line. Leonard covered and was spiked for his trouble by a vengeful Cobb in the play at first. There was no love lost between the Tigers and Red Sox in those days, and near the end of the 1915 season, both teams were in a fierce pennant battle, tied at ninety wins apiece. In a head-to-head game on September 16, Boston relief pitcher Carl Mays repeatedly threw at Cobb, finally nailing him on the wrist. Cobb retaliated by winging the bat at Mays and the Fenway crowd reacted by tossing bottles at Cobb, who ultimately left under police escort.

Cobb could not restrain himself, even in exhibition contests. When Detroit played an exhibition game against the Giants in 1917, Cobb cut up second baseman Buck Herzog's leg with a high slide, causing an immediate fistfight that was renewed later that same night in Cobb's room. Cobb could not even control himself at social events, let alone during games. In 1935, during a dinner with writer Grantland Rice at the Detroit Athletic Club, retired Indians catcher Jay Clark joked about how he had gotten Cobb out over ten times at the plate with a sweeping phantom tag that fooled the umpires. Cobb went ballistic, accused Clark of costing him ten runs, and had to be pulled off the surprised ex-catcher.

In 1922 Cobb lost two more batting average points in a separate league mishap reminiscent of the 1910 Lajoie debacle. One scorer credited Cobb with a May 15 hit, while the AP scorer called it an error. The league used the hit version in the records, and by season's end Cobb was perched at .401. The New York writers complained so forcefully that Fred Lieb, the scorer who had called it a hit, reversed his decision. Even though both scorers then called it an error, the league kept it as a hit, giving Cobb a .401 finish instead of .399. No titles or cars were at stake: Browns star George Sisler won the batting crown easily that year with a stellar .420 average.

Without question Cobb was one of a kind, the fiercest competitor of his day, if not of all time. He was probably respon-

sible for more skullduggery than any other player, taunting the
opposition, stealing home, spiking second basemen and pitchers alike, and even inspiring others to do the same, including
the bizarre 1910 episode where the batting title was stolen not
once, but three times. In the end, Cobb may have symbolized
the chip-on-the-shoulder, no-holds-barred character of Major
League Baseball more than any other single player, owner or
commissioner in the game's mischievous history.

13
HAL CHASE: MALIGNANT GENIUS

IN AUGUST OF 1920, Hal Chase, a former first baseman and
one-time Yankees manager, was officially banned from all Pacific Coast League games for attempting to bribe a pitcher.
That same month, William Veeck, the Cubs president, received a telegram warning of a possible fixed game against Philadelphia on August 31. Veeck benched Claude Hendrix, his scheduled starting pitcher, and then released Hendrix altogether.
Nonetheless, the *Chicago Herald and Examiner* reported on
September 2, 1920, that the Cubs-Philadelphia game had indeed been fixed with the then-considerable sum of $50,000
placed on the Phillies. Five days after that report, a Cook County
grand jury convened in Chicago to investigate the Cubs-Phillies
fix, but in an historic decision, the presiding judge asked the
grand jury to investigate also the possible manipulation of the
1919 World Series between the Cincinnati Reds and the Chicago White Sox. The eventual Black Sox trial would lead directly to Hal Chase.

Baseball gambling had grown to endemic proportions in
those days. And Hal Chase was involved in much of it. Chase
had been a top-fielding first baseman for the Yankees and White
Sox, but he could never resist throwing games for quick profits.
Although a talented fielder, one of the best of his day according
to many, he actually led the league seven times in errors com-

mitted—no doubt because of his talent for sniffing out gambler money. When he jumped to the young Federal League for more money, he clubbed the most league homers in 1915. He batted over .300 four times, and led the National League with a .339 average for the 1916 season.

In 1918, Chase was suspended by manager Christy Mathewson for throwing Cincinnati Reds games, and in 1919 the Giants' John McGraw tried to reform the wayward player but gave it up as hopeless. With his ties to the Reds, White Sox, and the gambling underworld, it is not surprising that on September 6, 1920, Chase was indicted on bribery charges in connection with the White Sox World Series loss to the Reds.

Less than three weeks later, on September 24, a Chicago grand jury heard riveting testimony from Giants pitcher Rube Benton that Hal Chase and the Cubs' Buck Herzog had bribed Benton to throw a game. Benton said that Chase had personally won $40,000 betting on the 1919 World Series, a revelation that still haunts baseball after more than eight decades. As early as 1910, Chase had been accused by his own manager of throwing games, but no one had foreseen the sweeping scope of gambling that would infest the game by 1920.

Gambling has probably been a part of sports for as long as sports have existed, including contests between Roman gladiators, between ancient Mayan Indians, and even between competitors in the original Olympic games, and gambling will always prompt efforts to rig the outcome. The entertainment value of sports lies first in the drama of the contest, which is wholly dependent on the uncertainty of the outcome. If games are perceived as choreographed, they become no more meaningful than a well-rehearsed ice show or exhibition, no different from the predestined games of the Harlem Globe Trotters—with one difference: the ice shows and the Globe Trotters present honest entertainment.

The modern baseball era has undergone more than its share of sports gambling. In Chicago in 1903, Jack Taylor was an opportunistic pitcher for the Chicago Colts, the predecessor to the Cubs. In the first-ever cross-town series between the Sox (then the White Stockings) and the Colts, Taylor had been brilliant in the first game, pitching the Colts to an 11-0 three-hit win on October 1, 1903. The Colts won the next two games for a commanding three-games-to-none lead in a seven-game series. But then Taylor not only lost his next start against the Sox, but two more after that as the White Sox pulled even. The Colts were convinced that Taylor lost those games on purpose and two months later he was gone, traded to the Cardinals on December 12 for a promising right-handed pitcher with fingers deformed from a farming accident, Mordecai "Three-Finger" Brown, who would be a north side superstar for years to come.

Baseball and gambling would prove a volatile mix of larcenous shenanigans jeopardizing the very existence of the game. Without the entertainment value of unfolding real-time drama, those games would be reduced to hollow exhibitions of hitting, pitching and fielding. In baseball more than any other major sport, there is a precedent for "good cheating" versus "bad cheating." Some elements of baseball mischief, though technically cheating, evolved as relatively acceptable under-the-table components of the game itself. Throwing spitballs, using corked bats, stealing signs, trash talking the batter, tossing pebbles at the hitter's shoes, faking the catch of a fly ball to hold the runners, employing the hidden ball trick, brush-back pitches and all the rest—these are the mischievous elements of the game invoked when necessary, all within the unwritten rules of baseball as the game is actually played. But gambling undermines the game itself, reducing it to a mere demonstration on a diamond devoid of character, drama and excitement.

Money and ego are the root of all sports evil, so gambling will never disappear altogether. Indeed, sports gambling is an established national industry, thriving on the NCAA tournament, Super Bowl, World Series, championship boxing and much more. Horseracing virtually depends upon gambling money for revenue.

According to baseball historian Bill James, as many as thirty-eight Major Leaguers were directly involved in gambling and related scandals in the notorious decade from 1917 to 1927, many of them incurring the wrath of Kenesaw Mountain Landis, the new commissioner who was appointed to save baseball from these criminal elements.

Dutch Leonard involved even icons Ty Cobb and Tris Speaker in a scheme to fix the last game of the 1919 season. Heine Zimmerman, who led the National League in both hitting and home runs in 1912, allegedly conspired with Hal Chase to bribe Fred Toney, Rube Benton and others. Buck Herzog was allegedly involved in attempting to fix the Cubs-Phillies game of August 31, 1920, the game that led to the grand jury indictment of the White Sox. In addition to the eight Black Sox players, including Eddie Cicotte and Joe Jackson, thrown out of the game forever, eleven other players received lifetime bans, including Hal Chase himself, along with Jean Dubuc, Jimmy O'Connell, Claude Hendrix, and Heine Zimmerman.

The two most famous players banned from the game in the past hundred years were Shoeless Joe Jackson and Pete Rose, who has admitted publicly that he gambled on baseball and lied about it. Shoeless Joe continued to maintain his innocence, but even he was not invulnerable to temptation in 1919, having taken $5000 from gamblers. What he denied was participation on the field; he insisted that he took no action to actually throw any of the 1919 Series games. But since he was involved in the conspiracy, he was banned "for life." (Perhaps Jackson should now be logically eligible for the Hall of Fame since he necessarily completed his lifetime sentence when he died.)

Buck Weaver was a Black Sox victim of a different sort. He was banned from baseball simply because he knew about the Series fix. He took no money, hit .324 in the 1919 Series, committed no errors, and maintained his innocence until his dying day on the streets of Chicago. His niece by marriage, eighty-six-year-old Marjorie Follett, a baseball fan extraordinaire, said as recently as 2000, that "Uncle Buck died of a broken heart."

Although there could hardly have been a more fitting name for the 1919 Chicago team, the "Black Sox" nickname did not result from the World Series fix, but was indirectly related to some of the probable causes of the conspiracy. The stinginess of team owner Charles Comiskey has been well documented and is often mentioned as one of the reasons the Sox players were vulnerable to gamblers. Although the team was loaded with star players, their salaries were far from competitive, and since the players were not free to switch teams, they either had to play for the Sox or not play in the majors.

Comiskey's penny-pinching was petty to the point of being counterproductive. He skimped on the little things that made a big difference, like meal money, and even refused to pay for the cleaning of team uniforms. The players, already underpaid, had little incentive to pay their own cleaning bills, so their uniforms became dirtier and grimier—the original reason they were called the Black Sox. Once the gambling conspiracy surfaced, this negative nickname took on a deeper significance.

The annual salary of the highest paid among the eight Sox players involved was $6,000, so the $80,000 bribe, divided among the eight, represented more than double their collective salaries at the time. First baseman Chick Gandil, the leader of the plot, took the largest share at $35,000. The other seven divided $45,000, of which $5,000 went to Shoeless Joe.

Although Eddie Cicotte had finished the season with twenty-nine wins and a sparkling 1.82 ERA, his game one Series start brought a 9-1 Cincinnati win, including a fielding error on Cicotte himself. The Reds won game two with a big fourth inning against pitcher Lefty Williams, but Sox starter Dickie Kerr, who was not in on the scheme, pitched a two run shut-out victory for Chicago in game three. The Sox lost the next two, one featuring a two-error performance by Cicotte; then Kerr delivered again in ten innings for the second Chicago win. Perhaps

feeling the heat for his obvious substandard play, Cicotte contributed a four-hit win to bring the Sox within one game of the
Reds. It was a best-of-nine World Series in those days, so the
Reds had two chances left to take the championship.
Lefty Williams, who had already lost his first two starts, 4-
2 and 5-0, was scheduled to start game eight. The gamblers
were in no mood to take the Series to nine games, so they threatened both Williams and his wife, to make sure he would be
knocked out of the game in the first inning. Williams obliged
with a woeful first, yielding three runs on four hits in one-third
of an inning pitched. The Reds went on to take the Series with
a 10-5 game eight victory.

The 1919 Series fix was blown open at the end of the 1920
season. All eight players were indicted and suspended, even though
there were three games left in a barn-burner pennant race with
the Indians. Eventually five more conspirators were indicted, including Hal Chase and Bill Burns, both of whom were the con-
nections between the gamblers and the players. In those rough
and tumble days, Hal Chase and gambling were nearly synonymous, and Chase was in perpetual trouble with the leagues and
the law, one judge calling him a malignant genius.

When the case went to trial in Chicago, all eight players
were acquitted. Some people say that the players and the jurors
celebrated the verdict in the courtroom; they certainly celebrated
together in a Chicago restaurant after the trial. However, the
players could not foresee that the appointment of no-nonsense
federal judge Kenesaw Mountain Landis as baseball's first independent commissioner would end their careers. Landis banned
all eight of them from baseball for life, and none was ever reinstated, although efforts to do so on behalf of Shoeless Joe and
Buck Weaver continue even today.

Most of the banned Sox players eventually opened taverns,
with the exception of Gandil, who became a plumber. Weaver
continued to insist on his innocence, but over the years he lost
appeals to two different commissioners. The lynchpin of the

conspiracy was the notorious underworld gambler Arnold Rothstein; after his murder in 1928, files and papers were discovered implicating many others in the affair.

Three of the players signed confessions, and all three confessions mysteriously disappeared before the trial. Even the court papers and transcripts of the Black Sox trial itself somehow disappeared from the Cook County court system, never to be found again. In 1960 an exhaustive but futile search was made of the archives, leaving a gaping void in baseball history. It would neither be the first nor the last time that this sort of thing would happen in the history of America's chip-on-the-shoulder game.

14

THE ROGER MARIS ASTERISK

Sixty, count 'em, sixty. Let's see some other SOB *match that.*
—Babe Ruth, September 30, 1927

ON OCTOBER 6, 1961, the soul of baseball's past vanished into Yankee Stadium box 163D as Roger Maris ripped his record sixty-first home run into Major League destiny. Embattled, bruised and betrayed by the most famous asterisk in sports history, Roger Maris would never be the same. Neither would big league baseball.

Both Roger Maris and Mickey Mantle had tried to best Ruth's record sixty home runs that fateful season. Maris made it, although he might not have clubbed his famous sixty-one homers if Mantle hadn't batted just behind him in the impressive Yankees lineup. Mantle was a golden-haired favorite, the pride of the Yankees and possibly of America, and Ruth himself was the favorite of then commissioner Ford Frick who was proud of knowing Ruth personally. As Mantle and Maris closed in on the long-ball milestone, Frick feared that a baseball icon was about to be toppled. And he took it personally.

Frick did more than fear the outcome, he chose to intervene to preserve Ruth's revered mark—or really to steal it back from Maris by discounting Maris's 162-game season. Even before Maris pulled past Ruth on the last day of the season, Frick announced that any new home run marks logged in the 162-game season would be distinguished in some way as being derived from the longer season, and thus in fact tarnished. When Ruth played, the Major League season was 154 games. Ironically, Ruth himself needed more—155 games, to be exact, to set his own record. Earlier in the year a rainout game did not count in the standings, but the individual statistics from that game were retained, so Ruth actually benefited from 155 games. Even more notably, the same thing happened to Maris in 1961 when his 162-game record really took 163 contests.

But Frick was consumed by his loyalty to Ruth and a blind adherence to the past, almost to the point of fanaticism. As home runs were launched in record numbers, Frick went so far as to publicly support the return of the spitball to help the pitchers counter the explosion of baseball offense. But contrary to Frick's belief, baseball offense had not exploded. The number of runs scored per game in 1961 were almost identical to the number of runs per game in 1927, the year of Ruth's memorable milestone, at just over 4.5 per contest. The 1927 American League runs were materially higher than in 1961—4.92 to 4.53—and the 1927 ERA for the entire American League was 4.14, but in 1961 it was only 4.02. So why all the fuss?

Frick, like the public at large, was blinded by the 1961 barrage of home runs. Even though teams were scoring about the same, they did it differently, swinging for the fences rather than playing small ball in the infield. As a result, 1961 American League batting averages were actually lower than their 1927 averages, .285 to .256. But home runs mounted, even as strikeouts rose and averages sagged. Indeed, not only did Maris and Mantle assault Ruth's record, but the 1961 Yankees launched more home runs than any team in history, including the 1927 team of Ruth and Gehrig: 240 vs. the Murderers' Row total of 158. The Murderers' Row squad struck out only 610 times, but scored 948 runs, while the Mantle-Maris version in 1961 struck out 785 times and scored only 827 runs.

Frick was either unaware of the facts or he ignored them. He not only tinkered with the past by attempting to qualify the Maris mark, but he proceeded to change the game itself. What upset the commissioner was the prospect of Mantle or some other slugger topping Ruth at the 154-game mark of any given season. Although Frick did not actually bring back the spitball as he threatened to do, he did lobby for rule changes to protect the pitcher at the expense of the hitters. He succeeded after the 1962 campaign when the strike zone was expanded vertically, going from "between the armpits and the top of the knees" to a much bigger "between the shoulders and the bottom of the knees." One year later, in 1963, league ERA dropped to about 3.5 per game, and pitching style changed dramatically. Suddenly high heat was in, and the likes of Don Drysdale, Bob Gibson and Tom Seaver had a virtual field day at the expense of big league batters who could not catch up to the high hard fastballs.

Still, today the late Mickey Mantle is universally admired, even loved, especially by aging Yankee fans. But except for his miracle year of 1961, hardly anyone remembers all of Maris's accomplishments—although Roger Maris was a legitimate force in his own right. After being acquired from Kansas City, he debuted for the Yankees on April 19, 1960, in a road game at Fenway Park with an impressive display of offense. Not only did Maris have a four-for-five day, he clocked not one, but two home runs, propelling New York to an 8-4 victory, and one month later he was already in the big league record books. On May 30, 1961, Maris, Mantle, and Moose Skowron *each* slugged two home runs in one game, tying the Major League record for most multi-homers in a single contest.

Maris's spectacular year in 1961 may not really have been better than Mantle's season. The Mick batted .317 to .269 for Maris, and he stole twelve bases out of thirteen attempts, while Maris had no attempts at all. Maris did drive in more runs (142 vs. 128) in addition to his sixty-one home runs. But Mantle's fifty-four homers made it one of the best years ever—considering, for example, that the great slugger Henry Aaron never hit as many as fifty even once in his long, storied career. Mantle's on-base percentage was noticeably higher at .452 to .376, partly due to Mantle's 126 walks compared to ninety-four for Maris, and the Maris home runs notwithstanding, Mantle's overall slugging percentage was higher at .687 to .620. However, history should give Maris his due, for he was not a one-season wonder. In fact, in 1960, he clubbed only one homer fewer than Mantle and actually won the league MVP award.

In 1960 the Yankees slugged 193 homers, and in 1962 they hit 199. It was this emerging pattern during 1961 that disturbed Ford Frick, who saw that someone would soon break the longstanding mark of a baseball icon. Although Frick never legitimized the spitball, he did expand the strike zone, but too late to influence the dramatic home run contest of 1961. However, he did his best to influence history. The Maris asterisk never actually appeared in the record books; this was fortunate because the asterisk would have set an extraordinarily bad precedent, demeaning almost every record in the 162-game era. Aaron had more games per season to set his career mark than Ruth had in his day; Rose had more games that caught up to and surpassed Ty Cobb; and then there were the spectacular long balls of Sosa, McGwire and Bonds.

It is certainly odd that Roger Maris, who achieved one of the most important landmarks of the modern baseball era to top off one of the most famous seasons ever, is not in the Hall of Fame. To be sure, his career numbers did not equal those of other players in the Hall. He had a lifetime average of .260 with 851 RBIs and 275 lifetime home runs—far short of the accomplishments of elite 400 and 500 homer members—but it is perhaps the Hall of Fame criteria that are at fault rather than Maris himself. There might be a lingering grudge against Maris, not so much for besting Ruth—that has been done on several occasions since, three times by Sammy Sosa alone—but perhaps for taking the 1961 season from favorite Mickey Mantle. But whatever the reason for his exclusion, Maris deserves to be in the Hall of Fame. Nothing symbolizes the miscreant spirit of baseball more than the efforts to discredit Roger Maris.

Only 23,154 fans showed up for Maris's last game of 1961, even though the contest was held on a Sunday afternoon and offered one last shot at surpassing the magical sixty—against the hated Red Sox, no less.

Much of the crowd was squeezed near the right field fences, where a lefty power hitter might plant the next long ball. In the first inning, Maris tagged a Tracy Stallard pitch deep to left, but the fly ball died short of the fences and wound up in the glove of left fielder Carl Yastrzemski. Stallard was still pitching in the fourth when Maris again stepped to the plate. The exuberant crowd may have changed history that day, booing loudly when Stallard pitched two straight balls to Maris, and fell behind 2-0. Rather than risk a breaking pitch—and incite the already hostile fans—Stallard gave in with a low fastball over the plate. It was history waiting to happen and Maris obliged, clocking the ball high and deep to right field—just where the crowd had expected, and right at the short Yankee fence.

Sam Gordon, a wealthy restaurateur, had offered $5000 for the defining ball—how times have changed—so both the crowd and the Yankee players in the right field bullpen just in front of the stands were anxious to cash in. "We all wanted a crack at the ball and getting the five thousand dollars," said Whitey Ford, ace of the Yankees' staff. The ball sailed over his head, into the stands, where it reached Sal Durante, a nineteen-year-old from Coney Island. Maris's teammates ecstatically welcomed the embattled slugger as he rounded the bases for one last time. Maris came to the plate two more times that day, but came up empty. Still, his solo shot on the fourth was enough, producing the solitary run of the game, the 109th Yankees win of the year. Only the 1927 Yankees and the 1954 Indians had won more games in a season—and, of course, no one had smashed more home runs than the quiet, unassuming Yankee, Roger Maris.

Not even Ruth. And that, of course, was what motivated Ford Frick.

Mickey Mantle played in sixty-five World Series games for the Bronx Bombers, a total that not only bested Maris, but was almost as many as Ruth (41) and Gehrig (34) *combined*. The Mick would smash 536 career home runs, the highest total of any switch hitter in history. Indeed, only two switch hitters exceeded 500 career homers, the other being Eddie Murray with 504. In 1956, Mantle won the vaunted Triple Crown with fifty-two long balls, a .353 average, and an impressive 130 RBIs. It was the year Mantle would set a new record for hitting at least one home run from each side of the plate (left-handed and right-handed) in each of three different single games during one season, and then he did it again several times during his illustrious career. No doubt the Mick had a more impressive career than Roger Maris, and he may have even had a more impressive 1961—but Maris deserves his due, for it was one year Mantle could not out-slug him.

Of course Ruth had a more memorable career than both of them, leading the league in home runs during every full season that he played, a remarkable feat in a remarkable career. The Babe hit the first home run ever at Yankee Stadium, and he never stopped until number 714 had been logged. Ruth and Gehrig may have had the best one-two punch careers, but even though the Ruth-Gehrig combo tied for the league lead in 1931 with forty-six each, no single-season one-two delivery was better than the magical home runs of Maris (61) and Mantle (54) in 1961.

But no baseball record was assailed and tarnished as Maris's was during and after the 1961 season. Not Mark McGwire's, not Hank Aaron's, not Pete Rose's. It was an emotional season that took a toll on Roger Maris, who, when asked by a reporter whether he could break the Babe's record, replied, "How the fuck should I know?"

He did break it, of course, despite Ford Frick's futile effort
to prop the Babe up. But, the record sixty-one remains oddly
tarnished, even now.

15
The Village Idiot

An empty car pulled up and Bowie Kuhn got out.
—Red Smith

BOWIE KUHN WAS A magnet for controversy during his tumultuous 1969–84 reign as commissioner of Major League Baseball. He drew legal fire from team owners, especially the Braves' Ted Turner and the Athletics' Charles O. Finley, as well as from players like pitcher Ferguson Jenkins and outfielder Curt Flood, and even from Melissa Ludtke, a *Sports Illustrated* reporter who successfully sued to gain locker room access to interview players.

Kuhn was a high-profile, powerful figure whose stiff demeanor and rigid approach provoked derision. He took himself much too seriously, and was no match for the witty gamesmanship of such strong personalities as Ted Turner, or the renegade union man Marvin Miller. But Kuhn fought back, setting the stage for two decades of unending baseball wars and shenanigans.

Kuhn was elected commissioner in 1969, and set out to be a peacemaker, telling both owners and players much of what they wanted to hear. But the times were changing rapidly and he could not have it both ways for long. He immediately became embroiled in the Curt Flood antitrust lawsuit, when Flood, who played for the St. Louis Cardinals, didn't want to be traded to the Philadelphia Phillies and decided in 1970 to sue Major League Baseball over the reserve clause dictating that a player was the property of the team holding his contract. The case eventually reached the Supreme Court, which on June 18, 1972, upheld a lower court ruling that exempted baseball from antitrust laws and upheld the reserve clause. But the decision left loopholes and by the end of 1972 the owners agreed in effect to end the reserve clause.

In that same year there was a players' strike, and then in 1976 the owners lost a key arbitration when Andy Messersmith sought free agency from the Dodgers. Player strikes and free agency were explosive questions, and soon the players hated Kuhn, while many owners despised him for allowing too much controversy—and scrutiny—in the big leagues. The press had a field day. When the players went on strike in 1981, writer Red Smith frequently lashed out at the commissioner, finally capturing the essence of Kuhn's painful lack of personality when he wrote one of baseball's most acerbic lines: "This strike wouldn't have happened if Bowie Kuhn were alive today."

Charles Finley had tried his own hand at semi-pro ball in the 1940s until he contracted tuberculosis. Finley survived, but his baseball career did not. He went into the insurance business, made millions and was able to return to his baseball roots with the purchase of the Kansas City Athletics in 1960. Like fellow Chicagoan 0, Finley loved innovation, especially if it meant tweaking the commissioner or other baseball owners, and he lost no time in getting started.

The colorful new owner feuded openly with his players and managers, even firing his best hitter, Ken Harrelson, who would lead the American League in RBIs the following year. Angry at Finley's management style, Harrelson publicly called his former employer a menace to baseball. Manager Alvin Dark, who also incurred Finley's wrath, was let go too. Finley not only juggled his players and quarreled with them, he made them wear white shoes—a flashy, even outrageous innovation at the time—and dreamed up catchy nicknames for them. Pitcher Vida Blue refused to be called "True" Blue, but the "Catfish" nickname stuck to the mustachioed pitcher Jim Hunter.*

Some of Finley's innovations worked; some didn't. Finley introduced ball girls, orange baseballs, a mascot mule named after himself, and his own version of franchise free agency when he moved the A's to Oakland. And he may not have invented the practice of dumping his star players after big wins, but he certainly used it on numerous occasions. Finley threatened, demeaned or even demoted his players—in addition to Hawk Harrelson, Reggie Jackson, Vida Blue, and Lew Krauss. This infuriated Kuhn, who frequently intervened in these unproductive spats. Finley and Kuhn did agree about night baseball, especially for the World Series, because Kuhn was always looking for ways to increase ratings and pad baseball coffers. But this single point of agreement was not nearly enough to insure a harmonious relationship.

It rankled Kuhn to watch Finley, whom he considered a buffoon, build the Athletics into a national power. The players wore their hair long, grew mustaches and stubble, put on white shoes with pastel green and yellow uniforms, and men like Reggie Jackson, Catfish Hunter and Blue Moon Odom exploited their cocky personalities. Even worse, Finley won games—lots of them, while Kuhn fumed. Oakland pulled off three consecutive World Series titles in 1973, 1974 and 1975. Finley had made stars of his players, his manager, and himself. He made money, too, but that was in serious jeopardy. Many of his stars were approaching free agency, and he would have lost them, either because he was cheap or just because they simply hated him, and Finley the entrepreneur could not stand losing these valuable players and getting nothing in return.

---

* This was not Finley's only encounter with unique nicknames. He employed a young runner in his Chicago offices whose round, cherubic face was reminiscent of home run slugger Hammerin' Hank Aaron. The runner became known as the Hammer, a moniker that stuck through the youngster's entertainment career as "M.C. Hammer."

So he impulsively jumped the gun, taking the upper hand and enraging Kuhn in the process. Before the 1976 season, Finley traded his brash slugger Jackson to the Orioles, then, just ahead of the June 15 trading deadline, cut deals to sell off three of his major stars for cash: Joe Rudi, Rollie Fingers, and Vida Blue, the latter to the Yankees, the others to Boston. Kuhn, fed up with Finley's irascible antics, intervened, vetoing the cash transactions and thus stripping $3.5 million—then a huge sum—from the pockets of Charles O. Finley, who counterattacked with verbal jabs and an army of lawyers.

Kuhn had invoked his far-reaching powers as commissioner to void the sale as being contrary to the "best interests of baseball," a vague clause in the Major League agreement that gave the commissioner almost limitless power. But one of the restrictions imposed on those powers by the courts was reasonableness. If Kuhn were to invoke them arbitrarily or, worse, as part of a vendetta, then Finley would have a chance to overturn Kuhn's actions. So in June of 1976, Charles O. Finley sued Bowie Kuhn in federal court in Chicago for $10 million in damages. Finley did not do it quietly; he embarked on a public assault, openly calling Bowie Kuhn the "village idiot." He followed this up by "apologizing to village idiots everywhere." To rub salt in the wounds, and while the final court decision was still pending, Finley sold yet another player, pitcher Paul Lindblad, for $400,000, on February 19, 1977.

A month later federal judge Frank McGarr ruled in favor of Kuhn and Major League Baseball, finding that the commissioner had not abused his "best interests" powers. Not surprisingly, Finley appealed to the Seventh Circuit Court of Appeals in Chicago, arguing that "the action of Kuhn was arbitrary, capricious, unreasonable, discriminatory, directly contrary to historical precedent, baseball tradition, and prior rulings and actions of the Commissioner."

The appeals court scrutinized Kuhn's rulings and reflected upon precedents in years of baseball history, including the extensive unilateral actions of first commissioner Kenesaw Mountain Landis. Just as the cash deal negotiations were concluded, Kuhn sent a message to all relevant parties conveying his concern "for possible consequences to the integrity of baseball and public confidence in the game." The hearing on that issue was immediately consummated involving seventeen different parties and witnesses. Kuhn expressed concern that the cash sales would be harmful to the competitive capacity of Oakland; that they reflected an effort by Boston and New York to purchase star players and thus to "bypass the usual methods of player development . . . traditionally used in professional baseball."

The appeals court agreed, concluding on April 7, 1978, that Kuhn had acted "in good faith, after investigation, consultation and deliberation, in a manner which he determined to be in the best interests of baseball."

The relentless Finley then turned to the United States Supreme Court, which refused on October 2, 1978, to hear his case, thus ending the saga of Finley and Kuhn.

While his various appeals were pending, Finley made an effort to sell the Athletics to oilman Marvin Davis who planned to move the team to Denver. The deal fell through; Finley kept trying and was able to resurrect it, but the deal ran aground again when the Oakland Coliseum board rejected an American League offer to buy out the remaining years of the team's stadium lease for $4 million, making a planned move to Denver economically unattractive.

Finally, on August 23, 1980, Finley sold the club for $12.7 million to the Haas family of San Francisco, inheritors of the Levi Strauss Company, who kept the team in Oakland.

But Finley was not the only rogue owner who fought against Kuhn. There was another who was much richer and was in the right place at the right time, building his fortune on the new electronic broadcasts of sports and news. Was Kuhn about to meet his match?

16

THE THEFT OF GARY MATTHEWS

Bowie Kuhn is out to kill me.
—Ted Turner

ATLANTA BRAVES OWNER Ted Turner was even more brash and more of a challenge to Bowie Kuhn than Charlie Finley had been. Turner, founder of cable superstations TBS and CNN, was a free spirit with a public persona, a self-made media mogul with money to burn. When Turner purchased the Atlanta Braves in January, 1976, Kuhn and Finley were locked in battle over Finley's antics as owner of the Oakland Athletics. But if the persistently annoying Finley was a thorn in Kuhn's side, Turner took his own level of antagonism a quantum leap forward, vexing the commissioner both publicly and privately.

It was Turner who signed the first official free agent, Dodger pitcher Andy Messersmith, soon after an arbitrator ruled against the baseball reserve clause. Turner had originally bought the Braves as dependable cheap programming for his local Atlanta television station that was relying on third-run television shows. Aware of the promise of cable, he soon converted the local station to WTBS, and began to broadcast Braves games nationwide.

Turner was about to become a dangerous force in the baseball free agent market. That same year he made a big play for offense, courting Giants star slugger Gary Matthews, the National League Rookie of the Year in 1973. Matthews had made a splash batting .300 in his very first season. A speedy out-fielder who stole seventeen bases that year, Matthews was part of a stellar Giants outfield that also boasted slugger Bobby Bonds (better known as Barry's father), as well as Garry Maddox, a lightning-fast fielder known for his agility in chasing down fly balls. Maddox's speed had become almost legendary, inspiring the quip: two-thirds of the earth is covered by water, the other third by Garry Maddox.

Matthews was under contract with the Giants and protected by baseball's anti-tampering rules. But in 1976, a new collective bargaining agreement included a Rube Goldberg free-agency system calling for a re-entry draft later that year. This gave Turner and other owners the possibility of acquiring Matthews. In the meantime, Kuhn had issued an edict preventing owners from tampering with each other's potential free agents prior to the time of the re-entry draft scheduled for November 4. Turner would have to compete for Matthews with the other owners. Or would he?

Turner could not resist defying the Kuhn order, dramatically. In October, Turner crashed the Yankees hospitality suite in the Waldorf Towers, accosting Giants owner Bob Lurie at a private cocktail party. Although Turner had been fined earlier in the season for approaching Matthews, he proceeded to provoke Lurie by inviting him to a surprise party he planned to throw for Matthews, saying, "I'm putting a big message up on the signboard at the airport, 'Welcome to Atlanta, Gary Matthews.'" Turner not only annoyed Lurie, he made headlines that infuriated Kuhn.

But Turner had just begun. Weeks later he was standing on the concierge desk at the L.A. Hilton bellowing for all to hear, "The commissioner of baseball is going to kill me. Bowie Kuhn is out to kill me. My life is over." Both Turner and Kuhn were in the city at the time, attending the annual baseball winter meetings. For three days Turner kept this up, even telling the *L.A. Times*, "Kuhn's going to gun me down in this hotel like a dog."

The ranting had grown so intense that his own people were finally forced to grab Turner when they spied him strolling though the lobby with a striking blonde, and shove him into the back booth of a sparsely attended bar. "Do you think I've convinced him I'm crazy?" inquired Turner calmly. When they enthusiastically responded in the affirmative, Turner surprised everyone by halting his harangues immediately, and behaving normally throughout the rest of the winter meetings. Turner shut off his tirades as easily as he turned them on.

What was Turner up to? Given Kuhn's run-ins with Curt Flood, Finley and Marvin Miller, executive director of the Players' Association, Turner must have known his outrageous taunts would provoke the staid commissioner. Predictably, Kuhn took only two weeks to suspend Turner from baseball for the entire forthcoming season. Turner feigned shock and reacted as Kuhn must have known he would, by rushing to the federal court for the northern district of Georgia, to challenge Kuhn's exercise of the "best interests" powers of the office.

Turner had first contacted Gary Matthews in September of 1976 through overtures from the Braves general manager, a clear tampering transgression in Kuhn's eyes. By the time Turner was taunting Giants owner Bob Lurie at the October party in New York, Kuhn had already slapped the Braves on the wrist with a $5000 fine and forfeiture of the their first-round draft pick. In November, the Braves signed Matthews, igniting Kuhn's already smoldering anger. When Turner exploded at baseball's winter meetings, he was intentionally throwing gas on the flames. But why?

Turner sued Kuhn to test the commissioner's unilateral "best interests" powers in the light of the new collective bargaining agreement that had grown out of the Finley battles. But Turner was aware that, for the first time, what constituted the controlling Major League Agreement was not a unilateral document, but rather an amalgam of both the agreement among the owners and the collective bargaining agreement with the players.

With ample resources, legions of New York lawyers, and history all on his side, Kuhn was a formidable foe. But Turner had money too, and a street fighter's guts and instincts. Kuhn was facing a new kind of enemy. Turner launched gutter assaults on Kuhn, in court, in the media, at the winter meetings. It was a campaign not just of pinstriped lawyers, a skirmish which Kuhn probably would have won, but an exercise in which Turner turned the weight of the commissioner's office against itself. Major League Baseball became something like a massive aircraft carrier with extraordinary firepower but limited maneuverability, suddenly confronted by a swift, unpredictable PT boat spinning circles at close range and slamming torpedoes into its hull from every direction.

The court eventually ruled that Kuhn had not exceeded his powers leveling the fine because such punishment was specifically contemplated by the Major League agreement, but that he had overstepped his bounds with the draft forfeiture because he had, quite simply, made that one up on the fly. The court thus dealt Kuhn an embarrassing blow:

> That the Commissioner's authority in [certain prior] cases went unchallenged does not persuade this court of the Commissioner's unlimited punitive powers in light of contractual language and established rules of construction to the contrary. If the Commissioner is to have the unlimited punitive authority as he says is needed to deal with new and changing situations, the agreement should be changed to expressly grant the Commissioner that power. The deprivation of a draft choice was first and foremost a punitive sanction, and a sanction that is not specifically enumerated under section 3 [of the Major League Agreement]. Accordingly, the court concludes that the Commissioner was without the authority to impose that sanction, and its imposition is therefore void.

So there it was. Curt Flood had not been able to crack baseball's reserve clause with his 1969 antitrust case against Kuhn and the owners, and Charles Finley had come up short in his claim about arbitrary conduct. But in 1976 pitcher Andy Messersmith had finally defeated the baseball lords with a key arbitration decision springing himself, and ultimately others, to free agency, an effort that was also a Turner victory since it was the Braves who had signed Messersmith to help launch baseball free agency as it is known today. A year later, in 1977, Turner won another victory in the battle over Gary Matthews, this time defeating the previously impregnable best-interests clause. But even then, the Turner-Kuhn wars had not ended.

The issue of the season-long suspension remained, and Kuhn may well have wondered why Turner had behaved so irrationally in public. When the smoke cleared, the Matthews signing was left unchallenged, so Turner managed to keep the slugger Gary Matthews for the Braves, but he himself had been cut off from baseball for a year. He took the time to win the America's Cup in his yacht *Courageous*.

But the citizens of Atlanta wanted vindication and the return of their famous baseball leader. Mayor Maynard Jackson and Georgia governor George Busbee flew, courtesy of Atlanta-based Delta Airlines, to lead a delegation of citizens straight to the commissioner's office in New York. Both houses of the Georgia legislature passed supporting resolutions signed by no fewer than ten thousand fans. The Burger King regional marketing people also got into the act, distributing 100,000 postcards to local patrons, to be signed and forwarded to the baseball commissioner's office, no doubt inundating his New York staff.

This was precisely the type of chip-on-the-shoulder attitude that had characterized big league baseball in the first place. The game had become staid and corporate under Kuhn, and Turner shook it to its foundations. But not without a dose of mischief. According to at least one Turner biography, Atlanta's "Mouth of the South" managed to infiltrate Kuhn's offices with a few well-placed bribes to get the names of the people who had sent in the postcards. The Braves organization thus had a unique mailing list of Atlanta supporters.

Kuhn took comfort in the one-year Turner suspension, but Turner had stolen Gary Matthews from under Kuhn's nose. And the commissioner hardly knew what had hit him.

17
THE UEBERROTH CABAL

WITH MARVIN MILLER'S UNION nipping at the owners' heels, arbitrators dismantling the sacrosanct reserve clause, and rogue owners like Ted Turner signing the new breed of free agents, the lords were rapidly losing their grip on the game as the 1970s wore on. Understandably vexed by the erosion of power over their players, the owners reacted in genuine baseball style. Led by then-commissioner Peter Ueberroth, the owners conspired to regain control in 1984, hatching a brazen plot to depress player salaries.

They did not foresee that their conspiracy was doomed and would soon rock the game with a one-*billion*-dollar claim that would backfire against Major League Baseball. Their action proved to be one of the greatest blunders in the history of the game, an ill-fated twenty-year odyssey that began not in a back room, but on the playing field with a 382 strikeout season in 1965.

Decades earlier, when the 1904 Major League season was drawing to a close, pitcher Rube Waddell of the Philadelphia Athletics had mowed down 349 batters on strikes, a big league record that remained unscathed by such pitching icons as Cy Young, Walter Johnson, Grover Cleveland Alexander, Christy Mathewson, Carl Hubbell, and dozens of others. Waddell's total was so remarkable that even *half* his strikeouts would have led the majors in many later years. In 1948, for example, the legendary Bob Feller led both leagues in strikeouts with just 164 (Harry Brecheen of the Cardinals had notched 149 for the National League), and in 1952, Warren Spahn's 183 led the National League, while Allie Reynolds of the Yankees topped the American League with a mere 160.

Waddell's mark would stand for sixty-one years, until Dodgers prodigy and emerging Hall of Famer Sandy Koufax rang up 382 strikeouts in 1965. The left-handed Koufax was a hard-throwing power pitcher when he first signed with the Dodgers in 1955 at age nineteen, but his control was suspect. As Koufax matured, he modified his style to deliver with stunning control, and in 1960 he managed to strike out 197 batters, even with a losing record. Just one year later Koufax was an eighteen-game winner who led the National League with 269 K's, launching a remarkable string of six consecutive seasons of dominance, a span that would find Koufax leading the league in both wins and shutouts three times apiece and topping the league in strikeouts four times.

The Koufax numbers grew even more impressive, almost legendary, as the years passed. He led the league in ERA for five straight years but, more remarkably, Koufax tossed a no-hit game in each of four straight years from 1962 through 1965. Koufax took home the Cy Young Award three times in four years, including a league MVP after his 25-5 mark in 1963, inspiring this lament from baseball sage Yogi Berra: "I can see how [Koufax] won twenty-five games, but I can't understand how he lost five." Then Koufax won a stunning twenty-seven games for the Dodgers in 1966, but he retired suddenly at the close of the season, citing too many shots and pain killers for his overworked arm. Still in the prime of his career, Koufax opted to save his deteriorating left arm and walked away at the top of his game.

As fate would have it, the year after Koufax was first inked, the Dodgers signed another live arm in right-hander Don Drysdale, forming one of the most dominant pitching duos in baseball history. As a member of the old Brooklyn Dodgers, Drysdale was one of the original "boys of summer" and, like Koufax, he smashed a long-standing record from 1904: Cy Young's forty-five consecutive shutout innings. The tall, imposing power pitcher threw fifty-eight straight scoreless innings in 1968. That same year he established himself as a legitimate hitter as well, slugging .591, belting two home runs in one game against the Cardinals. Overall, Drysdale became a master of shutouts, compiling forty-nine during his big league career.

Koufax's cerebral pitching relied on finesse, while Drysdale was a mean-spirited, aggressive power pitcher who led the National League in hit batters five times, setting a league career mark of 154. Drysdale started the first World Series game ever played at Dodger Stadium in Los Angeles, shutting out Jim Bouton's Yankees on October 4. Two days later Koufax finished the task, shutting New York down with a two-to-one complete game victory as the Dodgers swept the still formidable Yankee team of Roger Maris, Whitey Ford, Elston Howard and Joe Pepitone.

Two years later, the Dodgers were back in the Series, this time taking on the Minnesota Twins of Tony Oliva, Harmon Killebrew, and Jim "Mudcat" Grant. The Series would go seven games, with Drysdale or Koufax starting five of them. Claude Osteen filled in with two other starts, going 1-1, including a game-three complete game shutout win. Although the Dodgers eventually won it all, the 1965 Series is better known for what did *not* happen, for this was also the year that Sandy Koufax, observing Yom Kippur, sat out the World Series opener in Minnesota, leaving Drysdale to take the loss as Mudcat Grant threw a one-hitter against the Dodgers.

Drysdale and Koufax not only pitched the Dodgers to two world titles, leaving a string of shattered records in their wake, they *were* the Dodgers in those years. The 1965 team had no .300 hitters at all, their top hitter being the speedy but diminutive Maury Wills who batted just .286. Indeed, the whole team batted a mere .245, the lowest ever for a National League pennant winner until the 1969 Miracle Mets managed just .241 behind Tom Seaver and Jerry Koosman. And no one slugged home runs on those Dodgers, either: the team leaders Lou Johnson and Jim Lefebvre tied at only twelve each. With respective 1965 ERAs of 2.04 and 2.77, Koufax (twenty-six wins) and Drysdale (twenty-two wins) had become nothing short of the bedrock of the Dodgers franchise.

Drysdale and Koufax would have dominated any era, ranking with the top pitching combos of big league history, including players of the modern era like Curt Schilling and Randy Johnson, Greg Maddux and John Smoltz, Jim Palmer and Dave McNally, and of course Seaver and Koosman. They were among the most valuable tandems in the history of the majors, but they never pitched in the free-agent era. If they had, they probably would not have stayed together for as long as they did. Even though they got top dollar for their day, neither of them earned the staggering million-dollar salaries paid now. It was not, however, for lack of trying.

After the 1965 Series victory, Drysdale and Koufax became a player tandem of a different sort, this one a danger not only to the Dodgers organization, but to the league as a whole. At a time when five-figure salaries were the norm, Koufax and Drysdale announced a joint contract demand of $1.05 million. Even though the seven-figure deal, divided evenly, was to be spread over three years, amounting to $175,000 each per season, it was a quantum leap that shocked the owners, not the least of whom was Walter O'Malley of the Dodgers. The demand was unprecedented, not only for its size, but in two other important and ominous respects: first, the players used an agent, a relatively new phenomenon in the world of sports in 1965; second, it morphed into acrimony that caught the attention of the media, fans and baseball insiders.

The Koufax-Drysdale "strike" went on for thirty-two days, lasting the entire month of March when spring training was in its home stretch before the 1966 season. Ultimately the players caved in, failing to reach the million-dollar plateau, but still managing to nail down substantial annual raises of $60,000 each. Although their use of an agent may have been a sign of more bitter negotiations to come, the owners were most disturbed by the prospect of joint-player negotiations.

There was no viable players' union in place, baseball still benefited from its bizarre antitrust exemption, and the Messersmith arbitration was eleven years away. But the lords of the game saw clearly the dangers of joint star-power demands. What if other pitching tandems were to negotiate jointly? And what about hitting combos—like, say, the recent one-two punch of Mantle and Maris? The prospects constituted an unprecedented economic threat and were nothing short of frightening to the owners.

They had successfully fought off Curt Flood's antitrust lawsuit with a Supreme Court victory in 1972, so they were able to keep a lid on free-agency until a labor arbitrator ruled against the perpetuity interpretation of baseball's reserve clause, allowing pitchers Andy Messersmith and Dave McNally to become free agents in 1976. Shocked into action, the owners mustered enough power to get a ban on joint negotiating as part of a new labor agreement. The players may not have resisted as strenuously as they could have because they saw a future in having a strong official union that would render individual tandems unnecessary. But the new labor agreement helped the owners maintain stability by regulating free agency and holding off full freedom for players until after the sixth contract year.

Stability reigned until the early 1980s, but then the full impact of free agency began to hit the owners hard. Newly installed commissioner Peter Ueberroth saw a geometric growth in average player compensation from $50,000 in 1976 to $370,000 by 1985, an amount that more than doubled even the top demands of Dysdale and Koufax. The owners were profoundly disturbed, so Ueberroth called an urgent meeting of clubs to combat the surge in player salaries by taking advantage of baseball's antitrust exemption, but the plan backfired, leaving the owners with egg on their faces, a hole in their wallets, and a billion-dollar headache.

Immediately after the Ueberroth cabal hatched its plan to quash competition, the movement of free agent players nearly dried up. Before the 1985 season, twenty-six free agent players switched teams, more than half of those eligible, but after 1985 the owners signed only four players to new teams out of a possible thirty-two, causing almost ninety percent of the players to stay put. As the owners dug in still further the average salary of veteran players not only failed to increase, it actually went *down* by six percent. A year later, after the 1986 season, seventy-nine big league players were eligible for free agency including a cache of stars like Andre Dawson and Tim Raines, but *not one* of them was signed to a new team for more money.

The Drysdale-Koufax tables had clearly been turned; the players were now exposed to the inherent dangers of owner collusion. With the antitrust exemption insulating the owners from their anti-competition conspiracy, what could the players do? They could in fact do plenty. All they had to do was read the collective bargaining agreement that had been installed after the Messersmith free agency, especially the "Koufax-Drysdale clause" inserted by the owners themselves:

> The utilization or non-utilization of rights under this Article XVIII is an individual matter to be determined solely by each player and each club for his or its own benefit. Players shall not act in concert with other Players *and Clubs shall not act in concert with other Clubs* [emphasis added].

The players' union filed a grievance. The owners may have been protected from the Sherman Act antitrust laws, but they were bound by their own collective bargaining agreement. The irony was that the leagues had expended considerable time, money and psychic energy fighting Curt Flood to preserve their unique antitrust exemption, only to give it back voluntarily with a "no collusion" clause in the labor agreement. Perhaps they had become complacent or arrogant because they had always won, until 1976.

Peter Ueberroth was a charismatic businessman who had made millions in the travel business in California. He virtually invented corporate sponsorship of the Olympic Games, helping to present the enormously profitable Los Angeles Olympics of 1984. When he was appointed baseball commissioner, he did much to publicize baseball and increase revenues through television and corporate promotions. Unfortunately his aggressive stand against the players became too ambitious, ultimately causing the majors to be involved in a landmark arbitration suit and a very costly settlement. By the time the settlement began in 1991, nearly eight hundred players had filed claims against the owners amounting to more than a billion dollars. It all took three years to sort out, but when the first awards were made in 1994, many players received a million dollars or more apiece, including Andre Dawson and Tim Raines, Jack Clark, Lance Parrish, Tom Seaver, and Carlton Fisk. Average payrolls continued to rise as well, with the mean salary skyrocketing from $430,000 in 1988 to over $1,000,000 by 1991.

Just as the Sandy Koufax and Don Drysdale demands ended in ultimate failure—Koufax had a great year in 1966, but it was his last season, and the Dodgers were swept by the World Series pitching of the Orioles' Palmer and McNally—the collusion of the owners blew up in their faces and pocketbooks. The owners may have tried to work a salary scam, but they ended up with a collective black eye that rivaled, in some ways, the Black Sox collusion debacle of 1919. "Say it ain't so, Peter—and Sandy and Don."

18

A Rose is a Rose

*Voting shall be based upon the player's record,
playing ability, integrity, sportsmanship, character, and
contributions to the team(s) on which the player played.*
—Rules for Election, National Baseball Hall of Fame

PETE ROSE ADMITTED TO betting on baseball and blatantly lying to cover it up until, as part of a last-ditch book promotion, he confessed in the January 12, 2004, issue of *Sports Illustrated*. He was a great competitor, an habitual liar—and a victim.

Rose is certainly dishonest, but he cannot be relegated to a footnote to baseball history as the National Baseball Hall of Fame would like. He has been victimized by himself, to be sure, as well as by the Baseball Hall of Fame, the latter a self-appointed gatekeeper to baseball immortality, a private association with overblown credentials, officially unrelated to the Major Leagues.

The rule cited at the beginning of this chapter has existed for years, but had another rule not been added midstream, the Hall may have been forced to recognize the scoundrel Rose. Instead, its rules were rewritten, and the Hall doors were slammed shut against the all-time hits leader.[*] Ironically, the record holder Rose had replaced was none other than the equally

---

[*] Hall of Fame Rule 3E reads: Any player on Baseball's ineligible list shall not be an eligible candidate.

great Ty Cobb, a nasty, disdainful miscreant in his own right who, as we have seen, had lied, cheated, stolen, spiked, fought and insulted his way through baseball annals a century ago, long enough for his behavior to fade into the distant shadows of baseball nostalgia.

Cobb was probably the greater impact player, although Rose was not far behind. Cobb was a virtual malefactor of the game, but he is installed within the venerable Hall of Fame, and Rose only haunts it. So who cares? Baseball—or at least it should. Hall of Fame Rule 3E did not exist when Rose bet on baseball or even when he was shipped off to prison for tax evasion, but it was hurriedly enacted by the Hall just as Rose was released from prison in 1991. Cobb was disliked by most players of his day, notably Nap Lajoie who nearly wrested the 1910 batting title from him. Rose was not especially disliked, although his aggressive play bruised a few egos as well as bones, including Indians' catcher Ray Fosse, who was bowled over by Rose in a violent collision at the plate in a dramatic twelfth-inning play of the 1970 All-Star Game that left Fosse with a fractured shoulder.

Rose's name will be found in the top ten of seven different offensive categories, not the least being his perhaps unbreakable record for career hits at 4256, besting Cobb's 4191 and Hank Aaron's 3771 lifetime hits.[**] Cobb still holds the record for lifetime batting average at .367. Rose's lifetime mark was a highly respectable .303, a very good average considering that in Rose's era there were few legitimate .300 hitters and no .400 hitters at all. Cobb also bests Rose with 2245 runs scored, second in history behind Ricky Henderson. Rose is not far behind, checking in at 2165. Rose was practically a clone of Cobb in many ways, barely besting him in doubles, good for second place all-time with 746 over Cobb's fourth place 723; Cobb still bested him in triples with 297, a tribute to Cobb's speed and tenacity.

[**] Hank Aaron's overall hitting prowess is often overshadowed by his career home runs, but Aaron's 3771 hits were good enough for third place all-time, and he did it in one year less than both Cobb and Rose.

Rose belted 160 career home runs. In all his years in the game he clubbed only one grand slam, part of a 6-RBI game on July 18, 1964, but he leads the majors in lifetime singles at 3215.

Rose need not be loved or even liked to qualify for the Hall of Fame; his baseball record speaks for itself. And if the character rule is meaningful, what was the point of adding the new rule 3E concerning baseball's ineligible list? Did the Hall not trust the baseball writers who do the voting? It seems that the new rule was a hedge against Rose, just in case someone noticed his baseball accomplishments and felt they overshadowed his black marks on the game. Although Rose's accomplishments on the field are indisputable, he himself can inspire little genuine sympathy.

Perhaps the most remarkable chapter in the Rose odyssey arises from his legal battles with Commissioner Bart Giamatti, who mandated Rose's lifetime ban from the game. Although the Rose lifetime sentence is now legendary, few realize that for a brief but important moment, Rose had actually won his case against Bart Giamatti. And given the relentless travails of Rose in the ensuing years, it is even more astonishing that it was Rose himself who gave it all back.

In February of 1989, Commissioner Giamatti invoked baseball's well-known best interests clause found in Article 1, Section 2(b) of the Major League Agreement and retained high-powered Washington lawyer John Dowd to investigate the spreading rumors of Rose's gambling exploits. The result was a thorough account of gambling misadventures, including a history of baseball betting, the charge Rose vehemently denied until his tell-all book in early 2004. Based upon the Dowd Report, Giamatti had no choice but to suspend Rose. But the hearing that followed revealed a striking flaw in the commissioner's actions.

In gathering evidence against Rose, a deal had been cut with Ron Peters, a government witness who had turned on Rose in exchange for lenient treatment for his own crimes. As part of the deal, Giamatti wrote a letter to prosecutors on Peters' behalf, commending the witness for his forthright, truthful testimony. But the commissioner stumbled badly in thanking the witness for his "truthful" testimony: Giamatti seemed to be admitting his bias in the Rose case still pending before him. He may have prejudged the case—how else could he have accepted the testimony before the Rose hearing was concluded?

The law affords much latitude for private associations to govern their own affairs without court intervention, leaving such diverse institutions as the NFL, American Red Cross, New York Stock Exchange, and Major League Baseball to manage and resolve their own internal differences. But in so doing, the conduct of such associations must be fundamentally fair—sort of a "due process" standard for the private sector. Among other things, such standards do not allow an arbiter like Commissioner Giamatti to act arbitrarily or capriciously—or to prejudge a case. So there it was: the lawyers had Giamatti in a trap, and Rose had the strong potential for victory based upon the commissioner's pre-judgment which he had admitted in written correspondence.

But then Rose essentially gave it all back. He entered into a deal agreeing to the lifetime suspension. What could possibly have been the reason for this? One need only examine the context of the times in general and the Rose suspension in particular to develop a credible hypothesis. At the time, Rose was also under investigation for tax evasion related to the same incidents of alleged gambling, which could result in hard jail time. While this federal investigation was going on, Rose could hardly afford to prejudice his criminal case with testimony before Giamatti, so to avoid the possibility of dangerous admissions, he may have cut a deal. There is almost no other explanation for his sudden acceptance of a lifetime ban without getting something in return. But was that all? Could there have been more?

Given Rose's relentless zeal in fighting the suspension over so many years, it would appear he did not expect to be suspended forever. The Hall of Fame rule change may have had something to do with it, but that rule only keeps him out of the Hall—the suspension keeps him out of baseball, a much harsher sentence economically. If Rose had been free to manage a ball club all these years, especially the Reds or Phillies, he could have made millions of dollars. Until he is reinstated, that will remain an impossibility.

Chances are Rose may have received more in the Giamatti deal than meets the public eye. Giamatti was a great fan of the game, but he was behind the eight-ball where Rose was concerned and had little choice but to pursue a suspension. Rose needed to get out of a jam, but he certainly did not need or desire to relinquish baseball forever. Most serious settlements have, by definition, much to offer each side. Given all the circumstances, the parties and stakes involved, and the subsequent facts over the ensuing years, it is possible—even likely—that Rose may have had a secret "gentleman's handshake" deal with Giamatti allowing him to get back into the game. Even lifetime suspensions can be lifted upon reapplication after a year, and Rose and Giamatti may have anticipated just that. Baseball would prevail, Rose would preserve his legacy, and both parties would win. Based upon the history of most major settlements, that would probably have been the crux of a plausible settlement. Everyone should have been—and probably was—happy, at least under the dubious circumstances.

And then suddenly the unthinkable happened: less than three weeks after Rose's apparent acquiescence to the ban, Bart Giamatti dropped dead of a massive heart attack. Rose was already suspended for life, and if he and Giamatti had any secret understandings about reinstatement, those died just as swiftly. Rose was not only out of baseball: on April 20, 1990, he pleaded guilty to two counts of felony tax evasion, and on August 8, 1990, began serving a five- month prison sentence at Marion, Illinois, the penitentiary built to replace the facility at Alcatraz. When he was released, the Hall of Fame unanimously voted to shun candidates on baseball's ineligibility list. Although

Pete Rose is hardly a sympathetic figure, two wrongs still do not make a right.

The character rule that heads this chapter is laudable, but its implementation is hypocritical at best. It is used only to ban unpopular players or to rewrite baseball history at the whims of the Hall. There is no reason to keep Black Sox player Buck Weaver from the Hall, the only genuinely innocent member of the eight men out. There is even less reason to ban Shoeless Joe Jackson who, unlike Rose, was a very sympathetic figure—an illiterate farm boy. Moreover, Shoeless Joe has served his sentence. He was banned for life and, of course, has been dead for decades. Would putting Shoeless Joe in the Hall of Fame now suddenly corrupt him? Would keeping him out teach him a lesson? And then there is Pete Rose. Just in case the character rule was not effective, the new "eligibility" rule was pushed through just when Rose was released from prison. Banning Rose from baseball makes perfect sense. He is a known gambler, a liar, and a convicted felon—such malefactors should be kept out of baseball not just to punish them, but to preserve the integrity of the game. Rose, being very much alive and very guilty, could harm baseball just by association, or even more seriously if he were once again in a position to influence the game. But hanging his picture in the Hall of Fame would do no harm at all—it would simply admit that he was a part of baseball history, which ought to be an objective of any viable institution devoted to the legacy of the game.

But what about that troublesome character rule? It is invoked arbitrarily at best, virtually ignored when the Hall's version of history does not coincide with the facts. Take the late great Ty Cobb, the player Rose not only deposed in the all-time hits category, but perhaps the one player in the Hall of Fame who was most like Rose himself. They were similar players with similar records and achievements, and both played the game with the same intensity on and even off the field. And both were gamblers. Yes, both. The only difference is that Cobb is in the Hall and Rose is not.

On November 3, 1926, Ty Cobb suddenly resigned as manager of the Detroit Tigers, and then announced his retirement from the game altogether. Less than four weeks later, his motives became clear. On November 29, Tris Speaker resigned as manager of the Cleveland Indians, amidst rumors of gambling and game-fixing between Speaker and Cobb. Commissioner Landis held hearings at which witnesses, including pitcher Dutch Leonard, produced evidence to substantiate these rumors. Cobb and Speaker were said to have fixed a game in late September, 1919, to help Detroit win third-place money in the league standings. The 1919 season was, for more than one reason, a bad year for baseball and gambling.

A private meeting of American League officials was held, the result being the quiet resignations of Cobb and Speaker. As the matter escalated, public sentiment overwhelmingly supported the players. Then Dutch Leonard failed to appear and testify for the open hearings, while the parties claimed that all the evidence concerned only horse racing, not fixing baseball games. On January 27, 1927, Landis issued a finding that cleared both Cobb and Speaker, citing in part Leonard's refusal to participate in the hearings. The sudden turnabout had all the earmarks of a whitewash, a revisionist ploy that lives on today in and out of the Baseball Hall of Fame.

It is hardly surprising that baseball would become the revisionist national sport. After all, it steals bases, signs, games, records, and even history. But some such mischief is a part of the unwritten rules that infuse the game with the American pioneer spirit. Corking bats, tossing the spitter, and stealing signs are bits of mischief that, if discovered, are punished, but are expected as an integral part of baseball's character. Nevertheless, pretending to protect the game's integrity with revisionist lies is hardly respectable behavior.

Pete Rose is not only the career leader in number of hits, he had the most at-bats with 14,053 as well as Major League games played at 3562. In 1963, Rose was the National League Rookie of the Year, and he garnered 100 hits in each of his first twenty-three consecutive seasons, a remarkable accomplishment. *The Sporting News* even named him player of the decade for the 1970s, and in 1978 he accumulated a forty-four-game hitting streak, the longest for a National League player in the twentieth century, and the last serious assault on Gehrig's fifty-six-game streak.

With sluggers like Johnny Bench, Tony Perez, Joe Morgan, George Foster, Ken Griffey, Sr., Rose's 1975–76 Reds team was one of the best hitting teams in baseball history. It has been compared to such juggernauts as the great Yankees teams of 1927, 1936, and 1961, plus such memorable teams as the 1910 Athletics, the 1949 Dodgers, and 1952 Indians. To figuratively erase Rose from that team, the "Big Red Machine" that defeated the Red Sox in one of the greatest of all the World Series, is unacceptable.

To be sure, Rose himself committed the central larcenous act by betting, lying and stealing his own slice of history, and since the time of his suspension and conviction, he has done little to redeem himself. He has attacked the credibility of the Dowd Report, denied gambling on baseball, shamelessly hawked memorabilia on television—indeed, he has worn multiple uniforms and used multiple game bats just to increase his inventory of saleable items used while he managed the Reds in his later years. Only when all else failed did Rose confess and apologize. It was too little and too late. But that does not justify the continued twisting of baseball history by the Hall of Fame.

In the January 12, 2004, *Sports Illustrated*, he was quoted as saying, among other things, "There hasn't been a day in my life when I didn't regret making those bets." But his ultimate admission sums up the whole sordid mess, his candid reason for all the bets, gambling, fraud and lies in the first place: "I didn't think I'd get caught."

Part IV
Had Satchel Been White:
The Truth About Racism and Baseball

19

THE LEGEND OF CHARLIE GRANT

RUBE FOSTER WAS A thrower, and at 6'4" he was a behemoth for his time—the era of Ty Cobb. To complement a wicked arm and dogged personality, Foster developed a heartless fadeaway screwball—a reverse curve that, when thrown by a right-handed pitcher like Foster, actually breaks away from a left-handed hitter. Foster's screwball was so challenging that it was adopted and relied upon by superstar Christy Mathewson, who then dominated the league so convincingly that he became one of only two pitchers elected to the Hall of Fame on the first-ever induction ballot on February 2, 1936. Walter Johnson was the other, and both beat out pitching icon Cy Young, who was not inducted until the following year. Mathewson was a right-hander like Foster, and although Foster was a magician with the curve and screwballs, he never had a chance to pitch in the Major Leagues as did protegé Mathewson and other disciples of the screwball like Carl Hubbell.

Rube Foster was a black ballplayer, and so was relegated to perhaps the greatest asterisk in baseball history, the Negro Leagues. Foster was discovered by, among others, the legendary John McGraw, who managed the turn-of-the-century New York Giants for over thirty years, a span that saw nine Giants pennants and three World Series titles. After scouting Foster in spring training, McGraw was convinced that black players were the future of baseball, but he was unable to overcome the color barrier by himself. Instead, McGraw convinced Foster at least to tutor the white pitchers he could not officially join, one of whom was Mathewson, and so began decades of black player influence over the evolution of the white man's game.

Foster signed on with the Chicago Union Giants of the Negro Leagues and managed to pitch a shutout in his first outing. The novice pitcher soon slumped, but he played through it and eventually roared back, becoming the best black pitcher in the country by 1903. One season Foster apparently won over fifty games, but scant records have prevented verification, although the legend Honus Wagner could and did personally proclaim Foster "one of the greatest pitchers of all time." The Negro League star hurler had occasional success against traditional big leaguers and pitched effectively against the likes of Rube Waddell,* Three-Finger Brown and Cy Young. Foster led the Chicago Leland Giants to a stunning 110 wins against only ten losses during the 1907 campaign, after which he challenged the 1908 world champion Cubs to a three-game series. Foster pitched the second game, but lost a three-run lead in the ninth inning. Two years later, his Negro League team rang up a 123-6 record, and when he again challenged the Major League teams to a short series, there were no takers, perhaps for good reason.

The savvy Rube Foster never played in a Major League game, and no black ballplayer would, from Moses Fleetwood Walker in 1884 until Jackie Robinson donned a Dodgers uniform in 1947. Quite possibly, the beginning of the Major League color barrier may have involved Fleetwood Walker himself, for it was during an 1883 contest between Chicago and Toledo that superstar Cap Anson expressed his attitude toward Walker with a blunt ultimatum, "If you want me to play, you'll have to get that nigger off the field." Thereafter legend and fact began

---

* Foster allegedly acquired his nickname "Rube" when he once beat opposing pitcher Rube Waddell in an exhibition game.

to blur, but apparently Walker had suffered an injured hand and could not play, thus avoiding a direct confrontation with Anson.** Walker remained on the team and would eventually play forty-two games for the Toledo Blue Stockings, and his brother Weldy appeared in a few contests for the same team.

There were other instances of blacks in the majors from time to time, some of them presented as Cubans or Mexicans or even Native Americans. One of the more provocative baseball stories concerned one such ruse. John McGraw, the manager who would soon try to hire Rube Foster and other black ballplayers, signed a supposed Cherokee Indian, Chief Charlie Tokohoma, in 1901 during McGraw's stint with the Orioles. But the chief's Major League career was short-lived—he never took the field. Charles Comiskey of Chicago recognized Tokohoma and announced that he was Charlie Grant, a black ballplayer with the Columbia Giants, a local Negro team. Thus the story of Charlie Grant became a brief footnote to black baseball history, but Grant may have been the first black ballplayer signed in the twentieth century.

The rogue personality of baseball can neither be stilled nor corralled, and the greats of the game continue to be those who defy the status quo: Branch Rickey, Casey Stengel, Bill Veeck, Charles O. Finley, Ted Turner, and even George Steinbrenner. Charlie Grant was more than a footnote, he was the future.

The true beginning of baseball is the subject of debate, for it probably did not grow from cricket as sometimes believed, but from "rounders," another British game. The first suggestion of a "baseball" game in America may have come from the diary of a Revolutionary War soldier who scribbled mention of a "game of base" enjoyed by some of the troops dug in at Valley Forge. The first direct reference to the game may have been made in Jane Austen's *Northanger Abbey*, published in 1818.

** Cap Anson is in the Hall of Fame, providing one of many exceptions to the "character" criteria for Hall eligibility.

The reference is not only to "baseball" but to a girl playing the game: ". . . it was not very wonderful that Catherine should prefer cricket, base-ball, riding on horseback and running about the country, at the age of fourteen, to books." In 1834 a book of rules for various sports included specific rules for one called "baseball," but the rules were identical to the rounders game described in a book published in London in 1829. Abner Doubleday is said to have "officially" invented baseball in 1839, but most modern baseball historians question that.

In September, 1843, the New York Knickerbockers Base Ball Club was organized, adopting a series of rules that largely resemble the twentieth century game. On June 19, 1846, the New York Ball Club and the Knickerbockers squared off in a four-inning game which the Knickerbockers lost 23-1. Some accounts suggest the Knickerbockers lost deliberately to inspire their opponents and help raise interest in the new game. If true, the roots of baseball were truly steeped in skullduggery.

Whenever baseball may have begun, the Major Leagues did not emerge until much later, probably in 1871. The National Association of ten original teams was formed in a New York saloon on St. Patrick's Day, 1871. This suggests that heavy drinking may have played some part in the birth of the leagues. Sober or not, nine of the ten teams played that first season, three of them bearing familiar names: the Boston Red Stockings, the Chicago White Stockings (precursors to the Cubs and not to the current White Sox), and the Philadelphia Athletics.

With the National League under way in 1871, it was to be expected that the players would be all white, but over the years blacks would occasionally slip in and out of teams, playing a few games here and there. With loose records and even looser rules on who could play and when, tracking down the first black player was not easy. According to the SABR, the Society for American Baseball Research, the first was William Edward White, who played one game for the Providence Greys on June

21, 1879. White would also then become the first black player to earn a hit (he got one), get on base, and score a run.***

White's career of a solitary game piqued the curiosity of the SABR researchers because White's performance had been highly praised by the *Chicago Tribune*. Moreover, White had filled in on an emergency basis for the Greys' first baseman who had broken his thumb. If the Greys' roster was short-handed and White had debuted well, why was his career so short?

White had played for neighboring Brown University in the same period, so a search for Brown team photos turned up the 1879 team, a picture that included White, who looked noticeably darker than the other team members though with a lighter complexion than Satchel Paige, Jackie Robinson and Hank Aaron. White had identified himself as Caucasian in Brown University records which, if false, was an unnecessary deception since Brown had a practice of admitting black students. Historical records suggest that White was one-quarter black, enough to qualify as "Negro" in most states at that time. A determined search of Georgia records by SABR researcher Peter Morris turned up White's father's will, in which he left a bequest to three children of "my servant Hannah," including William Edward White.

It is probable that White's race cut off his baseball career. Filling in to play a single game was one thing, but being a regular team member was something else again. Since he had obviously played well and the Greys would continue to need help at first base pending the return of their injured regular, it is certainly odd that White simply disappeared from the team—and from the game itself. But in any case, it seems clear that William Edward White was probably the first black player to play a game in the Major Leagues. And it is more than possible that bigotry destroyed his career.

*** See Steve Fatsis, "Mystery of Baseball: Was William White Game's First Black," *Wall Street Journal*, Jan. 20, 2004.

But there is no question about Charlie Grant, Satchel Paige, Josh Gibson and Jackie Robinson: they were big-league caliber players banned from the Major Leagues for one reason only: racism. Witty and entertaining, lanky Satchel Paige was one of the dominant pitchers of his era—and actually a few eras to follow, given that he pitched in the Negro Leagues for twenty-two years, from 1926 to 1947, followed by Major League stints with the Indians in 1948, three seasons with the St. Louis Browns in the 1950s, barnstorming and exhibitions into the 1960s, and, finally, three innings for the big league Oakland Athletics in 1965.

Paige, then, pitched professionally for five decades, and was listed as fifty-nine years old during his last appearance with Oakland, but he may actually have been as old as sixty-five at the time, according to his old pitching buddy from the Negro Leagues, Ted "Double Duty" Radcliffe. As a youth, Paige spent five years in an Alabama reform school for shoplifting and, of all things, truancy. As a young man he worked as porter at the Mobile, Alabama, train station where he used a long pole and rope to tote many bags and satchels at once, earning one of baseball's most famous nicknames—Satchel.

Even after success in the Negro Leagues, Satchel had to hone his baseball skills the hard way in Mexico, Venezuela, and the Dominican Republic. Although banned from the majors for most of his career, Paige nonetheless faced numerous big league stars during his barnstorming days between seasons, winning four of six direct contests against Dizzy Dean's contingent of All-Stars. At 6'3" Satchel was tall, thin and wiry, and he used his unique physical traits not only for pitching leverage on the mound, but also to deceive and intimidate batters. He had an unnaturally high, and distracting, leg kick, plus a hesitation pitch that kept hitters off balance. He also used an annoying, sweeping windmill style to deliver a menagerie of oddball pitches, including his "two-hump blooper," which was a moving changeup. And he had not one but two different fastballs, including a hard blazing pitch named "Long Tom," but Satchel's hesitation pitch may have been his trickiest. He would sometimes slip a hitch into the delivery, causing just enough delay to throw off the hitter's timing. The "hesitation" complemented Paige's gangly leg kick in which his toes were higher than his eyes—in some ways like the Scarecrow in the Wizard of Oz—followed by a fleeting pause that gave the motion a confounding jerk when viewed from the batter's box.

Satchel Paige had everything—except a Major League uniform. He had a catchy nickname, an affable personality, blazing fastball, tricky delivery and a clever, relentless will to win. With all that, Paige became a folk and cult hero in his own time and beyond. For example, he enjoyed the controversy over his age, one of his many winks at baseball history. His friend "Double Duty" Radcliffe swore Satchel was born in 1900, which would make the pitcher six years older than officially listed. That would mean Satchel played his last Major League game at age sixty-five, a remarkable feat that was quintessential Satchel Paige.

Ted Radcliffe played for over fifteen Negro League teams during his own long and storied career, including three of the greatest teams from the late 1920s and very early 1930s: the St. Louis Stars, Homestead Grays and Pittsburgh Crawfords. He was a star pitcher who frequently doubled as a catcher. The writer Damon Runyon saw Radcliffe do both in one day during a 1932 Negro League World Series double header when Ted caught Paige in the first game, then shed the catcher's gear to pitch a shutout in the second. Deeply impressed, Runyon dubbed Radcliffe "Double Duty." His friends came to call him "Duty."

Duty and Satchel grew up together in Mobile, Alabama, where Satch earned his own nickname. Radcliffe was born in 1902, and played with Paige and others when they were boys, so if Duty says Paige was born in 1900, Duty should know. Duty eventually pitched in no less than five Negro League All-Star games, but true to his name, he also caught in nine All-Star contests.

Duty went on to manage in the Negro Leagues, including the Memphis Red Sox in the late 1930s, followed by the Chicago American Giants in the 1940s. One of his players on the Giants in 1948 and 1949 was Morgan Park High School's Johnny Washington, a lefty pitcher who went on to play with the Houston Eagles where he also played first base and the outfield. By 1951, Johnny's ball career had been interrupted by the Korean War, during which he was wounded twice and awarded two Purple Hearts and a Silver Star. His injuries included severe damage to his leg, and doctors told him not to expect to play again, but by 1955 Johnny was back at it. He found himself in the minor leagues in the Boston Red Sox organization, but the Red Sox were still reluctant to accept black players in the majors, so in 1959 Johnny retired and returned to his family in Chicago. But by 1963 he was back in baseball uniform, and he played semipro ball until 1990, the year of his sixtieth birthday. Washington may not have made it to the show, but longevity certainly was not a problem. Johnny says he can still pitch, even at seventy-four and counting.

From 1948 to 1952 Hank Presswood, another Chicagoan, played shortstop and third base for the Cleveland Buckeyes and Kansas City Monarchs. His manager for a time was none other than Satchel Paige. When asked if he could still get a hit off his friend Johnny Washington, Hank will say the only way he couldn't is if Johnny "never takes the ball out of his pocket." Presswood once played with Jackie Robinson in winter ball and, like Johnny Washington, he is full of Negro League stories, one about Cool Papa Bell, reputedly one of the fastest runners in Negro League history, who could turn off the light switch and be in bed before the room was dark. This clearly stretches the imagination, but legend insists it happened at least once when there was a short in the switch.

Short circuits or not, Cool Papa Bell was one of the great stars of baseball. Although he eventually declined the opportunity, Bell, at age forty-eight, was offered a roster spot in 1951 by St. Louis Browns owner Bill Veeck. Many remember the time Bell hit one up the middle and was hit by his own ball while sliding into second. Even if the grass were long enough, such a feat is definitely more legendary than factual. But Bell did really pull off at least one miraculous baseball act, scoring from first base on a sacrifice bunt against an exhibition roster of Major Leaguers, breezing past Indians catcher Roy Partee to score just as Partee was releasing the ball to first base. A frequent .400 hitter in the Negro Leagues, the swift Cool Papa reportedly once stole 175 bases in one 200-game season.

In an inspired fit of mischievous benevolence, an aging Cool Papa once intentionally forfeited a season batting title to enhance the chances of Negro Leaguer Monte Irvin to follow Jackie Robinson to the majors. Irvin made it to the "Show" at age thirty, played for eight seasons and batted .458 in the 1951 World Series. Sometimes the end does justify the means.

Perhaps the most explosive hitter of all time in any league was Josh Gibson, a powerful 215-pounder with a massive upper body, strong hands and quick wrists. Legend credits him with perhaps nine hundred career home runs, a prodigious total that would dwarf that of any other star from Ruth to Mantle, Mays, Aaron, Sosa, McGwire and Bonds. True to the baseball continuum of myth and fact, the story most frequently repeated about Gibson never really happened. With all its sluggers including Ruth, Gehrig, Mantle, Maris, Reggie Jackson and others, Yankee Stadium has never seen a ball launched completely out of the park. Josh Gibson supposedly was the only exception, said to be the only player to hit a fair ball out of the stadium. Historians disagree about that, but Gibson really did club the longest home run in the history of Yankee Stadium with a monster blast against the Lincoln Giants in 1930. Even that was not his longest—Gibson himself long pointed to a different home run as his most distant, a tape measure jack that left Farmers Park in East Orange, New Jersey and cleared a two-story structure across the street.

Adding to the Gibson mystique was the position he played: catcher. The strain on a catcher's legs and stamina is extraordinary, and playing hundreds of games at the position takes its toll. Josh Gibson had the endurance, but that may have been his downfall as he played through fatigue and even pain for seventeen professional seasons, in nine of which he led the Negro Leagues in home runs. Gibson had it all, including speed, a rarity for catchers as a whole. As a youth he was a track star, and his speed no doubt contributed to his home-run total, for many games in those days were played in parks without outfield fences. But he pushed himself hard, perhaps too hard, for when he was only thirty-five years old, Josh Gibson suddenly suffered a stroke and died hours later at his mother's home.

Baseball had been robbed. Gibson's untimely death was in 1947, just prior to Jackie Robinson's Major League debut. If he had still been playing at age thirty-six, Gibson surely would have been signed to the Major Leagues, if not by Branch Rickey, then by Bill Veeck whose Indians and Browns rapidly built a roster of Negro League stars, including Larry Doby and Satchel Paige. Had he slammed 25-30 homers in perhaps five twilight years at the Major League level, he still would have been among the best sluggers of his time. But it was not to be.

Still, the limited years Gibson gave to baseball were among the most productive of all time. In 1933, he slugged fifty-five home runs in just 137 games for the perennial champion Pittsburgh Crawfords, followed by an even better 1934 season when he cannoned sixty-nine jacks before amazed spectators. As a teenager in 1930, Gibson had caught the attention of Cum Posey, the famed manager of the Homestead Grays, a dominant Negro League franchise. When the team's starting catcher injured a finger, Gibson was summoned from a cross-town team and the rest became history—lots of history. In his rookie season, Gibson hit for a stunning .461 average and slammed a five-hundred-foot-plus home run into the Yankee Stadium left-field bullpen, still one of the longest balls ever clubbed at the House of Ruth.

After his intervening stint with the Crawfords, Gibson was back with Posey and the Grays in 1936, the beginning of a nine-year championship run. But the more Gibson played, the more stressed were his weary knees and body. Sometimes his shoulder would dislocate, but he would continue to play after a teammate jerked it back into place. The pain wore him down; in 1943 Gibson had to be hospitalized with an emotional breakdown. He revived to play for three more seasons, but the pace was catching up with him. Perhaps because of the physical pain, he drank heavily and, according to many, slipped into a dangerous drug habit.

It may have been a stroke that took Gibson on January 20, 1947, but teammates and others believed it was despair that killed perhaps the greatest big leaguer who never was. The man was quiet and suffered mostly alone, and, like many of his colleagues, never talked about the segregation that relegated so many stars to the Negro Leagues. As Johnny Washington would say decades later, the players didn't think a lot about it, they just played and did their job—one day at a time.

One of Gibson's most intriguing plate appearances had been a strikeout—at the hands of none other than Satchel Paige himself. For years, Paige taunted Gibson that one day the rangy pitcher would strike the slugger out with the bases loaded. Finally, on June 3, 1942, at Forbes Field in Pittsburgh, Paige's Monarchs faced Gibson's Grays. With one man on, two outs, and Gibson up third, the table was set for Paige to make good. The quirky pitcher then walked the next two batters to intentionally load the bases to face Josh Gibson. As a stunned crowd gasped, Paige proceeded to announce the next three pitches— all fastballs. And so they came, Paige's Little Toms and Long Toms exploded from Satchel's herky-jerky leg kick and all the mighty Gibson could do was strike out on three pitches. Some called the feat a stunt, some said it was reckless, but most would acknowledge that it was essentially Satchel.

Perhaps Josh Gibson's single greatest swing of the bat symbolized his situation and the situation of all other great black players at that time. On June 3, 1937, Gibson cannoned the most prodigious long-ball shot of his life when he connected on a drive clunked just two feet from the top rim of Yankee Stadium nearly six hundred feet away. Those who saw it believed the ball would have sailed a full seven hundred feet if it had cleared the roof that day. Alas, it just missed clearing the roof before caroming back to earth. What might have been, had the lords not stupidly tried to pretend that black ballplayers were inferior.

In baseball more than any other sport, defiance has become subversion, and the tool of that defiance has been deception. Pretending blacks were inferior. Pretending the makeup and substance of the ball does not change. Pretending that steroids have not been a big part of the contemporary game. Pretending that the weather on the first night World Series game was not cold, as Bowie Kuhn did by enduring frigid temperatures without an overcoat just to fool the television cameras. Pretending that bats are not corked, signs are not stolen, umpires are infallible. Pretending the spitter is dead—or that the hapless and disingenuous commissioner Bud Selig, labeled by the acerbic *Chicago Sun-Times* columnist Jay Mariotti as the "Mr. Magoo of baseball," is not hapless and disingenuous.

Baseball mirrors the American heritage, good and bad, like no other sport. When cheating is an unwritten part of the accepted rules of the game, expected by most and perceived by all, it perpetuates the dishonest legacy of the game. When deception is used as a tool for illicit agendas from racism to steroids, the greatest weapon against it is the truth. And baseball, like America, has plenty of both.

When Bill Veeck signed forty-eight-year-old Satchel Paige to a Major League contract with the 1948 Cleveland Indians, *The Sporting News* publicly deluded itself, condemning the deal as a damaging publicity stunt: "Were Satchel white, he would not have drawn a second thought from Veeck." *The Sporting News* was promptly rebuffed with one of the great self-evident truths of sports history:

Had Satchel been white, he would have been in the majors twenty-five years ago.
                                              —Bill Veeck, July 14, 1948

20

RICKEY AND ROBINSON: STEALING HISTORY

Luck is the residue of design.
—Branch Rickey

AS THE "STAR SPANGLED BANNER" was sung before thousands of fans at the opening of the 1947 World Series, it not only symbolized a triumph for African Americans in general, but specifically for Jack Roosevelt Robinson, a young man carrying the burden both of his historic achievement and of responsibility for a new era.

A fortuitous series of events had brought Jackie Robinson to the brink of destiny. It was partly luck, to be sure, but Robinson's mentor, Branch Rickey, maintained that luck naturally flows from planning and effort. William White, Charlie Grant, Josh Gibson, Satchel Paige and others made their unique mark on history, all of them inching the baseball world forward toward a better place. But it was Jackie Robinson's 1947 "trial by public ordeal" that genuinely integrated the game, leading to the eventual acceptance of minority players like Willie Mays, Juan Marichal, Orlando Cepeda and Roberto Clemente, Fernando Valenzuela, Alex Rodriguez, and Hideo Nomo. Interestingly, Robinson was once called the Jim Thorpe of his race, a well-meant comment that probably grossly underestimated black athletes in general. Thorpe, a Native American who starred in football and baseball and dominated the 1912 Olympics, was considered one of the greatest all-round athletes in history, but the comparison seems to imply that both men were somehow racial aberrations.

Nothing could be further from the truth. Robinson's overall impact was of course profound—and that is precisely the point. Jim Thorpe was certainly a credit to his race, but he did not put Native Americans on the sports map as a group. Robinson benefited and inspired an entire race, opening the doors to legions of talented athletes. As great a player as Robinson was, his real impact can be measured by all those who have come after him.

From sometime after Cap Anson's "no niggers" ultimatum in 1883 to the death of Commissioner Kenesaw Mountain Landis on November 25, 1944, baseball maintained a policy of racial segregation, a policy that proved its own fallacy. If blacks had no talent, they couldn't have reached the Major League level on their merits: only if they were capable of playing big league ball would the game have felt it needed to exclude them. There certainly is no NBA rule against midgets, to take an extreme example—and even if the NBA were predisposed to discriminate against small people, a segregationist rule would be hardly necessary for they would never make a team anyway. But baseball, like much of America, did not see it that way.

From 1920 to 1944, Kenesaw Landis was the gatekeeper, and in that quarter century no black ballplayer set foot on a big league field. Exclusionary policies were ubiquitous in twentieth-century America, so perhaps baseball should not be singled out in hindsight. On the other hand, sports offer a unique measure of the value of a participant. A pitcher—black or white—can throw a ninety-five mph fastball or he can't. A batter can hit the curveball or he can't. So baseball doesn't deserve a free pass because of ignorance or a perverted culture—there was plenty of evidence that Satchel Paige could mow down big leaguers as well or better than even the great white pitchers of the day. Baseball swept the obvious truth under the rug of ignorance.

Baseball should have known better. Undoubtedly, baseball did know better, for many human reasons, some of which were Josh Gibson, William White, Satchel Paige—and Jesse Owens. In fact, an argument could be made that Jesse Owens was really the "first" Jackie Robinson. Robinson proved that black ballplayers could successfully compete against whites, but Owens proved on a grand world stage that athletes of color were formidable international competitors.

Fortunately, neither Ohio State University nor the U.S. Olympic team discriminated against Jesse Owens, a young man with a big future. Owens, whose first name was really James ("Jesse" was the blend of his real initials, J.C.), was destined to validate the black athlete in the most dramatic fashion possible: four gold medals at Hitler's 1936 "Aryan Olympics." As a nineteen-year-old track star at Ohio State, Jesse had already run a 9.4-second 100-yard sprint, setting a world record that would last for twenty-one years.

Three years later, Owens found himself under a world spotlight in Nazi Germany, forced to prove himself in one of the most hostile sporting environments of all time. Owens was not entirely alone: his African American teammate Ralph Metcalf would make history by his side, winning his own preliminary heat in making the finals. The German sprinters, Osendarp and Borchmeyer, had been in the first heats, running 10.5 and 10.7 in the 100 meters. A crowd of one hundred thousand watched Owens fly to first place in a blistering 10.3 preliminary heat. But a second round of heats, and the finals, still awaited.

Borchmeyer and Metcalf won their final round of heats at 10.5 each, but Owens exploded to a 10.2 finish that would have broken the world record again if it were not for a minor tail wind that negated the official record status. Before the games were over, Owens would break or tie a total of nine Olympic records, taking four gold medals in the Nazi heartland: the 100 meters in an official time of 10.3; the 200 meters; the 400 meters relay, and the long jump. Ralph Metcalf finished second in the

100 at 10.4 seconds, and years later he would excel at another type of race—politics—becoming a member of Congress from Chicago.

Germany actually beat the United States that year with a total of eighty-nine medals to America's fifty-six. But the Owens gold medal sweep at Berlin was a necessary bridge to genuine integrated sports. Immediately on the heels of Owens' international victory came Joe Louis, the heavyweight "Brown Bomber" who took the world boxing title in 1937 and held it longer than any other heavyweight fighter: eleven years, eight months. Louis was a popular "people's" champion, taking the case of black athletes to yet another level of achievement and acceptance. But baseball was another story, a difficult old-boy network of white tradition and entrenched power.

Owens had been forced to leave Ohio State early to help support his family, but earning money from his fame and great talent would prove remarkably difficult. There were no endorsement opportunities for him, so he ran professionally where he could, but he had to improvise to make ends meet. He was even reduced to running sprints against thoroughbred racehorses, which he did at the invitation of the Negro Leagues. More significantly, Owens also made a practice of racing the star Negro League players, reinforcing both the potential for blazing speed in baseball and emphasizing the ability of some black athletes to deliver in a big way. Owens not only beat his baseball counterparts, but he did so after giving them a ten-yard head start.

Completing a full-circle connection to the great Jesse Owens, it was Jackie Robinson's brother Mack who had finished second to Jesse's gold in the 1936 Olympic long jump competition. If that were not enough, Jackie himself went on to win the 1940 NCAA long jump title and was on track for the 1940 Olympics if the games had not been cancelled because of the war. Thus the Owens connection and influence on the game of baseball is not idle speculation—there was a personal connection that could only have inspired the Robinson family.

There were legions of black ballplayers in the Negro Leagues who could have excelled at the big league level, but the eventual choice of Robinson was no random act of history. As an athlete, Jackie possessed great speed, competitive instincts, and all-round athletic ability, averaging an astonishing eleven yards per carry as a running back during his junior year at UCLA. Also while at college, Robinson led the old Pacific Coast Conference in basketball scoring two years in a row, although he was left off the first, second and even third strings of the all-conference team, undoubtedly because of race.

Robinson could have been signed several years before his 1947 debut. He and a Negro League companion, Nate Moreland, had requested a workout with the Chicago White Sox as early as 1942 and, surprisingly, the Sox obliged with a spring training tryout in March, although nothing came of it at the time. Young Bill Veeck was on the horizon, perhaps the first true rogue owner in the modern vein of Charles Finley, Ted Turner and basketball's Mark Cuban. Veeck, recognizing the value of black ballplayers, attempted to buy the struggling Phillies franchise as early as 1943; he intended to stock the team with talented Negro League players, but Landis got wind of it and killed the deal.*

With Landis standing in the way, the future of blacks in baseball was little more than a dream. But tyrants cannot live forever, and in November 1944 Landis died from a heart attack at seventy-eight. On April 16, 1945, three black players, including Jackie Robinson, had workouts with the Boston Red Sox, but the Sox backed off, going, as it were, "0-for-2" in retaining perhaps the most influential ballplayers of the twentieth century: Ruth and Robinson. But the value of Robinson and the opportunity he represented were not lost on baseball icon Branch Rickey, the Dodger executive who had had his disagreements with Kenesaw Landis over the years, including a battle over Rickey's conception of the baseball farm system.

---

* Some historians dispute the accuracy of that particular story, but Veeck's ultimate contributions to baseball integration are not subject to debate.

Fortunately for Robinson and baseball, Branch Rickey saw the world differently from most of the baseball establishment. As manager of the last-place Pirates in 1953, Rickey shamelessly cut slugger Ralph Kiner's salary. When Kiner protested that he was demoting the team's true star, Rickey responded with the now famous justification, "We could have finished last without you." So it is little wonder that as team president of the Dodgers in August, 1945, Rickey found himself in a cutting-edge private meeting with Robinson and Dodgers scout Clyde Sukeforth. Robinson feared that the skipper wanted a timid player, but Rickey told him, "I want a player with the guts not to fight back." Less than two months later, Rickey shocked the sporting world by signing Robinson to the Dodgers minor league system, giving the black player the greatest opportunity and the greatest responsibility of his life.

Rickey could have made no better choice. At twenty-six, Jackie was much more mature than the average rookie, he had great character, and he was the consummate ballplayer. *The Sporting News,* however, was less than impressed, predicting, "The waters of the International League will flood far over his head." It took one day for Robinson to rebut that. Playing second base for Montreal, Robinson debuted on April 18, 1946, against Jersey City, clubbing a home run and three singles in his first game of the season. Jackie never looked back that year, leading the International League in hitting at a blistering .349 pace. The floodwaters may have been rising, but it was hardly Robinson who was sinking.

In April the following year, during a home exhibition game at Ebbets Field, the Dodgers announced to the crowd that the team had purchased the minor league contract of Jack Robinson from Montreal. Although things had already been set in motion in 1945 when Robinson signed the Dodgers' minor league deal, history was made on April 15, 1947, when Jackie Robinson strode onto the big league field against the Braves. Known largely for his play at second, Robinson debuted at first base to keep star veteran Ed Stanky at second base, and responded with eleven successful fielding chances on the first day. His initial plate appearances were unimpressive, with an 0-for-3, but that was unimportant: the hits would come, often in bunches, sometimes raining down on the opposition like a summer downpour.

At the end of the day, Rickey and Robinson had changed baseball and sports forever, successfully integrating big league baseball seven years before the Supreme Court, in 1954, mandated the same basic right for the children of our state school systems in *Brown v. Board of Education*.

Rickey had known it would not be easy. He had chosen Robinson for his superior talent, of course, but also because of his stable temperament. For the first year, Rickey tried to make things easier for Robinson by refusing, with Jackie's consent, to comment publicly on his choice. As anticipated, problems mushroomed immediately, starting at home. Even Jackie's new Dodgers teammates tried to launch a petition drive against him, but that was quickly quashed by the team's acerbic, strong-willed manager, Leo Durocher. Once the season began, the Cardinals planned, but never carried out, a strike protesting Robinson's signing. It was Phillies manager Ben Chapman who probably launched the nastiest verbal assaults, mercilessly attacking Robinson when the Phillies visited Ebbets Field in April. Harold Parrott, the former traveling secretary for the Dodgers, said that Chapman spewed venom about "thick Negro lips" and skulls, and about the skin diseases the other players would contract from sharing Jackie's combs and towels.

Robinson later confessed that Chapman's baiting had had a terrible effect on him, but he held up and even cracked the winning hit in a one-run pitchers' duel that day. If anything, Chapman's vitriol had a positive effect on the season, unifying the Dodgers players against the other team. On the second day, Chapman's verbal abuse caused a direct confrontation between the Phillies manager and many of Robinson's teammates that almost ended in an exchange of blows. One Dodger,

Eddie Stanky, called Chapman a coward and challenged the Philadelphia manager to a fight. When the Dodgers took offense as a group and embraced Robinson as a teammate, a significant line had been crossed in baseball history. Notwithstanding pockets of discontent and hatred, Americans ultimately rallied behind Robinson, who at year's end was second only to Bing Crosby in a national popularity poll. On April 15, 1947, Jackie Robinson had showed up at old Ebbets Field in the Pigtown section of Brooklyn, and by the end of the season, had led the Dodgers to the World Series against Joe DiMaggio's crosstown Yankees. Robinson debuted with a .297 season average, led the league in stolen bases with twenty-nine, and then won the first-ever Rookie of the Year Award. But it wasn't easy—making history never is.

If Joe Louis and Jesse Owens spelled the beginning of the end for sports segregation, the final step in baseball integration may have begun with a Dodgers pennant in 1941. Managed by the irascible Leo Durocher, those Dodgers would nab a hundred regular season wins, but they ran into a post-season buzz saw, yielding the World Series to the hated Yankees in five games. Frustrated as much as inspired, Durocher announced the following year that he would sign black ballplayers, prompting a hypocritical statement from Commissioner Landis. "There is no rule," Landis said, "formal or informal, or any understanding—unwritten, subterranean, or sub-anything—against the hiring of Negro players by the teams of organized baseball." Thus only two possibilities existed: either Landis was lying, or black ballplayers were so inept that they couldn't snare even the final roster spot on the worst teams of the day.

In May of 1942, an exhibition game won by Satchel Paige drew an impressive 29,000 fans to Chicago's Wrigley Field, catching Landis's attention. A week later, on May 31, Paige pitched another exhibition game, this time thumping Dizzy Dean's cadre of all-stars before an expectant crowd of 22,000. Paige and Dean were scheduled to lock horns again for a Fourth of July showdown, but Landis nixed the game because the first two contests were outdrawing Major League games.

Paige's center stage successes, coupled with Durocher's brash announcements, spelled trouble for the all-white national pastime, and Landis dug in. But Branch Rickey knew what he wanted and was willing to wait. On November 25, 1944, Kenesaw Mountain Landis died.

Five months later, two Negro League players turned up for spring training at the Dodgers facilities in upstate New York. Terris McDuffie, a pitcher, and "Showboat" Dave Thomas, worked out before Rickey, who eventually took a pass on both of them. That same month, Jackie Robinson and two other Negro League stars tried out for the Boston Red Sox at Fenway, and the Sox turned them all down. Just before the end of that April, a Major League owners' meeting resulted in an announcement that "the use of Negro players would hazard all the physical properties of baseball." It's not clear whether this meant that integration would cause riots and violence, or whether the "physical properties of baseball" referred literally to the players' skin color. Either way, the owners' attitudes were clear. Four months later a determined Branch Rickey sat down with Jackie Robinson to discuss their inevitable date with baseball destiny. In October, the Dodgers announced Robinson's arrival in a minor league role. But the Dodgers' mandate was clear.

The newly elected commissioner, Albert "Happy" Chandler, a former United States senator and governor of Kentucky, did not stand in the way of the impending Rickey and Robinson revolution. When Robinson first took the field in a Major League uniform on April 15, 1947, black baseball fans expressed their own recognition of the new social and economic reality—they showed up in force. Of the 25,000 fans at Ebbets Field, over half, an estimated 14,000, were African American. Baseball had a whole new fan base.

Once past the opening day test, Jackie Robinson quickly made a splash, jerking his first of many home runs on April 18,

1947. But the relentless big-league pressures took their toll, and by April 30 Jackie was mired on an 0-for-20 slump. He would explode out of it the next day with a leadoff double, but it would still be a long, though certainly rewarding, season.

The largest single-game paid attendance at Wrigley Field, a record that still stands, was set when Robinson's Dodgers came to Chicago on May 18, 1947. More than 46,000 fans (about 6,000 over the current listed stadium capacity) saw the Dodgers whip the Cubs 4-2, although Robinson struggled with an 0-for-4 performance that brought a promising fourteen-game hitting streak to an abrupt halt. But the crowds kept expanding. Nine days later, 51,780 people watched the Dodgers down the Giants at the Polo Grounds. Robinson kept hitting and the crowds kept coming for exactly ten years until Robinson announced his retirement before the 1957 season. Even then, after a decade of integrated ball, three teams still were all white: the American League's Red Sox and Tigers and the National League Phillies.

Three years later, in 1960, the last significant Negro League folded, although only eight percent of the Major League players were African American. No American League MVPs were black then, but, remarkably, black ballplayers won the National League MVP award with regularity. As of the beginning of the 1960 campaign, nine of the National League MVP awards had been won by black ballplayers, beginning with Jackie Robinson in 1949 and including Robinson's Dodgers teammate and three-time winner Roy Campanella. Ernie Banks had already won twice for the Cubs, with Willie Mays, Hank Aaron, and Don Newcombe checking in with one each.

Both of the 1960 MVPs were white: Dick Groat for the Pirates and Roger Maris of the Yankees. Although Maris repeated in 1961 on the strength of his record home-run year, Frank Robinson took the National League award. White players continued to win the award in the American League until the Yankees' Elston Howard finally broke the ice in 1955. Howard, an outstanding but not fleet-footed catcher, became a nine-time All-Star during his career. On Howard's debut, Yankees manager Casey Stengel commented, "When they finally get me a nigger, I get the only one who can't run." The black catcher who couldn't run went on to play for the Yankees in ten World Series.

Integrating the Yankees was not easy. In 1953, six years after Robinson was signed, the team's traveling secretary said: "No nigger will ever have a berth on any train I'm running." Later that same year, the Yankees traded away their top minor-league black player, Vic Power, who was equally candid about being dumped. "They were waiting to see if I could turn white, but I couldn't do it."

The Tigers did not ink their first African American player until 1958, when they acquired journeyman caliber infielder Ozzie Virgil in a multi-player swap with the Giants. By then the Red Sox were the lone holdout, enduring charges of racism from the NAACP. Then Pumpsie Green debuted for the Red Sox on July 21, 1959, as a pinch runner against the White Sox.[**]

Johnny Washington was a wily veteran pitcher in the Red Sox organization in those days, but he could not outlast the racial barriers of Boston to make the majors. Before signing with the Red Sox, Johnny had played in the Negro Leagues for the Chicago American Giants and the Newark Eagles, better known as the Houston Eagles. They traveled the country by bus, and, since he was very light-skinned, his teammates sometimes sent Johnny into white-only diners to buy sandwiches for everyone. Johnny said that the guys on the bus amused themselves by betting on whether he would get thrown out before he could get the food. He did fail once, but later said he had an affable relationship with the proprietor anyway, and had no trouble at that same restaurant in following months and years.

With its high-profile Yankees and Red Sox clinging to segregation, the American League as a whole was slow to embrace

---

[**] Pumpsie's brother Cornell Green would become a defensive back for the Dallas Cowboys.

black ballplayers. One historic exception was Bill Veeck's Cleveland Indians. Unlike Boston, which fought against the tides of racial change until 1959, in March of 1947 Veeck was building a spring training camp in Arizona where the racial climate was relatively friendly. The Giants followed suit, adopting Arizona for their spring training, and the Dodgers moved from Florida to Havana, Cuba.***

Veeck signed Larry Doby, a young star from the Negro National League who was hitting at a .414 pace at the time. Veeck personally escorted Doby into the Stadium for his Cleveland debut on July 5, 1947. Doby struck out that day as a pinch hitter with two men on base, but he was destined for stardom. There was no American League Rookie of the Year at the time—the National League was just then inventing the honor—but Doby would be a force in the Indians' lineup. By 1954 he would lead the league in both home runs and RBIs.

In the summer of 1947, the subtle tides of change became raging torrents, and on July 20 two black ballplayers appeared in the same big league lineup, when Home Run Brown and Hank Thompson took the field for the St. Louis Browns. The Browns swept a double-header that day against the all-white Boston Red Sox, who would take another dozen years to field Pumpsie Green. By August, the Dodgers were again making history, showcasing Dan Bankhead, the first black pitcher in Major League history, who made a relief appearance against the Pirates. It was an auspicious debut for Bankhead, who yielded no fewer than eight runs in just over three innings, and added another footnote to history when he became the first pitcher, black or white, ever to homer in his first big league plate appearance.

*** Fidel Castro was twenty-one years old at the time. As a star pitcher for the University of Havana, Castro displayed a modest level of baseball talent. Although the Dodgers had roots in Havana, it was the Giants who offered Castro $5,000 to sign. The future dictator declined, opting for law school instead. Castro made a few cameo appearances on the mound over the years, but never really played big league winter ball as legend sometimes suggests.

On July 9, 1948, Negro League legend Satchel Paige became the first black pitcher in American League history, yielding two hits and no runs in a relief effort against the Browns; he may have been forty-eight years old at the time. Paige's start in the majors came soon after when player-manager Lou Boudreau tabbed him to take the mound against the Senators on August 3. It was a day to behold before a stunning 72,434 energized fans packed into the cavernous Cleveland stadium, Paige winning his first start 5-3. Pushing fifty, Paige would help pitch the Indians to a pennant that year, going 6-1 in August and September with a stellar 2.48 ERA. When he took the mound on October 10, 1948, he became the first black pitcher in World Series history and, although Paige pitched very little, the Indians went on to win the title in six games over the Boston Braves.

The following 1949 season found Paige a year older but no less impressive: the nearly ageless pitcher appeared in thirty-one games. Bill Veeck sold the Indians before the 1950 season, and Paige was released—a remarkably uninspired move given the pitcher's popularity. Veeck went on to buy the St. Louis Browns, and the Browns signed Satchel in 1951, a big season for Veeck and the Browns. That was the year midget Eddie Gaedel debuted, and Veeck offered a contract to forty-eight-year-old Negro star Cool Papa Bell. Bell, whose game depended largely upon speed, declined.

Paige pitched for three years with the Browns, including 1952 when he notched a winning big-league record at 12-10. Even more remarkably, Satchel would lead the league in wins earned in relief with eight such victories tacked onto ten saves. Released again in 1954, Paige turned up with Bill Veeck's Miami Marlins, an International League team, where he pitched for three more years. Paige went on pitching well into the 1960s. It wasn't until September 25, 1965, that Satchel Paige pitched his final contest, starting a game for rogue owner Charley Finley's Oakland Athletics. At age sixty-five or fifty-nine or somewhere in between, he went three innings, gave up one hit to Boston's

Carl Yastrzemski, allowing no runs. Then Leroy Robert Paige quietly walked off the mound and into Major League history.

It is difficult to imagine baseball without its black stars, from brash Reggie Jackson to upbeat Ernie Banks, sullen Barry Bonds, colorful Sammy Sosa and legions of other stars and superstars. In 1951, when Bobby Thomson launched—stole—his famous home run against Ralph Branca, Jackie Robinson was there. When St. Louis gunned down the star-studded Red Sox for the 1967 title, Bob Gibson was there for three dominant Cardinals wins in the Series. On August 15, 1951, newcomer Willie Mays chased down a line drive at the Polo Grounds, caught it, wheeled and rocketed the ball home to shoot down the Dodgers' Carl Furillo trying to score from third.

Hank Aaron, one of the greatest of all time, first played pro ball in 1952, for the Negro League Indianapolis Clowns. In 1953, he became the first black player in the South Atlantic League. It wasn't easy. When Hank's father first saw him play pro ball in Montgomery, Alabama, there were frequent hateful racial slurs. "When Henry came up," said Herbert Aaron, Sr., "I heard the fans yell, 'Hit that nigger, hit that nigger.' Henry hit the ball up against the clock. The next time he came up, they said 'Walk him, walk him.'"

Aaron's first baseman on the Milwaukee Braves was Joe Adcock, known for clubbing four home runs in a game on July 31, 1954, and totaling eighteen bases that day, a big league record. He had a simple, earthy view about pitching to Aaron. "Trying to sneak a pitch past Hank Aaron is like trying to sneak the sunrise past a rooster."

Aaron had been called up to "The Show" with the Braves in 1954 to replace injured outfielder Bobby Thomson, and he never left the team, snaring Rookie of the Year honors after his first season. He led the league in hitting in 1956 and won the MVP award the following year. And every year Aaron relentlessly clubbed home runs, eventually eclipsing Babe Ruth's career mark with homer number 715 in 1974, then extending the record to

755 by the end of the 1976 season. Aaron himself had mixed emotions about the feat; he felt cheated by the baseball pundits who may have failed to recognize the significance of the record, sometimes lamenting that Ruth's all-time mark was the greatest record of all time until Aaron broke it, after which Joe DiMaggio's fifty-six-game hitting streak became the greatest.

In 1974, during Hank Aaron's season-long chase of Babe Ruth's ghost, racists fought his efforts at every turn in every city. Mail poured in from everywhere, some supportive but most laced with venom by those who couldn't accept the breaking of Ruth's record at all, let alone by a black man. During most of 1974, Aaron received more than 3,000 letters a day, over 900,000 by the end of the year. Indeed, with the advent of Aaron's record, the greatest of all baseball records may have "become" DiMaggio's. When Roger Maris broke Ruth's single-season home-run mark of sixty, he experienced the same phenomenon with the alleged asterisk, and even tasted a little hatred along the way.

Hank Aaron, Satchel Paige, Jackie Robinson and all those others who came before them endured a special brand of exclusion by those who sought to steal their achievements by pretending that black ballplayers were inferior and relegating them to the Negro Leagues. But the truth gradually slipped out, with Paige mowing down big leaguers in exhibition play, Jesse Owens embarrassing Hitler at the 1936 Olympic Games, and Jackie Robinson enduring a quantum-leap season of skeptics and detractors. Before it was all over, Robinson would be the first Rookie of the Year, a six-time All-Star, the 1949 MVP and league batting champion, and a 1962 inductee into the Hall of Fame. He retired with an impressive career batting average of .311 with thirty-eight World Series games under his belt.

Robinson died prematurely at 53 in 1972. But his legacy continues. In 1999 the postal service issued a commemorative stamp for him, and he is remembered every day of the baseball year, season after season after season.

21

THE GREENBERG CONSPIRACY

JACKIE ROBINSON WAS THE idol of millions of African Americans, not just ballplayers, but of all walks of life. When baseball's first black star was asked who his own idol might be, the answer could have been Satchel Paige, Josh Gibson, Joe Louis, or Jesse Owens. In fact it was none of those. Jackie Robinson's idol was an affable, gangly, determined white boy from the Bronx, the son of Rumanian immigrants and a reject from both the Giants and the Yankees of Babe Ruth and Lou Gehrig.

On May 6, 1933, the engaging Jewish rookie named Hank Greenberg strode to the plate in a Tigers uniform to face the Senators' Earl Whitehill in Detroit. The ball was soon cannoned deep into the distant stands, the first of many memorable home runs by Hank Greenberg, an even-tempered but relentless competitor who in his own right paved the way for Robinson and all those who followed from Paige to Larry Doby, Roy Campanella, Mays, and Hank Aaron.

Baseball was in Greenberg's blood from the time he was a tall, awkward student at Monroe High School in the Bronx. He was twelve years old when the House that Ruth Built was completed in 1923, and an impressionable sixteen when the 1927 Yankees, the most celebrated baseball team of all time, took the field in his own backyard, New York City. Modest and sincere, Greenberg was a natural on and off the field, although at 6'4"

he was sometimes uncoordinated and ungraceful, often pain-
fully so. Giants manager John McGraw was impressed with
Greenberg's bat, but he did not trust the reliability of the young
player's running and fielding, so the Giants ultimately took a
pass, a disappointing setback to the aspiring young slugger.

The Yankees obstacles to Greenberg can be summarized in
two words: Lou Gehrig. Hank Greenberg's natural position was
first base, but by the close of the 1920s, Gehrig had long been
established as a genuine superstar, playing first for the Bronx
Bombers. The feared Murderers' Row team of 1927 that regis-
tered a stunning 110 victories had also produced the American
League MVP, but it was not Babe Ruth, as many might sup-
pose, but instead the iron man, Lou Gehrig. Even though that
was the historic season of the Babe's sixty homers, Gehrig had
knocked in an extraordinary league-topping 175 runs. If Ruth
was the marquee star of the team, Gehrig was its soul, a relentless competitor who would play 2164 career games for the Yankees, 2130 of them in a row, all the while notching a .340 lifetime average. So if Hank Greenberg was going to make his Major
League mark at first base, it certainly would not be in Yankee
pinstripes.

In 1930, nineteen-year-old Hank Greenberg was signed by
the prescient Detroit Tigers. Whether Detroit saw things the
Giants had missed or whether it was just plain luck is a question no one can answer now. Greenberg was slow afoot, sometimes looked ungainly, and he soon suffered a setback when he
broke his wrist. But that wouldn't be the biggest blow:
Greenberg's big league career would endure a tidal wave of anti-
Semitic hate and abuse that would not just challenge the emerging superstar, but might even have motivated his hallmark
achievements. It was this ordeal that would offer inspiration
and perspective to Jackie Robinson fourteen years after
Greenberg's inaugural season encounter with vicious bigotry.

Greenberg played during the twilight of Ruth's career and
although Hank's own star shone brightly, his share of the lime-

light in Detroit was darkened by the sparkling media images of
Ruth and Gehrig, and perhaps by the lords of the game.

These were the Depression days, when baseball was king
and the owners ruled the game at will, usually through the
strong-arm tactics of Kenesaw Mountain Landis, its flamboy-
ant, egocentric commissioner. A former federal judge from Chicago, Landis was thick-skinned and resolute, seen by many as a
virtual despot, an arrogant sovereign who ruled with no meaningful constraint. He was certainly a bigot, with probably the
motive as well as the power to intervene in one of the grandest
home run chases of the twentieth century. It is possible, indeed
it is likely, that Landis had a hand in stealing a milestone slice of
immortality from Hank Greenberg, the consummate gentleman
of the game and hero to the disenfranchised, including legions
of Jewish immigrants and at least one young man with a dream:
Jack Roosevelt Robinson. Such a Landis intervention would
certainly have altered the slugger's defining career year—1938,
the season of Greenberg's valiant assault on Ruth's unbreakable Murderers' Row sixty-homer record, achieved just eleven
years before.

Greenberg set the stage for his date with destiny and consequent confrontation with Landis. His rookie season saw the
burgeoning power hitter collect a respectable twelve home runs
and thirty-three doubles to complement his solid .301 average.
It was a salutary effort, although somewhat obscured by the
established stars of the era, including a career year for the Athletics' Jimmie Foxx, the American League MVP. All Foxx did
was rip league pitching for a .356 average, forty-eight home
runs, and 163 RBIs. But the steadfast Greenberg was coming.

In his sophomore campaign, Greenberg batted a formidable
.339 and led the league in doubles with sixty-three, adding an
impressive twenty-six home runs and 139 RBIs. Most importantly, Greenberg led his Tigers to the 1934 pennant and into
the World Series. Even though the Tigers would lose the championship that year to the Gas House Gang Cardinals, Greenberg

would hit a respectable .321 for the Series. He would also strike out nine times over the seven games, a reminder that he shared the occasional weakness of many great power hitters before and after him.

Those strikeouts were no accidents, perhaps having less to do with Greenberg's shortcomings than Dizzy Dean's laser pitching. Apparently the young hitter, still just twenty-three years old, could be fooled with breaking pitches, so at a key moment in game one with two Tigers on and Greenberg at the plate, Leo Durocher shouted to the ace starter Dean, "Don't waste your fastball. Throw the son of a bitch a ham sandwich." Greenberg struck out and the Cardinals prevailed 8-3.

The disappointment of the 1934 Series loss would partly inspire his return to the fall championship a year later against the Cubs, but the close of the 1934 regular season also presented a much different defining moment—and image—for Greenberg. With the American League pennant in sight and the relentless Yankees nipping at Detroit's heels, Hank was confronted by a groundbreaking September dilemma a full thirty-one years before a similar high-profile issue was faced by Dodger pitcher Sandy Koufax: the Jewish holidays.

With Rosh Hashanah falling on September 10, the Tigers facing Boston and the Yankees lurking, Greenberg elected to play, and clocked not one, but two home runs that day driving in and scoring both the Detroit runs in a narrow 2-1 victory. With the public blessing of a Detroit rabbi who reminded everyone of the joy represented by the Jewish New Year, Greenberg answered baseball's call to duty.

But eight days later the issue, and the result, were much different. It was Yom Kippur, the highest of the holy days, a somber day of introspection and atonement. Just as Koufax would do at the threshold of the 1965 Series, Greenberg did the only thing a man of his faith could do: he sat out a crucial contest against none other than the implacable Yankees themselves—a laudable act of principle insisted upon by Hank's father. The baseball gods were in accord, and the Tigers prevailed, shutting the New York-ers down 2-0. When the pennant race was finally concluded, the surge of the relentless Tigers downed the Yankees by seven full games. But Greenberg had put his faith on the map, an act of character accepted by many, praised by some, but disliked by others, some of whom were in very high places.

The following 1935 season would be a milestone year for both Greenberg and the Tigers. But it would be a season of dis-content punctuated by a defining encounter with prejudice in an unlikely World Series venue: Chicago's Wrigley Field. The explo-sive power of Hank Greenberg's bat came alive with a vengeance as the slugger garnered a breathtaking 110 RBIs—not for the season, which even then would be a career year for many good-to- great players, *but by the midyear All-Star break!* It was a feat of incredible baseball prowess and the Tigers were stalking yet another pennant and date with World Series destiny. But possible unscrupulous shenanigans were beginning to influence events. Even with those mystical RBIs in a banner year that followed a 1934 pennant, Greenberg was left off the 1935 All-Star team. No one can question the obvious star power of those who were selected instead of Greenberg—the implacable Jimmie Foxx and Lou Gehrig—but nonetheless there remains a question about se-cret factors tied to the religion of the Detroit star.

Given the arguments to be made for Foxx and Gehrig, any speculation about ulterior motives for the All-Star snub is still guesswork, albeit reinforced by both the nature of the times in general and of Landis in particular. But there can be no doubt about the documented deluge of overt anti-Semitism that was spewed at Greenberg during the 1935 Series—on and perhaps even off the field. While the determined Tigers were again best-ing the Yankees for the pennant, this time by a narrow three games, Charlie Grimm's Cubs with Stan Hack and Gabby Hart-nett were piling up an impressive 100 wins to snare the Na-tional League pennant by four games over the Cardinals, pro-pelling both teams toward a notorious incident of bigotry.

When the Tigers met the Cubs at Wrigley Field for game one of the World Series on October 2, 1935, the Jewish holidays had just concluded. And Hank Greenberg was an immediate lightning rod for storms of ethnic insults pouring out not from subversive hate groups or even from the fans that day, but directly from the Cubs bench. According to Greenberg's memoirs, documented by witnesses and many other sources, the Cubs began to scream insults, including "Jew bastard" and "Christ killer" at Greenberg. The stream of venom from the Cubs' Charlie Root, Billy Herman and others was so abhorrent that the home plate umpire, George Moriarty, was forced to intervene.* Moriarty sternly chastised the Cubs dugout and threatened ejections if the verbal assaults continued, drawing his own line of fire from the vengeful Cubs. The umpire, repelled by this public desecration of both Greenberg and the game itself, would later tell the press, "No ballplayer can call me the names they did and get away with it." Published accounts disclosed the brunt of the umpire's anger. "I told Grimm and Chicago, if I heard any more such profanity as they yelled at Greenberg that I'd chase five of them off the bench with Grimm leading the procession."

Commissioner Landis was appalled, too—but apparently in a different way: *Landis fined the umpire.*** It was yet another defining moment for Landis, but his unbridled power met with little moral resistance, even when his ugly bigotry was clearly evident.

Two days later, in game two of that 1935 Series, Greenberg went on to make his own statement, in his own way: on the field. He calmly jacked a two-run smash off the pitcher Charlie Root—the leader of the Cubs' hate-filled diatribe—in the very

---

* A minor but interesting note: the actor Michael Moriarty is a direct descendant of umpire George Moriarty.

** Landis also fined some of the Cubs players, but whether doing so reflected real outrage or was just a sham to hide his true feelings is irrelevant. The fining of a respected home plate umpire who not only maintained order and avoided an ugly escalation, but admirably defended the integrity of the game, speaks volumes for itself regardless of any feigned mitigation or obfuscation by the bigoted Landis.

first inning, leading the Tigers to an 8-3 win to tie the Series at one game each. But fate was not kind to Greenberg that day: the relentless first baseman broke his wrist, and was sidelined for the rest of the Series. The Tigers prevailed despite this, over-whelming the Cubs in six games.

Greenberg had led the league with a staggering 170 RBIs that year of 1935 and, broken wrist or not, he was awarded the league MVP ahead of rivals Foxx and Gehrig. The easy-going Greenberg probably did not see the honor as reparation, though later in life he grew to appreciate awards, for others as well as for himself. "When you're playing," he observed in 1988, "awards don't seem like much. Then you get older and all of it becomes more precious."

Nineteen-thirty-six seemed full of promise. It began with another torrid RBI pace that found Greenberg garnering six-teen in only twelve games, but in an on-field collision he broke his wrist again, abruptly snuffing his entire season. It wasn't the Tigers' year. The Yankees quashed a good Indians team to run away with the pennant and then take the Giants in seven games to snare the 1936 Series.

The pundits believed Greenberg's twice-broken wrist would end his big league career altogether, but they failed to take into account his characteristic determination and competitive drive. Greenberg took little time to prove them wrong with a vengeance, putting together a stunning career year in 1937 and earning his second MVP award. He drove home no fewer than 183 runs, the third highest total in modern baseball history, belting forty home runs and notching a .337 average. The Tigers failed once more to best the Yankees, but it was nonetheless a remarkable year for baseball. Rogers Hornsby finally retired at age forty-one, Lou Gehrig and Joe DiMaggio terrorized the American League, and Hank Greenberg became the first player in history to clock a home run into the distant center field bleachers of Yankee Sta-dium. But when the season dust had cleared, it was the 102-win Yankees left standing to face the cross-town Giants in the World

Series. It proved to be no contest, with the Yankees taking the title in five games for their second straight world championship. In spite of yeoman efforts by Greenberg and others that year, Detroit finished thirteen games behind the champs, but there was always next year. Of course.

In the autumn of 1938 the nation, or at least the East Coast, had a brief Martian-invasion scare when radio actor Orson Welles and his Mercury Theater of the Air broadcast an adaptation of the H.G. Wells' novel *The War of the Worlds,* to celebrate Halloween. So it was a strange year in which Greenberg, the affable Detroit star, chased the most sacred Ruthian mark of them all—the sixty-homer milestone.

It might have been less disruptive if the sixty-homer season had been a fluke by a lesser ballplayer like, say, Roger Maris, whose 1961 plateau never seemed to rouse the near-religious fervor surrounding Ruth. But any assault on a god will generate a firestorm, and in those days Babe Ruth was an American idol. Greenberg's 1938 long-ball achievements would have enraged Ruth's innumerable followers in any case, but his religion added a poisonous element to the ensuing uproar.

On May 25 Greenberg clubbed two home runs in a Detroit victory over the Yankees, and two days later he became the first player ever to jack one into the distant seats at Chicago's Comiskey Park. On July 26 he had another two-homer game, followed by still another the very next day, both against the Senators. Remarkably, all four home runs were in a row, two in closing the first game followed by two more to start the second, and with that Greenberg tied a Major League record shared by only a handful of players. On September 27, Greenberg had another two-homer game, his last of the season, marking a record-setting eleven multi-homer games on the year, besting even the immortal Ruth and propelling the Detroit star to fifty-eight dingers with five games to go.

The multi-homer mark undoubtedly forced Kenesaw Landis and his cronies to recognize that baseball's marquee sixty milestone was vulnerable. This must have been a shock to the dogmatic commissioner who single-handedly kept the game racially "pure" literally until the day he died in office. Having to purge Ruth's season from the record books was a ghastly enough prospect, but replacing him with a likeable, high-profile Jewish player was simply unthinkable.

As the summer and fall of 1938 wore on, Greenberg continued to charge forward—on the field and in the batter's box. By September 9, he had slugged forty-seven shots into the seats and sometimes beyond. On September 11, Greenberg slammed two more in a double-header sweep over the White Sox. The nation was energized by Greenberg's performance. With forty-nine home runs, he had already clubbed more than Gehrig's 1931 league-leading forty-six, Jimmie Foxx's 1933 forty-eight, the thirty-six Greenberg and Jimmie Foxx each slugged in 1935, and DiMaggio's 1937 mark of forty-six.

Greenberg had already tied Gehrig's 1934 forty-nine, but, more importantly, he was on the way to top Foxx's own stunning fifty-eight round-trippers of 1932. Even more remarkable, he was maintaining a neck-and-neck pace with Ruth himself, who by September 11, 1927, had clocked his fiftieth. Two days later, Ruth had launched two more in a double header against the Indians to reach fifty-two; on September 17, 1938, Greenberg smashed two more in one game for his fifty-third of the year. Although still keeping even with Ruth according to the calendar, Greenberg had played more games than Ruth had done in 1927. All this must have been slow torture for Landis.

On September 23, the unstoppable Greenberg slammed still two more in one game, homers fifty-five and fifty-six; then he did it again on September 27—one was an astonishing 440-foot line-drive rocket that never left the park as Greenberg motored around the bases and survived a close play at home. Perched at fifty-eight with five games to go, the nation held its breath—as Landis squirmed. The next day Greenberg slammed a blast onto the roof in St. Louis, but the ball was foul. With three games left, all in Cleveland, Greenberg needed just two more to reach Ruth's record of sixty.

Two of those Cleveland contests were scheduled for League Park, a small bandbox where the right-field porch was only 290 feet from home plate, but one was slated for the cavernous Municipal Stadium where left center was a distant 450 feet from home and deep center was even farther. Ruth's record escaped unscathed from the first game at tiny League Park, but then the powers intervened. Suddenly the second contest was moved to the mammoth Municipal Stadium where now the final *two* games of the season would be played, instead of only one. With a record-setting eleven multi-homer games under his belt already that year, Greenberg was certainly capable of tying or breaking Ruth's mark in just two games, especially if one or both of them had been at League Park. But Municipal was something else.

Years later, Bill Veeck, who owned the Indians during their 1948 pennant drive, saw an outfield pasture so vast that he half-expected a range war. Veeck installed temporary fences, shortening the outfield to 410 feet and the lines to 310, but Greenberg did not have that advantage in 1938. It may be no coincidence that Greenberg was a confidant of Veeck and invested $100,000 of his own money to be a joint owner and front-office VP for those same Indians. If nothing else, Greenberg had to have remembered that outfield, for that is where he faced Bob Feller in the next-to-the-last game of his record 1938 campaign.

By September 27, 1927, Ruth had clubbed fifty-seven homers, raised to fifty-eight and then fifty-nine on September 29, the latter a grand-slam monster against the Senators, and then, finally, on the last day of the season, Ruth launched the famous number sixty at home in Yankee Stadium, helping lift the Yankees to a 109-win Murderers' Row year. The final day of Greenberg's season was October 2, a double header in the vast Cleveland cavern. Making matters worse was hitting against fireball Hall-of-Famer Bob Feller, who struck out an American

League record eighteen Tigers that day. Even so, Greenberg managed a spectacular double off Feller, a 420-foot shot that never found the distant outfield walls—a sure home run in any other park of the day, especially in the diminutive League Park where the game could have been played.

When game two began and ended, Greenberg was still stuck at fifty-eight home runs, even though he managed three singles in the nightcap. He may have had yet another at-bat to tie Ruth, but darkness settled in. Ironically, umpire George Moriarty, who had been fined by Landis for defending Greenberg in Chicago, was forced to call the game.

"I'm sorry, Hank," he said. "But this is as far as I can go."

"That's all right, George," Hank replied. "This is as far as I can go, too."

Greenberg was emotionally and physically drained, and Ruth's record remained intact.

Some call it just bad luck—but others believe it was big league intervention by powers intent upon preserving the Ruth legacy. One of those was Tigers' teammate Billy Rogell who felt the deck was stacked against Greenberg both because of his religion and because of the deep-rooted reverence for Ruth. Still, it was hardly a wasted season for Greenberg. He had not only broken Ruth's record for multi-homer games, but he set a single-season record for home runs in one stadium with thirty-nine clubbed in Detroit's Briggs Stadium, more than Ruth ever hit in the Polo Grounds or Yankee Stadium. Even with all that, the MVP award went to Boston's Jimmie Foxx, who hit .349 and drove in 175.

Perhaps it was Greenberg's competitive spirit that appealed to Jackie Robinson, or maybe it was that he had played in Ruth's shadow. But it would have been fitting that Greenberg won his place in Robinson's heart because Jackie felt an affinity for someone else who had suffered from hateful bigotry. Landis had been there to taint Hank's assault on Ruth. And if Landis had not died, Robinson would never have made history.

Greenberg endured far more than his share of abuse, but the years were not all bad. Most fans loved him, not only in Detroit. He had a spectacular ball career interrupted by four years of service in World War II, and then he was a part of the Indians miracle in 1948 that brought black ballplayers to the American League under the aegis of Bill Veeck.

Was Greenberg's home-run record stolen? We may never really know—but it was ironic that the disingenuous season-ending move to the giant Municipal Stadium enabled a bigger crowd to see Greenberg go for the record.

Only in baseball.

PART V
THE GREAT BASEBALL CONSPIRACY

22

THE GREAT BASEBALL BLUNDER

IN 1922, THE UNITED STATES Supreme Court, in a decision written by Justice Oliver Wendell Holmes, Jr., ruled that Major League Baseball was not a business engaged in interstate commerce and was therefore exempt from federal antitrust laws. The Sherman Act, passed in 1890, proscribed "contracts, combinations and conspiracies in restraint of trade."

This illogical decision changed the game of baseball more than any other single event, except perhaps for the Jackie Robinson revolution. And Baseball Commissioner Kenesaw Mountain Landis was involved in both these events.

Landis—named for the site of a famous Civil war battle—was born in Millville, Ohio, in 1866 and practiced law in Chicago from 1891 until Theodore Roosevelt appointed him to a federal district judgeship in 1905. As a federal judge, he presided over a key antitrust case, hitting Standard Oil with a whopping $29 million fine. In 1920, Landis became the first baseball commissioner and ruled every facet of the game with an iron fist for over twenty-four years.

There have been only nine commissioners since 1920. All have been wholly independent—none had any other formal allegiance to the game, like being owners, managers or players—with the exception of Allan H. "Bud" Selig who became "acting commissioner" on September 7, 1992, despite his ownership interest in the Milwaukee Brewers. Landis was more than independent; he was tyrannical. George Will has described some aspects of Landis's character:

> Landis was a grandstanding judge—in baseball lingo, a hot dog. . . . He tried to extradite the Kaiser because a Chicagoan died when a German submarine sank the *Lusitania*. Landis enjoyed stiff drinks of whiskey but handed out stiff sentences to people who violated Prohibition.

The dramatic and colorful influence of gamblers over the 1919 World Series has received much attention from sports commentators, pundits, and historians, but the equally significant Supreme Court ruling exempting baseball from antitrust laws has not been much discussed, even though its consequences influenced the game for the remainder of the twentieth century.

Even in 1922, Major League Baseball was an entertainment juggernaut, chugging legions of ballplayers from city to city and state to state to play highly profitable games supported by millions of fans from New York to St. Louis. Bigger-than-life players—Ty Cobb, Cy Young, Babe Ruth—performed in state-of-the-art stadiums of the day—the Polo Grounds, Fenway Park, Wrigley (then called Weeghman) Field and beyond; their exploits were broadcast over the interstate airwaves by a new entertainment medium, radio.

Created in 1913 by a consortium of wealthy businessmen, the Federal League of Professional Baseball Clubs was an upstart competing baseball league determined to take on Major League Baseball where others had failed. With franchise clubs in Chicago, St. Louis, Pittsburgh, Indianapolis, Cincinnati, Buffalo, Baltimore and Brooklyn, the new league was in a position to attract its own major stars. Major League Baseball owners were wary—and furious.

Also in 1913, Ty Cobb held out over a salary dispute that, although it was eventually resolved, highlighted the issue of player compensation and gave the owners something to think about. Then the Federal League took a bite out of the majors, signing Joe Tinker to play for the new Chicago Whales, owned by Charles Weeghman, who built what is now Wrigley Field, for his new team.

After landing Joe Tinker, the Federal League went on a shopping spree, raiding the Major Leagues of Hal Chase (who was to help fix the 1919 World Series), Mordecai "Three-Finger" Brown and many others—eighty-one Major Leaguers in all. This caused the Major League owners to invoke the reserve clause and sue to prevent players from switching leagues.

In 1914, the legal seeds of the antitrust dilemma were sown by a lower state court in Erie County, New York. Facing the issue of involuntary servitude with the baseball monopoly controlling its players, the judge refused to enforce the restrictive clause in the player contracts, expressly found that "organized baseball is now as complete a monopoly of the baseball business for profit as any monopoly can be made," and commented:

> The game of baseball, which began as an athletic sport of youthful players attending the schools and colleges throughout the country, has continued as the favorite athletic sport of America during the past half century, and has been commercialized and organized as professional baseball and developed into a big business conducted for profit under the name of "Organized Baseball."

The Federal League, rapidly establishing itself as a competing new professional consortium of rogue teams and wealthy owners, was raising salaries with its wholesale raid on established stars. When the Major Leagues attempted to retaliate with defensive moves of their own, the Federal League did just what the lords of the game had feared they would do: they filed an antitrust suit in 1915. The case was heard by Judge Landis, an unabashed baseball fan who regularly attended both Cubs and White Sox games, often sitting in the box with William Veeck and his young son Bill. Landis worked on the case for eleven months, and achieved a complex settlement that bought baseball peace but did not quite end the case. The Federal League was dissolved. Whales owner Charles Weeghman bought the Chicago Cubs and moved the team north to his new stadium at Clark and Addison streets; Phil Ball took over the Browns and Sportsman's Park in St. Louis; and a number of Federal League owners sold their ballplayers back to the Major Leagues. But the Federal Baseball Club of Baltimore refused to accept the settlement and vowed to fight on. Landis, revealing his bias, wrote, "Both sides must understand that any blows at the thing called baseball would be regarded by this court as a blow to a national institution."

In 1920, by dramatically boosting his home-run record from nineteen to fifty-four, Babe Ruth contributed to the growing popularity of baseball, increasing Yankee attendance to 1.289 million fans. Major League baseball was well on its way to re-juvenated fame and fortune, making its mark as a national entertainment phenomenon. But then the Black Sox scandal blew up in everyone's face. The game had to be saved, its mess had to be cleaned up, and the appointment of a respected authority, an independent commissioner, was the obvious way to go. Some of the biggest names in the country were considered for the post, among them General John J. Pershing, and former President William Howard Taft.

Taft was the owners' first choice, for obvious reasons. Not only did he wield extraordinary power in and out of Washington, he was one of the most enthusiastic baseball fans in the country. He had been a pitcher himself during his college years, his half-brother Charles had once owned the Cubs, and when he was president he had instituted the custom of throwing out the first pitch of Opening Day, assuring himself one Major League mound appearance annually. Taft also supposedly instituted the seventh-inning stretch, which he did by accident when he stood up mid-inning at a Pirates game. Although there is some question whether this latter contribution to the game actually occurred, it is clear that Taft's affinity for baseball itself is indisputable.

But Taft was Chief Justice of the U.S. Supreme Court, and chose to remain there. The owners then turned to Judge Landis, an antitrust expert in the city that was the heart of the Black Sox scandal. As commissioner, Landis maintained his offices at 333 N. Michigan Avenue, and, for the first few years, kept his federal judgeship. On January 20, 1921, *The Sporting News* reported:

> Judge Landis in accepting office outlined his plans for the government of the game, dwelling particularly on the big reason for his entering into it, which is to clean out the crookedness and the gambling responsible for it and keep the sport above reproach. The Judge made it plain he would have no mercy on any man in baseball, be he magnate or player, whose conduct was not strictly honest. They must avoid even the appearance of evil or feel the iron hand of his power to throw them out of any part of the game. The judge will be the absolute ruler of the game.

The case of *Federal Baseball Club of Baltimore, Inc. v. National League of Professional Baseball Clubs, et al* was tried in the Supreme Court of the District of Columbia, which found for the Baltimore club. The Major League then appealed to the D.C. Court of Appeals, which reversed the decision. Baltimore went to the U.S. Supreme Court, which, on May 29, 1922, in a ruling written by Judge Holmes, upheld the appellate court decision.

It is interesting to look at the Federal Baseball ruling in the light of other Supreme Court decisions of the time on other Sherman Act suits. Consider the following excerpts from the Supreme Court's Federal Baseball opinion itself:

> A summary statement of the nature of the business involved will be enough to present the point. The clubs composing the

Leagues are in different cities and for the most part in different States. The end of the elaborate organizations and sub-organizations that are described in the pleadings and evidence is that these clubs shall play against one another in public exhibitions for money, one or the other club crossing a state line in order to make the meeting possible. . . . Of course the scheme requires constantly repeated traveling on the part of the clubs, which is provided for, controlled and disciplined by the organizations, and this it is said means commerce among the States.

That seems cogently to support Baltimore's argument that Major League Baseball is engaged in interstate commerce. But then the Court comes to the opposite conclusion:

But we are of the opinion that the Court of Appeals was right. The business is giving exhibitions of base ball, which are purely state affairs. It is true that in order to attain for these exhibitions the great popularity that they have achieved, competitions must be arranged between clubs from different cities and States. But the fact that in order to give the exhibitions the Leagues must induce free persons to cross state lines and must arrange and pay for their doing so is not enough to change the character of the business.

The falsity of this reasoning is clear on its face, but it is even more surprising when we consider the other Supreme Court antitrust decisions of the day. On November 7, 1921, in *Pennsylvania Railroad Co. v. Weber*, the Supreme Court ruled that moving railroad cars from state to state was interstate commerce subject to federal antitrust laws The Court found that transporting livestock from state to state was also interstate commerce. And in *Butter Bros. Shoe Co. v. United States Rubber Co.*, the Court found that: "Importation, either of goods, persons, or information, into one state from another is the indispensable element, the test, of interstate commerce."

On February 27, 1922, just three months before the Federal Baseball decision, but a month *after* Federal Baseball had been argued before the Court, the same Court found that grain stored in elevators, even if it did not leave the state, was interstate commerce because it "affected" other grain that may or may not so travel from state to state. Thus, the Court found that professional baseball players traversing multiple states earning big salaries to entertain millions of fans in gargantuan stadiums were not engaged in interstate commerce, but that moving railroad cars *was* interstate commerce, as was *stationary* grain that was parked in elevators and did not cross state lines at all.

And on May 29, 1922, the very same *day* as the Federal Baseball decision itself, the same Court found that the tracks, bridges, roadbed, and equipment of a carrier in interstate commerce—a train—have a definite interstate character "and give such character to those employed on them." So the trains carrying ballplayers from state to state were engaged in interstate commerce, but the ballplayers riding on them for profit were not so engaged?

In *Hart v. B.F. Keith Vaudeville Exchange*, less than a year after the Federal Baseball decision, the Supreme Court considered the interstate impact of a traveling vaudeville show. Justice Holmes himself wrote this opinion, finding that the arranging and transporting of vaudeville performers was the conduct of interstate commerce. So, apparently Justice Holmes believed that hundreds of highly paid ballplayers chugging about the country on interstate railroads were not engaged in interstate commerce, but that small bands of jugglers and comedians were engaged in such commerce.

But, even so, why would a respected jurist like Holmes do such a thing? In his book *The Common Law*, Holmes offers a possible explanation:

The life of the law has not been logic: it has been experience. The felt necessities of the time, the prevalent moral and political theories, intuitions of public policy, avowed or unconscious, even the prejudices which judges share with their fellow-men, have had a good deal more to do than the syllogism in determining the rules by which men should be governed.

All in all, the Supreme Court rendered a preposterous decision to allow centralized power in Major League Baseball, using logic that the court itself did not even believe if one looks at its other antitrust decisions handed down in roughly the same time period.

The Federal Baseball suit landed on Landis's desk and would have ended there, too, if the Baltimore franchise had not pushed its case all the way to the eventual Holmes opinion which, remarkably, still stands, having endured later challenges, the most notable being outfielder Curt Flood's assault on the ridiculous exemption in 1972. In 1953, when George Toolson, a Yankees player, sued the club over the reserve clause, the Supreme Court found that when Congress passed the Sherman Act in 1890, its intention was to go after the monopolies and trusts of the robber barons, and did not intend it to apply to baseball. But the courts did deny the exemption to boxing, football, basketball, hockey and golf.

23
THE BUSINESS THAT ISN'T A BUSINESS

When the Supreme Court says baseball isn't run like a business, everybody jumps up and down with joy. When I say the same thing, everybody throws pointy objects at me.
—Bill Veeck

EXACTLY FIFTY YEARS AFTER the 1922 Federal Baseball decision, fate handed the Supreme Court a superb chance for redemption in a new battle waged by star outfielder Curt Flood. It would be a close vote, but in 1972 the Court eventually rendered the same preposterous ruling all over again.

When the St. Louis Cardinals rose up in 1964 to spank the great New York Yankees with a 4-3 World Series win, they did it on the backs of great pitching complemented by an outstanding batting order that featured speed and clutch hitting. The pitching staff was led by workhorse fireballer Bob Gibson (19-12) who pitched a remarkable 287 regular season innings capped by twenty-seven Series innings (the equivalent of three complete games, including ten full innings in game five) for two wins of the Cardinals' four Series victories; Ray Sadecki (20-11; 220 innings); and thirty-five-year-old veteran Curt Simmons (18-9; 244 innings). Those 1964 Cardinals won ninety-three games under Manager Johnny Keane with pitching, speed and the timely hitting of such name fielders as Lou Brock, Mike

Shannon, Ken Boyer, Julian Javier, catcher Tim McCarver, and center fielder Curt Flood. The fleet-footed Lou Brock led the team with a .348 average in 419 at-bats, but Ken Boyer led the entire league in RBIs (119) and was named National League MVP. Curt Flood, the mainstay of a fast outfield, led the Cardinals in plate appearances with an impressive 679 at-bats, hitting .311 and tying superstar Roberto Clemente for the National League lead in total hits with 211.

With key additions of Bobby Tolan, Roger Maris, and League MVP Orlando Cepeda, the Cardinals won a sparkling 101 games under Red Schoendienst in 1967, taking the World Series from Carl Yastrzemski's Red Sox behind Bob Gibson who started and pitched a six-hitter in Series game one, a five-hit shutout game four, and a three-hit game seven win. In 1968, the same Cardinals team won ninety-seven games and the pennant behind a staggering 305 innings from Bob Gibson who won twenty-two games with a stunning 1.12 ERA, the second lowest since 1893. Curt Flood led the 1968 Cardinals with a .301 average (fifth best in the league), following up his .335 in 1967. Lou Brock stole sixty-two bases that year, and Bob Gibson (League MVP and Cy Young winner) struck out a league-leading 268 batters. But even with all that, 1968 would eventually be the year of the Tigers with Denny McLain (thirty-one wins, AL Cy Young and MVP) and Mickey Lolich (three Series wins with a 1.67 ERA) pitching Detroit to a seven-game World Series title.

The following year, 1969, saw the first of two New York miracles by the Mets, who took the Braves in the newly devised National League Championship Series, then downed the Orioles to dominate the World Series in five games behind the pitching of Tom Seaver, Jerry Koosman, Gary Gentry, Nolan Ryan and Tug McGraw. But just after the close of the regular season, the proud but slipping Cardinals stunned baseball—and Curt Flood—with a blockbuster multi-player trade.

On October 7, 1969, St. Louis shipped Curt Flood, Tim McCarver, outfielder Byron Browne, and pitcher Joe Hoerner off to Philadelphia in exchange for marquee slugger Dick Allen, Cookie Rojas, and pitcher Jerry Johnson. Allen, who had clubbed thirty-two homers that year, publicly complained that "Baseball is a form of slavery." Flood followed that complaint with a refusal to go to Philadelphia. On December 24, 1969, Flood echoed Allen in a letter to Commissioner Bowie Kuhn: "After twelve years in the Major Leagues, I do not feel that I am a piece of property to be bought and sold irrespective of my wishes."

Curt Flood had played twelve seasons for the Cardinals. The speedy outfielder, who stood a slight 5'9", could play offense and defense both, winning the Gold Glove award seven years in a row, including in 1969. But Flood had misplayed a crucial fly ball in the 1968 World Series, a mishap that would haunt him for years, perhaps influencing that famous trade a year later. Flood, devastated by the trade, asked Bowie Kuhn to free him from the "slavery" of the baseball reserve clause, and when Kuhn refused, Flood filed suit in January 1970, for $4.1 million, alleging antitrust violations against the commissioner, league presidents and all the owners in Major League Baseball. The case found its way to the U.S. Supreme Court just as the Federal Baseball case had done a half-century before.

The 1972 Court ruled five to three against Flood with the ninth justice, Lewis Powell, having recused himself. The June 19, 1972, opinion, written by Justice Harry Blackmun, "a great baseball fan," according to Bowie Kuhn, included a five-paragraph summary of baseball history, followed by a bizarre list of Blackmun's eighty-seven favorite ballplayers. Curt Flood, who was black, was not on Blackmun's list, which began with Ty Cobb and ended with Lefty Grove. Ruth got second billing, and the rest included such names as Lou Gehrig, Honus Wagner, Jackie Robinson, Satchel Paige, Rogers Hornsby, Wee Willie Keeler, Fred Merkle, Three-Finger Brown, Cap Anson, Hank Greenberg, Nap Lajoie, and Cy Young. The written opinion meanders through a sentimental journey of baseball from an 1846 game in Hoboken to the 1869 Red Stockings and includes the famous baseball poem about the classic Cubs double play trio "Tinker to Evers to Chance."

Blackmun made sentimental references to Abner Doubleday, Al Spalding and Cap Anson, omitting all mention of gamblers, cheats, liars, and overt racists. Indeed, according to Bob Woodward's *The Brethren*,* Blackmun's initial list of great ballplayers included no African American players at all. When Justice Thurgood Marshall commented on this, Blackmun added Jackie Robinson, Satchel Paige and Roy Campanella to his list. Apparently Willie Mays, Hank Aaron, and Larry Doby were not up Blackmun's standards, while such dubious stars as Davy Jones, King Kelly, Big Dan Brouthers and Eppa Rixey were.

In any event, there seems to have been some strange behind-the-scenes maneuvering during the justices' private voting conferences.** Justice Powell abstained because he owned shares of stock in Busch Breweries, a company with family ties to Busch Stadium, the Cardinals ownership and the plight of Curt Flood himself. As the conferences progressed, some justices switched sides. Justice Marshall switched to Flood, causing a four-to-four tie. Justice Byron White considered doing the same, which would have changed baseball history, but Justice Powell's clerk— that same Justice Powell who was abstaining because of his Busch Brewery stock—seems to have persuaded White to leave the vote tied. Then Chief Justice Warren Burger shifted his vote to the ownership camp, resulting in the eventual five-to-three ruling against Flood.

This opinion was written during a time of great national unrest with two political assassinations, anti-Vietnam uprisings, racial protests, and the presidency of Richard Nixon. These justices had grown up with the bedrock dependability of baseball and such heroes as Ruth, Gehrig, Stan Musial, Ralph Kiner, Ted Williams, and even Ty Cobb and Tris Speaker. They were emotionally tied to the game, and apparently could not separate their romantic in-

---

* As quoted in Paul Weiler and Gary Roberts, *Sports and the Law*.
** See Marvin Miller, *A Whole Different Ball Game*.

volvement from the demands of the law, as seems evident from Blackmun's bizarre, self-indulgent stroll down memory lane. The decision against Flood was even more inexcusable than the Court's 1922 decision. The era of Federal Baseball was different; it was less sophisticated, and lacked the extreme interstate nature of commerce in America, not the least of which would ultimately manifest itself in the form of national television broadcasts. But the Flood opinion actually got the law and facts right, expressly finding that "professional baseball is a business in interstate commerce"; that the baseball antitrust anomaly is "an aberration that has been with us now for half a century"; and that "other sports operating interstate—football, boxing, basketball, and, presumably hockey and golf—are not so exempt [from antitrust legislation]."

But then, after correctly reciting the law, the facts, and essentially the stupidity of the prevailing antitrust exemption, the Court illogically ruled that since the aberration had been around so long, it could not be changed now unless Congress amended the law to make clear that it was not intended only to challenge robber barons.

Richard Nixon had appointed four of the justices deciding the Flood case. The four had all joined the Court between 1969 and 1971—three while the Flood case was pending in the courts, and one, Burger, in 1969 when the case was originally filed. Three of those four justices voted against Flood (Rehnquist, Burger and Blackmun himself), while the fourth, Powell, was the abstaining justice who nonetheless influenced White's vote.

In retrospect, Marvin Miller could not help but wonder what the outcome would have been if Hugo Black and John Harlan had not resigned from the bench in 1971, but had served just one more year.

Nixon himself was an unabashed fan of Major League Baseball; he, too, was weighed down by the sentimental past. In connection with the baseball All-Star Game in 1969—the same year the Flood case was filed—Nixon told a group of big league players visiting the White House, "If I had my life to live all over again, I'd have ended up as a sportswriter." The day after that year's All-Star Game, when the Apollo 11 astronauts splashed down after their lunar landing, Nixon asked them, "Were you told how the All-Star Game came out?" Clearly, this overwhelming fascination with big league baseball saturated the thinking of that administration and of those justices whom it had appointed.

Justices Marshall and Brennan, both of whom voted for Flood, reacted with a strongly dissenting opinion:

> Americans love baseball as they love all sports. Perhaps we become so enamored of athletics that we assume that they are foremost in the minds of legislators as well as fans. We must not forget, however, that there are only some 600 Major League baseball players. Whatever muscle they might have been able to muster by combining forces with other athletes has been greatly impaired by the manner in which this Court has isolated them. It is this Court that has made them impotent, and this Court should correct its error.

But ironically *Flood v. Kuhn* achieved some ultimate retribution for the players. Flood himself may have lost—and Flood never played baseball again—but the case inspired Marvin Miller to de-emphasize the antitrust angle in favor of what would prove a much more potent legal weapon: labor law.

Under Miller's stewardship, the baseball players refocused on the federal labor statutes, strengthening their union while the complacent owners sat on their laurels. Just four years after the Curt Flood debacle, the players' union challenged the Major League reserve clause with a labor grievance filed by Andy Messersmith against the National League with a companion American League challenge by Dave McNally. The Messersmith-McNally arbitrator read the text of the reserve clause itself and made a stunning discovery. The brief renewal clause had been interpreted for years as a perpetual renewal of the player's contract with his existing team, so that any failure to come to terms on a new deal for that player would have the effect of automatically renewing his old contract. The leverage this had created for the owners was extraordinary, but in truth the language did not really say what it was thought to mean. The arbitrator noted that the clause stated that the player's contract would be renewed just one time. The owners had insisted this meant that every time the contract was renewed, the "one time" renewal clause was also renewed—a self-serving loop of baseball logic that would renew itself into perpetuity.

But the owners had been too greedy. In addition to their clause allegedly renewing itself forever, they had inserted a stipulation that each and every time the renewal occurred, the player's salary would be reduced by twenty-five percent. The effect was to send the player's salary plummeting toward zero over time, an illogical and untenable result, according to the arbitrator. The arbitrator, therefore, ruled that the "one time renewal" could mean only what it says—one time—and that as a matter of logic and law it could not continue to renew itself "one time" forever.

Messersmith and McNally were thus sprung as free agents, and the surprised owners failed to react quickly as the union continued to gain power. The issue was not lost on some of the more progressive owners, however, like Ted Turner who had acquired the Atlanta Braves to provide good, consistent and cheap programming for his burgeoning TBS television empire. Turner seized the opportunity and signed the free-agent pitcher Messersmith, then exhibited his trademark flair for showmanship by giving Messersmith the number 17 on the back of his jersey to correspond with Turner's TV channel. Turner then outdid himself by printing "Channel 17" across the back of Messersmith's jersey, an advertisement that remained in full view of the outfield camera for so long as Messersmith was on the mound.

The arrogant owners were beaten at their own game and, even though they had their antitrust ruling, they lost everything else: the reserve clause, free agency, player strikes, and they suffered from exploding player salaries over the next twenty years.

24
SEARCHING FOR MUDVILLE

What visions burn, what dreams possess him
Seeker of the night?
The faultless velvet of the diamond,
The mounting roar of 80,000 voices
And Gehrig comes to bat . . .
—Thomas Wolfe, *You Can't Go Home Again,* 1940

BASEBALL IS THE CONSUMMATE American metaphor, with shared images that not only unite us, but connect our inner selves with a sense of past and purpose: Gehrig, the tragic figure; the bigger-than-life Ruth; the courage of Jackie Robinson; the anguish of Shoeless Joe; the rage of Cobb; the disillusionment of Roger Maris. Legends even as they played, the greatest of baseball icons still refuse to fade away, haunt us still: Hank Aaron, Ted Williams, Mickey Mantle, Joe DiMaggio, Satchel Paige, "Say-Hey" Willie Mays.

Football has its own legends—Walter Payton, Johnny Unitas and others—but somehow fails to pervade the American spirit. Even basketball's spectacular run from Chamberlain and Russell to Jordan, Bird and Magic falls short. Why is that?

The revealing answer lies somewhere in the depths of a nation's heart. Propelled by cultural forces, charmed by a distinct dash of American romanticism as old as Emerson and

Thoreau, the truth lies somewhere among the predilections of Grantland Rice, Ring Lardner, Ogden Nash and Sinclair Lewis, seasoned by the salty characters of Babe Ruth, Casey Stengel, Yogi Berra, Branch Rickey and the immortal Lou Gehrig. But that truth is not fungible; it is different for each of us, yet very real for all of us.

If nothing else, the history of baseball is a confluence of remarkable coincidences, luck and certainly mischief, reflecting America's own chip-on-the-shoulder attitude with remarkable acuity. Not to be outdone by deeds long past, baseball conjured yet another asterisk era with its steroid malaise of the new millennium, but thanks to Florida, the Supreme Court and a few hanging chads, an equally bizarre asterisk affixed itself to the White House, perhaps symbolizing baseball's inherent Americana.

There is no crying in baseball and there are no asterisks in football. When the football season moved from fourteen games to sixteen, it failed to evoke even a yawn, let alone a flurry of asterisks and consternation. When Jim Brown's career-rushing record was surpassed by Walter Payton, there was no uproar as there had been with Babe Ruth's record.

Mudville: it could be the metaphor for America's bonding to baseball, a place lodged nowhere at all but everywhere in time and permanently in our national soul.

The outlook wasn't bright for the Mudville nine that day;
The score stood four to two with but one inning to play.
And then when Cooney died at first, and Barrows did the same,
A sickly silence fell upon the patrons of the game.

Those immortal words of Ernest L. Thayer's were first delivered in a theater by actor William De Wolfe Hopper on May 18, 1888, and first appeared in print sixteen days later in the *San Francisco Examiner*. They have never gone away. Soccer may now be favored by our young people, while football pageantry dominates sports television, but baseball is an impres-

sionist painting, a work of art, a constant anchored by the spec-
ters of Ruth, all the Babe's men, and those that followed.

A straggling few got up to go in deep despair. The rest
Clung to that hope which springs eternal in the human breast;
They thought if only Casey could but get a whack at that—
We'd put up even money now with Casey at the bat.

Baseball, as we have said, probably evolved from the British game "rounders," rather than from cricket as has been generally believed. By 1900 the game was producing its own superstars: Christy Mathewson, Honus Wagner, Cy Young.

By 1904 the game had one World Series under its belt and
the Major League schedule was extended to 154 games. Its star
of the day may have been Napoleon Lajoie, who became the
prototype for the modern free agent, jumping leagues to escape
an "oppressive" team salary cap and land a $2600 deal with
Cleveland of the aggressive new American League. With
Pittsburgh's Honus Wagner dominating the National League,
Lajoie owned the American League for many years, with 3251
hits and a career .339 average. In 1901 he had not only won
baseball's unofficial triple crown, he had nailed a virtual "quin-
tuple crown," leading the league in no fewer than five categories: batting average (.422), slugging percentage (.635), home
runs (14), RBIs (125), and hits (229).

But in 1907 Lajoie was challenged by a nasty new kid on the
block, Ty Cobb, who knocked Nap off his perch. Slugging away
for the Detroit Tigers—sometimes even off the field—Cobb suddenly led the American League in batting (.350), slugging percentage (.473), RBIs (116), hits (212), and stolen bases (49). The
only major category he failed to win during the 1907 campaign
was home runs, which the Athletics' Harry Davis captured with
just eight. Duly impressed by the performance, a high-flying soft
drink manufacturer signed Cobb to an endorsement deal, launching decades of the sports imagery of Coca-Cola.

At the time, basketball, invented in 1892 by James Naismith to fill the winter months between football and baseball seasons, was still evolving, while football, though popular, was relegated to the college ranks. Michigan, Army, Yale, and Notre Dame provided the credible gridiron excitement of the day.

It was before Wrigley Field had been constructed. The Cubs still played in West Side Park, featuring the double play combination memorialized by a New York newspaperman: "Words that are heavy with nothing but trouble. Tinker to Evers to Chance." From Casey striking out to Tinker and Chance, from "Say it ain't so" to "Who's on First" and even Hemingway's *Old Man and the Sea,* baseball crept into American literature and pop culture, where it remains ensconced today. Striking out, swinging for the fences, throwing a curve, acting like a screwball, and coming from left field are all baseball's contribution to our language.

Then there was Eddie Bennett, a hunchback who had grown up in Brooklyn, in Flatbush, where he had worshipped the Polo Grounds ballplayers. By the time Eddie was fifteen, he had moved to the south side of Chicago and become a devoted fan of the White Sox players at Comiskey. One day Sox outfielder Happy Felsch couldn't resist touching Eddie's back for luck as he passed by the delighted youngster. That day Felsch ripped the Yankees for the White Sox, so for the following game he brought Eddie into the clubhouse where several teammates rubbed the boy's back with the apparent result that the Sox won their second straight game against New York.

With Eddie and the Sox going two for two, the youngster was adopted as an official mascot for permanent luck. Eddie was officially promoted to batboy as well as paid mascot, and the Sox went on to capture pennants in 1917 and 1919. But when the Black Sox scandal surfaced after the 1919 Series, Eddie's bubble burst and his luck was suddenly seen as black magic. Eddie was sent packing, and he went back to Brooklyn to work for his beloved Dodgers. As luck—or maybe Eddie—

would have it, the Dodgers won the 1920 pennant. Eddie was two for two in the pennant-luck department, and so again he was anointed as a magical merchant of baseball fortune.

In 1921, Eddie landed a job with the Yankees for the sole purpose of being a good luck charm again which, apparently, he was—although the acquisition of Babe Ruth the year before didn't hurt the team. Ruth played catch with Eddie every day before every game. Still, under the magical aura of Eddie Bennett, the Yankees nailed six pennants and three World Series titles between 1921 and 1932. Whatever forces may have been at work, everywhere he went, Eddie helped steal a little history.

The sorcery of Eddie Bennett propelled New York to a World Series sweep over the Cubs in 1932, the year the Yankees became the only team to go an entire season without being shut out. But Eddie's own magic abruptly ran out when he never fully recovered after being hit by a car during the year. He lost his mascot job and ended up in scant quarters at a rooming house in Manhattan, where he died alone three years later. The year following Eddie's accident, the great Yankees lost the pennant to the Senators by seven games, and they would go on to lose to the Tigers in 1934 and 1935.

Then from 5,000 throats and more there rose a lusty yell;
It rumbled through the valley, it rattled in the dell;
It knocked upon the mountain and recoiled upon the flat,
For Casey, mighty Casey, was advancing to the bat.

Babe Ruth reinvented baseball as the power game of today. He may have changed baseball even more than Wilt Chamberlain or Michael Jordan would influence professional basketball years later. Ruth's record sixty-homer 1927 season was a quantum leap for the Babe, although he had already changed the face of the game. Just twelve years earlier, in 1915, the American League home run leaders knocked a whopping seven over the wall. The following year Ruth was a pitcher in Bos-

ton where he led the league in earned run average at a stellar
1.75 pace.

In 1917, Yankee Wally Pipp, who would later gain greater
fame for "preceding" Lou Gehrig, led all comers with just nine
home runs. Then in 1919 Ruth raised the bar to a lofty twenty-
nine jacks. One year later Ruth was in Yankee pinstripes when
he belted an incredible fifty-four homers, six times Pipp's total
from just three years before. The Babe's 1927 record more than
doubled his 1919 record, nearly a full ten times the league leaders from just a decade earlier.

> Ten thousand eyes were on him as he rubbed his hands
>   with dirt;
> Five thousand tongues applauded when he wiped them on
>   his shirt.
> Then while the writhing pitcher ground the ball into his hip,
> Defiance gleamed in Casey's eye, a sneer curled Casey's lip.

Ruth hit his final home run as a member of the Boston Braves
on May 25, 1935, just a week before he left the game for good.
It was the third jack in the same game, Ruth having slugged
two-run shots in both the first and third innings against the
Pirates. Then came the great finale. Ruth's last blast, his record
home run number 714, was the first ever to clear the Forbes
Field stands and sail over the roof in right field, exiting the park
altogether. No one could measure the titanic blast, but the roof
itself was a full six hundred feet from the plate.

The opposing pitcher Guy Bush, who gave up Ruth's final
two homers that day, said later, "I never saw a ball hit so hard
before or since."

The Braves subsequently moved to Milwaukee and then later
to Atlanta. Almost thirty-nine years later, Hank Aaron, a member of the same Braves team, broke that record. "I don't want
them to forget Babe Ruth," Aaron said, later that year. "I just
want them to remember me." Aaron, a star slugger who launched

forty more homers, retired with the all-time career lead of 755 home runs. But he regarded his seminal moment as the day he bested Ruth with shot number 715 against Dodger pitcher Al Downing on April 8, 1974.

And now the leather-covered sphere came hurtling though the air,
And Casey stood a-watching it in haughty grandeur there.
Close by the sturdy batsman the ball unheeded sped—
"That ain't my style," said Casey. "Strike one," the umpire said.

In the new sluggers' age with such free-swingers as Sammy Sosa, Mark McGwire, Ken Griffey, Jr., and Barry Bonds, it is surprising to remember that Aaron, the all-time homer king for over three decades, never hit as many as fifty in a single season. Not once. In his best year he hit forty-seven, but he also faced an incredible array of National League hurlers all at once: Sandy Koufax, Don Drysdale, Ferguson Jenkins, Juan Marichal, Tom Seaver, Bob Gibson and Steve Carlton, plus a host of specialty relief pitchers later in his career, including Mike Marshall, Phil Regan, and Ted Abernathy. And Aaron averaged only sixty-three strikeouts per season and garnered three gold gloves along the way.

Then came the great home-run chase of 1998 when the Cardinals' Mark McGwire bested the Cubs' Sammy Sosa, seventy homers to sixty-six. McGwire was the first slugger to crack the seventy-homer barrier, and Sosa quickly became the first player to slam more than sixty in three different seasons. Aaron's explanation: "The athletes today, most of them, are much more superior collectively to when I was playing. They're bigger. They're stronger. They're healthier."

Aaron was right that weight training and nutrition played a part not only in baseball, but in basketball and football as well. However, he left something out: the scourge of the modern game. Steroids.

With their quick muscle-strength and bulk-building powers, steroids quickly became the choice of football players and world-class track athletes. Baseball players caught on to the habit, adding a new chapter to the shenanigans of the sport. But clearly separating baseball from the other sports was its stubborn reluctance to conduct steroid testing, a process adopted years earlier by both the NFL and the International Olympic Committee.

Now the Major League Baseball officials and union leaders have changed the steroids testing program, prompted by testimony from Jason Giambi and Barry Bonds that caused Senator John McCain to threaten legislation, mandating a new drug-testing policy, because the game could become "a fraud in the eyes of the American people."

The new rules call for testing all players at least once a year and also randomly in and out of season. It expands the list of banned drugs, but avoids action on amphetamines. The rules include the following penalties: the first time a player is caught, he gets a 10-day suspension without pay; the second failure brings a 30-day suspension, and the third failure, a 60-day suspension. If he is caught a fourth time, he will be suspended for a full year.

On January 15, 2005, the *New York Times* ran an editorial calling the penalties "absurdly light," contrasting them with the career-threatening two-year suspension and lifetime ban Olympic track athletes get the first and second times, respectively, they get caught.

> *From the benches black with people, there went up a*
> *   muffled roar,*
> *Like the beating of the storm waves on a stern and distant*
> *   shore.*
> *"Kill him! Kill him!" shouted some one in the stand;*
> *And it's likely they'd have killed him had not Casey raised*
> *   his hand.*

An August 2001 *Sports Illustrated* article described Cardinals slugger Mark McGwire as one of the most overrated players of the game. Although McGwire clubbed one homer for every ten at-bats during his career, he struck out a fourth of the time, was not much of a hitter as averages go, his fielding was limited, and even his home runs dropped off when they counted most—the playoffs, where he homered just five times in 118 plate appearances. The first man to reach the seventy-homer milestone, McGwire's record is nonetheless tainted by another aberration: questionable supplements. He admitted to using them; even though they were legal in baseball at the time, they were not legal in other major sports. Consequently McGwire's thunderous marks will always carry an implied asterisk. Taking drugs pushes the limits of baseball's quaint cheating. Throwing a spitter once in a while, framing a pitch to fool the umpire, striding off the mound to coax a strikeout call, stealing signs and growing the grass long—these are all part of the mischievous, colorful history of the American game. But ballooning up on steroids? This crosses the invisible line.

The whole sport may very well carry an asterisk for a two-decade span sandwiching the new millennium. In the April, 2004 *New York Times Magazine*, Stephen Metcalf bluntly asks, "Can drug-free baseball stars smash records?" The question itself is damning enough, but the answer is demoralizing: no— at least not according to a statistical phenomenon of evolution called the "Gould paradox." Named for the late paleontologist Stephen Jay Gould, the Gould Paradox says that in a healthy, affluent society more and more of the population approaches the outer limit of the human body's physical capabilities. Applied to sports, and in particular baseball, the paradox explains that over time, as fielding techniques and equipment become standardized, the gap between the average player and the superstar will close.

Individual performances in the early years of a sport, like Ruth's quantum leap home runs or Wilt Chamberlain's 100 points in a single game, reflect aberrations as the sport seeks a hypothetical norm. In the late 1960s, the baseball equilibrium became so refined that hitters could barely hit .300, let alone the .400 from the early days of Cobb, Lajoie, and even Ted Williams. Yet as the relative efforts of the stars seem to diminish, the norms stay the same, while the lesser players improve closer to the center. Although star averages are down, the baseball mean average of .260 stays relatively stable decade after decade.

The Gould Paradox in action presents the false impression of diminished quality of play, when in reality all that happens is that the standard deviation of such quality is narrowing. As a sport matures, the distances from the norm continue to narrow unless one of three things occurs: a) there is a fundamental change in the rules and/or nature of the game, b) something changes the players themselves, or c) an aberration occurs in the form of innovation or some other quantum leap.

An example of the latter phenomenon is the high jump. When Dick Fosbury jumped over the bar backward to break the Olympic record in 1968, he established a more scientifically efficient means to transfer force over the bar. Suddenly all the high jump records were in jeopardy from more and more jumpers imitating the "Fosbury Flop." And of course when Wilt Chamberlain stepped onto the basketball court, he was the first seven-footer, a quantum leap of basketball evolution.

Often great waves of change are brought about by rule modifications, like banning the spitball, lowering the pitchers' mound, or moving the outfield fences, or from innovations in equipment—fiberglass poles for vaulters, batting helmets, larger and more efficient gloves for fielders. But as a sport matures, innovations occur less frequently and the players achieve an optimum norm of height, weight and strength. Ruth, the aberration, smashed two to ten times the home runs of his contemporaries, and Oscar Robertson *averaged* the vaunted "triple double" for a whole season at one point in his NBA career. Those types of stand-out performances will occur less, if at all, in a mature sport.

Thus, it appears, mature sports have an ironic propensity toward predictability. Not much stands out, until something upsets the equilibrium—like steroids. Juice the hitters on muscle supplements and suddenly more force meets the ball and more balls leave the ballpark—not only from recognized power sluggers, but suddenly from Punch and Judy hitters who pop twenty dingers out of nowhere. Aluminum bats do the same thing for college and high school players, the trampoline effect propelling balls 500 feet and more. Aluminum has never been allowed in the majors, but it did not have to be, for apparently steroids became the clandestine "aluminum bat" of the big show.

Stephen Metcalf makes two salient observations, first noting that baseball "is an unusual sport in that it satisfies the poet in every accountant and the accountant in every poet." He then asks the question of the new baseball millennium: why have the owners and the players' union stood idly by while a suspicion taints their sport, to the point where the president of the United States feels compelled to mention it and Senator John McCain threatens intervention?

Baseball, the oldest and most mature of our major team sports, pushes the envelope the farthest and seems to appear tired or dull. Enter the Gould Paradox. The owners and the union almost certainly did not realize it, but one way to perk up the game is to change the equilibrium, and one way to accomplish that is to suddenly make the players bigger and stronger to achieve more star power. The home run season of 1998 was one of the most electrifying since 1961—and at least one of the participants was admittedly juiced on something.

But that begs the real question. There is precedent in baseball for legitimately altering the equilibrium. It has been done dozens of times with rule changes throughout the twentieth century. Bat size is now regulated, catchers' mitts are vastly improved, spitballs are banned, the strike zone has been modified, the mound lowered, the fences moved in and out, the seams on the ball raised. The real solution? Don't juice the players, juice the ball instead.

If baseball demands more marquee home runs, just juice the ball itself—make it tighter, cork it, do whatever is necessary to rocket it faster off a big league bat. But make sure the players are legit. The effect on history is the same, but the human effect is much different. When baseball juices the ball itself, all the players have the same advantage and disadvantages. But when under-the-table drugs are tolerated, the legitimate player is put at a disadvantage. He either sells out his own health by juicing up on 'roids, accepts relative mediocrity, or leaves the game— hardly a balanced set of choices and certainly not healthy for either the players or the game.

> With a smile of Christian charity great Casey's visage shone;
> He stilled the rising tumult, he bade the game go on,
> He signaled to the pitcher, and once more the spheroid flew;
> But Casey still ignored it, and the umpire said, "Strike two."
> "Fraud!" cried the maddened thousands, and echo answered
>   "Fraud!"
> But one scornful look from Casey and the audience was awed.
> They saw his face grow stern and cold, they saw his muscles
>   strain,
> And they knew that Casey wouldn't let that ball go by again.

Some images we create, some, like greatness itself, are thrust upon us. But others actually *become* us, shaping America rather than the other way around. Baseball is not just a national game, it defines us, teases our culture, creating history, not just reflecting it. For all its shortcomings, Major League Baseball became integrated in 1947, seven years before our schools even began to follow suit on the heels of 1954's *Brown v. Board of Education*. It provided genuine war heroes like Ted Williams and put controversial religious issues into play *à la* Hank Greenberg and Sandy Koufax. It gave us gamblers, greed and tyrants on and off the field, and it innovated the first true team sports superstar in George Herman Ruth. For whatever else it may be, baseball is not just a game, it is a symbolic microcosm of us all, framing our no-holds-barred approach to mischief, history and even a little larceny. Baseball's impish personality and sometimes naughty but true Yankee energy drives the fresh, often magical essence not just of America's baseball, but of baseball's America.

Sneer is gone from Casey's lip, his teeth are clenched in hate;
He pounds with cruel violence his bat upon the plate
And now the pitcher holds the ball, and now he lets it go,
And now the air is shattered by the force of Casey's blow.

Oh! Somewhere in this favored land the sun is shining bright;
The band is playing somewhere, and somewhere hearts are light,
And somewhere men are laughing, and somewhere children shout;
But there is not joy in Mudville—mighty Casey has struck out.

After decades of grit, legends, and mischief, Mudville lives on.

ACKNOWLEDGMENTS

MUCH HEARTFELT GRATITUDE is due many, including my wife Nan and legions of supportive family and friends; assistant Meghan, who helped with both research and advice—some of it even solicited; friends Mickey and Steve, sentenced to a lifetime of Cubs mystery and hope, who offered their extensive baseball library as well as their support; my alma mater Chicago-Kent College of Law, which believed in me not just once, but twice; and especially my publishing team of Jordan and Anita Miller, Joan Andreski, Ann Avouris and Doyle Olson, who, thankfully, harbor a not-so-latent affinity for baseball skulduggery and literary mischief.

Bibliography

Books

Abrams, Roger I. *The First World Series and the Baseball Fanatics of 1903*. Boston: Northeastern University Press, 2003.

Adair, Robert K. *The Physics of Baseball*. 3rd Ed. New York: HarperCollins Perennial, 2002.

Alexander, Charles C. *Our Game:An American Baseball History*. New York: MJF Books, 1991.

Asinof, Eliot. *Eight Men Out: The Black Sox and the 1919 World Series*. Evanston, IL: Holtzman Press, 1963.

Bibb, Porter. *Ted Turner: It Ain't as Easy as It Looks*. 1st Ed. New York: Crown, 1993.

Burns, Ken, and Geoffrey C. Ward. *Baseball: An Illustrated History*. New York: Alfred A. Knopf, 1994.

Dickson, Paul. *Baseball's Greatest Quotations*. New York: HarperCollins, 1991.

Fitzhenry, Robert I., ed. *Harper Book of Quotations*. 3rd Ed. New York: HarperCollins, 1993.

Helyar, John. *Lords of the Realm: The Real History of Baseball*. New York: Villard Books, 1994.

James, Bill. *The New Historical Baseball Abstract*. New York: Simon & Schuster, 2001.

Kuhn, Bowie. *Hardball: The Education of a Baseball Commissioner*. New York: Times Books division, Random House, 1987.

Lee, Bill, and Dick Lally. *The Wrong Stuff*. New York: Viking Press, 1984.

Light, Jonathan Fraser. *The Cultural Encyclopedia of Baseball*. Jefferson, NC, and London: McFarland and Company, 1997.

Lindberg, Richard. *The White Sox Encyclopedia*. Philadelphia: Temple University Press, 1997.

Miller, Marvin. *A Whole Different Ball Game: The Inside Story of the Baseball Revolution.* New York: Carol Publishing Group, 1991.

Myers, Doug, and Brian Dodd. *Batting Around: A Comprehensive Collection of Hitting Achievements, Ancecdotes, and Analyses.* Lincolnwood, IL: Contemporary Books, 2000.

Official Baseball Rules (2001 Edition). St. Louis: The Sporting News, Vulcan Print Media, 2001.

Okrent, Daniel, and Steve Wulf. *Baseball Anecdotes.* Oxford: Oxford University Press, 1989.

Reichler, Joseph L., ed. *The Baseball Encyclopedia.* 7th Ed. New York: Macmillan, 1988.

Shatzkin, Mike, ed. *The Ballplayers: Baseball's Ultimate Biographical Reference.* New York: William Morrow & Co., 1990.

Solomon, Burt. *The Baseball Timeline.* New York: Avon Books, 1997.

Spink, J.G. Taylor. *Judge Landis and 25 Years of Baseball.* St. Louis, MO: The Sporting News, 1974.

Thorn, John, Pete Palmer, and Michael Gershman, eds. *Total Baseball—The Official Encyclopedia of Major League Baseball.* 7th Ed. New York: Sport Media Publishing, 2001.

Veeck, Bill, and Ed Linn. *Veeck—As in Wreck.* Chicago: University of Chicago Press, 1962.

Weiler, Paul C., and Gary R. Roberts. *Sports and the Law: Text, Cases and Problems.* St. Paul, MN: West Group, 1998.

ARTICLES

Bamberger, Michael. "Mark McGwire." *Sports Illustrated,* August 27, 2001.

Barra, Allen. "Stuck on '61*'." *Wall Street Journal,* May 4, 2001.

Canadian Press. "Aaron Remembers Passing the Babe." April 6, 2004.

Chicago Tribune. "Hollow Achievement." June 4, 2003.

Conklin, Mike. "Watching the Ballgame? Expect Expectoration." *Chicago Tribune,* October 10, 2003.

Couch, Greg. "Face It: Baseball Cheating Far From Fleeting." *Chicago Sun-Times,* June 5, 2003.

Fatsis, Steve. "Mystery of Baseball: Was William White Game's First Black?" *Wall Street Journal,* January 30, 2004.

Glauber, Bill. "The World's Uniform." *Chicago Tribune,* July 11, 2003.

Golden, Daniel. "Bucky Dent Revisits the 'Monster,' to See if He is Still Reviled." *Wall Street Journal,* May 27, 2003.

Hersh, Philip. "The Ball—Sewing Circles." *Chicago Tribune*, July 15, 2003.

Holtzman, Jerome. "Courageous Flood Staked Career on Free Agency." *Chicago Tribune*, January 21, 1997.

Isaacson, Melissa. "Yankees' Return Stirs Memories, Passions." *Chicago Tribune*, June 7, 2003.

King, Bill. "Putting Together the Deal of the Century." *Street & Smith Sports Business Journal*, October 13, 2003.

Lieber, Ron. "How One Man Went From Regular Fan to a Cubs Legend." *Wall Street Journal*, October 16, 2003.

Newbart, Dave. "Historians Make pitch for Last-Minute Reprieve." *Chicago Sun-Times*, February 26, 2004.

New York Times. "Sick Boy Expecting Ruth 'Homer' Today." October 9, 1926.

———. "Grange's Football to Invalid Boy." October 10, 1926.

———. "'Dr.' Babe Ruth Calls on His Boy Patient." October 12, 1926.

———. "Boy Gets Tilden Racquet." October 14, 1926.

Popper, Steve, "Revelry at Wrigley as Cubs Win Division." *New York Times*, September 28, 2003.

Rose, Pete, and Rick Hill. "Pete Rose's Confession." *Sports Illustrated*, January 12, 2004.

St. John, Allen. "By the Numbers." *Wall Street Journal*, June 6, 2003.

Sports Illustrated. "Throwbacks." December 17, 2001.

Verducci, Tom. "Sammy's Second Season." *Sports Illustrated*, August 25, 2003.

Walker, Sam. "Baseball and Espionage." *Wall Street Journal*, September 19, 2003.

Wall Street Journal. "Another Bone-Headed Play." October 17, 2003.

Zeller, Tom. "Play Ball! Just Don't Get Caught." *New York Times*, June 8, 2003.

WEBSITES

The Ballplayers: Baseball's Ultimate Biographical Reference:
    http://www.baseballlibrary.com/baseballlibrary/ballplayers
Information on Davy Crockett:
    http://www.americanwest.com
Ballparks:
    http://www.ballparks.com/baseball

Rules of Election to the Baseball Hall of Fame:
   http://www.baseballhalloffame.org/hofers_and_honorees/
   rules.htm
Wrigley Field:
   http://www.cubs.mlb.com
Information on the 1936 Olympics—Berlin:
   http://www.infoplease.com
League Leaders: Major League Baseball Hitting, Career All Time:
   http://www.mlb.com
Mussill, Bernie, "The Evolution of the Baseball Bat,":
   http://www.stevetheump.com
New York Yankees Historical Statistics:
   http://www.yankees.mlb.com

COURT DECISIONS AND BASEBALL ARBITRATIONS

American League Baseball Club of Chicago v. Chase, 149 N.Y.S. 6
   (1914).
Atlanta National League Baseball Club & Ted Turner v. Bowie Kuhn,
   432 R. Supp. 1213 (1977).
Brown v. Board of Education, 347 U.S. 483 (1954).
Federal Base Ball Club of Baltimore v. National League, 259 U.S. 200
   (1922).
Finley v. Kuhn, 569 F.2d 527 (7th Cir. 1978).
Flood v. Kuhn, 407 U.S. 258 (1972).
Hart v. Keith Vaudeville Exchange, 262 U.S. 271 (1923).
Hooper v. People of State of California, 155 U.S. 648 (1895).
Lemke v. Farmers' Grain Co., 258 U.S. 50 (1922).
Pennsylvania Railroad Co. v. Weber, 257 U.S. 85 (1921).
*National & American League Professional Baseball Clubs v. Major
   League Baseball Players Assoc.* (Messersmith and McNally Griev-
   ances), 66 Labor Arbitration 101 (1976).
Rose v. Giamatti, 721 F.Supp. 906 (S.D. Ohio, 1989).
Toolson v. New York Yankees, Inc., 346 U.S. 356 (1953).

INDEX